Guardians of the Code: The Developer's Handbook to Secure Programming

Table of Content

Chapter 1: The Foundation of Security

- Brief overview of significant cybersecurity incidents.
- Exploring the CIA triad: Confidentiality, Integrity, and Availability.
- Shifting from reactive to proactive security approaches.
- Integrating security into each phase of the development process.
- Overview of legal frameworks related to secure programming.
- Introduction to industry standards (e.g., ISO 27001) and compliance requirements.
- Creating comprehensive documentation for security processes.
- Establishing a culture of security through training programs.
- Developing effective incident response plans.
- Exploring emerging technologies and trends in cybersecurity.

Chapter 2: Understanding Common Vulnerabilities

- Defining vulnerabilities in the context of software development.
- Understanding SQL injection and other common injection vulnerabilities.
- Exploring the types of XSS attacks and their consequences.
- The mechanics of CSRF attacks and potential risks.
- Identifying and avoiding common security misconfigurations.
- Risks associated with weak authentication and session management.
- Understanding the dangers of insecure direct object references.
- Debunking the myth of security through obscurity.
- Risks associated with file uploads and potential exploits.
- Securing APIs against common vulnerabilities.

Chapter 3: Coding Defensively: Best Practices

- Establishing and adhering to a set of secure coding guidelines.
- The importance of validating and sanitizing user input.
- Developing effective error handling mechanisms.
- Securing user sessions through encryption and tokenization.
- Overview of HTTP security headers and their significance.
- Incorporating security aspects into code review processes.
- Risks associated with outdated dependencies.
- Best practices for reading, writing, and storing files securely.
- Techniques for obscuring code to deter reverse engineering.
- Evaluating and selecting secure third-party libraries.

Chapter 4: Encryption and Data Protection

- Basics of encryption algorithms and their applications.
- Securing data stored on devices and databases.
- The importance of securing data during transmission.
- Best practices for secure key generation, storage, and distribution.
- Understanding the role of hashing in data integrity and password storage.
- The concept and applications of digital signatures.
- Implementing end-to-end encryption for secure communication.
- Exploring the impact of quantum computing on encryption.
- The role of random numbers in encryption and security.
- Overview of data protection laws and regulations.

Chapter 5: Secure Communication Protocols

- Overview of common communication protocols in software development.
- Understanding the fundamentals of SSL/TLS encryption.
- Common vulnerabilities associated with SSL.
- Implementing the latest TLS versions for enhanced security.
- Exploring protocols like SFTP and SCP for secure file transfers.
- Overview of security protocols for API communication (e.g., OAuth, JWT).
- Risks associated with insecure DNS configurations.
- Securing email communication through protocols like SMTPS and STARTTLS.
- Challenges and protocols for securing communication in the Internet of Things (IoT).
- Exploring new and emerging communication protocols.

Chapter 6: Authentication and Authorization

- Differentiating between authentication and authorization.
- The importance of MFA in enhancing authentication security.
- Understanding OAuth for authorization and OpenID Connect for authentication.
- The concept of tokens in authentication.
- Exploring the use of biometrics for user authentication.
- Implementing RBAC for fine-grained authorization.
- Understanding ABAC and its benefits in dynamic access control.
- Configuring and implementing secure authorization policies.
- Overview of SSO and its advantages in user experience and security.
- Challenges and best practices for authentication and authorization in microservices.

Chapter 7: Testing for Security: Penetration Testing and Beyond

- The role of security testing in the development life cycle.
- Exploring various security testing types (penetration testing, code reviews, etc.).
- Understanding the objectives and methodologies of penetration testing.
- Overview of popular security testing tools (e.g., OWASP ZAP, Burp Suite).
- The role of static and dynamic code analysis in security testing.
- Integrating security testing into continuous integration/continuous deployment (CI/CD) pipelines.
- Focusing on security testing specific to web applications.
- Challenges and strategies for testing the security of mobile applications.
- Ensuring the security of cloud-based applications and infrastructure.
- Responding to emerging threats and vulnerabilities post-deployment.

Chapter 8: Continuous Vigilance: Maintaining a Secure Codebase

- Recognizing the dynamic nature of security threats.
- Developing a robust strategy for timely application of security patches.
- Conducting regular code reviews for ongoing security assessment.
- Continuous education for development teams on emerging threats.
- Preparing for and responding to security incidents.
- Continuous monitoring for suspicious activities and security incidents.
- Integrating security into the DevOps culture.
- Establishing key performance indicators (KPIs) for security.
- Communicating security updates and best practices to end-users.
- Strategies for staying ahead of evolving cybersecurity threats.

Chapter 1: The Foundation of Security

Brief overview of significant cybersecurity incidents.

The landscape of cybersecurity has been marked by numerous significant incidents that have shaped the way individuals, organizations, and nations perceive and approach digital security. One of the seminal events was the Stuxnet worm's discovery in 2010, a sophisticated cyber weapon designed to target Iran's nuclear facilities. Its unprecedented level of complexity and ability to physically damage infrastructure underscored the potential of cyber threats to impact the physical world. The following years witnessed a surge in large-scale data breaches, with the 2013 Target breach being a notable example where hackers compromised credit card information for millions of customers. The scale and impact of such incidents prompted increased attention to cybersecurity on a global scale.

In 2017, the WannaCry ransomware attack spread across the globe, infecting hundreds of thousands of computers in over 150 countries. Exploiting a vulnerability in Microsoft Windows, the attack highlighted the risks posed by outdated software and the importance of timely security updates. The same year also saw the emergence of the NotPetya malware, which caused widespread disruption, particularly in Ukraine, and demonstrated the potential for state-sponsored cyberattacks to have far-reaching consequences.

The year 2018 brought the revelation of the Cambridge Analytica scandal, involving the unauthorized access of Facebook user data for political profiling. This incident ignited debates on privacy, data protection, and the ethical considerations surrounding the use of personal information in the digital age. In 2019, the City of Baltimore fell victim to a ransomware attack that paralyzed its systems, illustrating the vulnerability of critical infrastructure to malicious actors seeking financial gain.

As the world transitioned into a new decade, the SolarWinds supply chain attack unfolded in 2020, revealing the extent to which sophisticated threat actors could compromise trusted software vendors to infiltrate high-profile targets. The incident raised concerns about the security of software supply chains and the need for enhanced measures to protect against such attacks. The same year witnessed the emergence of the COVID-19 pandemic, which cybercriminals exploited through phishing campaigns and malware attacks capitalizing on the global crisis.

In 2021, the Colonial Pipeline ransomware attack captured headlines as a criminal group disrupted the critical infrastructure of a major U.S. fuel pipeline, highlighting the potential for cyber threats to impact essential services. This incident, along with the JBS meat processing cyberattack, emphasized the interconnectedness of cyberspace and the physical world, underscoring the need for robust cybersecurity measures across industries.

Amid the ongoing evolution of cyber threats, the emergence of the Log4j vulnerability in late 2021 marked a significant challenge for the cybersecurity community. Exploiting a widely used Java logging library, the vulnerability posed a widespread risk, prompting urgent responses from organizations and highlighting the constant need for vigilance in the face of evolving threats.

In conclusion, the past decade has been characterized by a series of landmark cybersecurity incidents that have reshaped the digital landscape. From state-sponsored attacks to ransomware campaigns and supply chain compromises, these incidents have underscored the importance of proactive cybersecurity measures, collaboration among stakeholders, and the continual adaptation of defense mechanisms in the face of evolving threats. As technology advances, the need for a comprehensive and resilient approach to cybersecurity becomes increasingly evident, with the lessons learned from past incidents serving as crucial guidance for the ongoing efforts to secure the digital realm.

Exploring the CIA triad: Confidentiality, Integrity, and Availability.

The CIA triad, an acronym for Confidentiality, Integrity, and Availability, forms the foundation of information security, guiding the principles and practices that organizations employ to safeguard their data and systems. Confidentiality, the first pillar of the triad, emphasizes the need to protect information from unauthorized access or disclosure. It encompasses measures such as encryption, access controls, and secure communication channels to ensure that sensitive data remains confidential and accessible only to authorized individuals. In an era marked by pervasive digital communication and interconnected systems, maintaining confidentiality becomes paramount to preserving the privacy and security of personal, financial, and organizational information.

Integrity, the second tenet of the CIA triad, centers on the accuracy and trustworthiness of data. Ensuring data integrity involves safeguarding information from unauthorized alterations or tampering, guaranteeing that it remains accurate and unaltered throughout its lifecycle. Hash functions, digital signatures, and data validation mechanisms are instrumental in verifying the integrity of data, offering a layer of assurance against malicious or unintentional modifications. As organizations rely on data to make critical decisions, preserving the integrity of information becomes vital for maintaining trust, regulatory compliance, and the overall reliability of digital systems.

Availability, the third dimension of the CIA triad, pertains to the accessibility and usability of data and systems. It underscores the importance of ensuring that authorized users can access information and resources when needed, without disruptions. Availability encompasses measures such as redundancy, backups, and disaster recovery planning to mitigate the impact of hardware failures, cyberattacks, or other unforeseen events that could jeopardize system accessibility. In a world where downtime can lead to financial losses, reputational damage, or even threats to public safety, prioritizing availability aligns with the imperative of providing uninterrupted services and maintaining operational resilience.

The interplay of these three principles is evident in the complex and dynamic landscape of information security. Organizations face the ongoing challenge of balancing confidentiality, integrity, and availability, recognizing that enhancements in one dimension may have implications for the others. Striking this balance requires a nuanced and context-specific approach, acknowledging that different types of data and systems may demand varying degrees of emphasis on each facet of the triad. For instance, while sensitive financial data may necessitate a strong focus on confidentiality, critical infrastructure systems may prioritize availability to prevent service disruptions.

The evolution of technology introduces new dimensions to the CIA triad. Cloud computing, for example, has transformed the traditional paradigms of data storage and processing. While offering scalability and flexibility, the cloud also raises concerns about data confidentiality and integrity. Organizations embracing cloud services must navigate the intricacies of shared responsibility models, encryption protocols, and access controls to maintain the desired level of security across all three dimensions of the triad.

Cybersecurity incidents often serve as poignant reminders of the interconnected nature of the CIA triad. Data breaches compromise confidentiality, malware attacks may corrupt data integrity, and denial-of-service incidents can disrupt availability. The SolarWinds supply chain attack in 2020, for instance, underscored the intricate relationship between integrity and availability as a sophisticated adversary compromised a trusted software vendor to infiltrate high-profile targets. This incident prompted renewed scrutiny of supply chain security and highlighted the need for organizations to extend their vigilance beyond traditional perimeter defenses.

In conclusion, the CIA triad encapsulates the fundamental principles that guide the practice of information security. As technology continues to advance and the threat landscape evolves, organizations must remain agile in their approach to confidentiality, integrity, and availability. By adopting a holistic and adaptive security posture, organizations can navigate the complexities of a digital world while upholding the principles of the CIA triad, thereby fortifying their resilience against the ever-changing landscape of cyber threats.

Shifting from reactive to proactive security approaches.

The evolution of cybersecurity strategies has witnessed a fundamental shift from reactive approaches to proactive methodologies, reflecting a growing recognition that anticipating and mitigating threats before they manifest is crucial in today's dynamic threat landscape. Reactive security measures, traditionally predominant, involve responding to incidents after they occur, often leaving organizations vulnerable to emerging and sophisticated threats. The rise of proactive security signifies a strategic transformation aimed at preventing, rather than merely reacting to, cyber threats. This paradigm shift encompasses various facets, including threat intelligence, risk assessments, and advanced technologies that collectively contribute to a more resilient and anticipatory security posture.

At the core of proactive security is the integration of threat intelligence into organizational defense mechanisms. Threat intelligence involves the analysis of data to discern patterns, trends, and potential risks. By staying abreast of the tactics, techniques, and procedures (TTPs) employed by threat actors, organizations can anticipate potential threats and vulnerabilities. This proactive stance enables the implementation of preemptive measures, such as patching known vulnerabilities, adjusting security policies, and enhancing incident response plans. The growing ecosystem of threat intelligence feeds, both commercial and community-driven, empowers organizations to proactively fortify their defenses against emerging threats.

Proactive security also entails a shift toward risk-based approaches that prioritize resources based on the potential impact and likelihood of threats. Conducting comprehensive risk assessments enables organizations to identify and prioritize vulnerabilities, allowing them to allocate resources efficiently. This proactive risk management approach involves continuous monitoring, periodic evaluations, and scenario planning to anticipate potential threats and vulnerabilities. By understanding the risk landscape, organizations can make informed decisions about where to invest in security controls, training, and technology to preemptively address potential issues before they escalate.

The advent of advanced technologies has played a pivotal role in facilitating proactive security measures. Machine learning, artificial intelligence, and automation have emerged as potent tools in analyzing vast amounts of data to identify anomalies and patterns indicative of potential security incidents. These technologies empower security teams to proactively detect and respond to threats in real time, reducing the reliance on reactive measures. Automated responses, such as isolating compromised systems or blocking malicious activities, contribute to a more agile and proactive defense posture.

Furthermore, the concept of "zero trust" has gained prominence in proactive security strategies. Zero trust assumes that threats can originate from both internal and external sources, challenging the traditional notion of a trusted internal network. This approach emphasizes continuous verification of user identity, device health, and network integrity, ensuring that access controls are dynamic and responsive to the evolving security landscape. By adopting a zero-trust mindset, organizations proactively minimize the attack surface and reduce the risk of lateral movement by threat actors within their networks.

Incident response, a critical component of any cybersecurity strategy, has also evolved from reactive to proactive models. Proactive incident response involves the development and rehearsal of incident response plans before a security incident occurs. Conducting tabletop exercises, simulations, and red teaming activities allows organizations to test their response capabilities, identify weaknesses, and refine their incident response procedures. This proactive approach ensures that when a security incident occurs, the organization is well-prepared to execute a swift and effective response, minimizing the impact and downtime.

The transition from reactive to proactive security is not without challenges. It requires a cultural shift within organizations, fostering a mindset that values prevention, continuous improvement, and adaptability. Proactive security also demands collaboration and information sharing within the cybersecurity community, as collective intelligence enhances the ability to anticipate and counter emerging threats. Additionally, the integration of new technologies and methodologies requires ongoing education and skill development for security professionals to effectively leverage these tools in a proactive manner.

In conclusion, the shift from reactive to proactive security approaches marks a critical evolution in the cybersecurity landscape. As organizations face increasingly sophisticated and persistent threats, the proactive stance becomes imperative for staying ahead of adversaries. By embracing threat intelligence, risk-based approaches, advanced technologies, zero trust principles, and proactive incident response strategies, organizations can fortify their defenses and significantly reduce the impact of cyber threats. This transformation represents a paradigm shift in the way cybersecurity is conceptualized and operationalized, emphasizing the importance of anticipation, prevention, and continuous improvement in the ongoing battle against cyber threats.

Integrating security into each phase of the development process.

The integration of security into each phase of the development process, often referred to as DevSecOps, represents a paradigm shift in the approach to software development. Traditionally, security was treated as a separate and often delayed consideration, leading to vulnerabilities and inefficiencies in addressing potential threats. However, recognizing the need for a more proactive and holistic security posture, organizations have embraced the concept of embedding security seamlessly throughout the entire development lifecycle.

In the initial phase of project planning and design, incorporating security involves establishing a clear understanding of the application's architecture and potential risks. Security architects and developers collaborate to perform threat modeling, identifying potential vulnerabilities and attack vectors. This proactive approach allows teams to design security controls directly into the architecture, laying the foundation for a more resilient and secure application.

As development progresses to the coding phase, integrating security practices becomes crucial. Developers adopt secure coding standards and best practices to minimize the introduction of vulnerabilities. Automated code analysis tools are employed to scan for common security flaws, such as injection vulnerabilities, cross-site scripting, and insecure dependencies. By catching and addressing security issues at the coding stage, developers can prevent the propagation of vulnerabilities into subsequent phases, reducing the overall risk and minimizing the effort required for remediation.

Continuous integration and continuous deployment (CI/CD) pipelines, integral components of modern software development, offer opportunities to automate security testing and validation. Security-focused automated tests, including static analysis, dynamic analysis, and security scanning, are seamlessly integrated into the CI/CD pipeline. This ensures that code changes undergo rigorous security checks before being deployed to production environments. Automated testing not only enhances the speed of development but also provides rapid feedback to developers, enabling them to address security findings early in the development process.

In the realm of containerization and orchestration, securing the containerized applications and their runtime environments becomes a priority. Container security tools are incorporated into the development pipeline to assess the security posture of container images, identify vulnerabilities, and enforce security policies. Container orchestration platforms, such as Kubernetes, offer security features that enable developers to define and implement security configurations, network policies, and access controls, ensuring a secure deployment environment.

In the deployment and runtime phase, monitoring and continuous security validation become pivotal. Security teams deploy tools for continuous monitoring of application behavior, system logs, and network activity. Intrusion detection and prevention systems, as well as security information and event management (SIEM) solutions, contribute to real-time threat detection. Additionally, runtime application self-protection (RASP) technologies enable applications to defend themselves against attacks by detecting and blocking malicious activities. This proactive monitoring approach allows organizations to identify and respond to security incidents promptly, reducing the dwell time of potential threats.

User authentication and access control are critical components of the runtime phase. Implementing strong authentication mechanisms, such as multi-factor authentication, and enforcing least privilege principles ensure that only authorized users have access to sensitive resources. Role-based access controls (RBAC) enable organizations to define and manage granular permissions, minimizing the risk of unauthorized access. Integrating security into access management is essential for protecting against insider threats and unauthorized external access.

The final phase of the development process involves ongoing maintenance, updates, and decommissioning of applications. Security considerations extend to patch management, vulnerability monitoring, and secure decommissioning practices. Automated tools facilitate the tracking and application of security patches, reducing the window of vulnerability. Regular vulnerability assessments and penetration testing help identify and address security weaknesses that may arise from changes in the threat landscape or updates to external dependencies.

The cultural aspect of DevSecOps is equally crucial in ensuring the successful integration of security throughout the development lifecycle. Fostering a culture of collaboration among development, operations, and security teams promotes shared responsibility for security. Security awareness training for development and operations staff enhances the understanding of security principles, threats, and best practices. By breaking down silos and fostering a collaborative culture, organizations create an environment where security is not seen as a bottleneck but as an integral part of delivering reliable and secure software.

In conclusion, the integration of security into each phase of the development process is a transformative approach that aligns with the principles of DevSecOps. By embedding security practices from project planning and design through coding, testing, deployment, runtime, and maintenance, organizations can proactively identify and address security issues, reducing the risk of vulnerabilities and enhancing the overall security posture of their applications. This holistic approach not only improves the resilience of software systems but also fosters a culture of collaboration and shared responsibility, ensuring that security is not an afterthought but an inherent and integral aspect of the development lifecycle.

Overview of legal frameworks related to secure programming.

Legal frameworks related to secure programming play a crucial role in shaping the landscape of software development by establishing guidelines, standards, and regulations to address cybersecurity concerns. One notable legal framework is the General Data Protection Regulation (GDPR), implemented by the European Union to protect the privacy and personal data of its citizens. GDPR emphasizes the importance of incorporating security measures into software systems, requiring organizations to implement "data protection by design and by default." This means that security considerations must be an integral part of the development process, ensuring that applications handle personal data securely from the outset.

In the United States, various laws and regulations impact secure programming, reflecting the country's multifaceted approach to cybersecurity. The Health Insurance Portability and Accountability Act (HIPAA) establishes standards for protecting the confidentiality and integrity of healthcare information. Software applications in the healthcare sector must comply with HIPAA's security requirements, emphasizing the need for secure coding practices to safeguard sensitive patient data. Similarly, the Gramm-Leach-Bliley Act (GLBA) imposes data protection requirements on financial institutions, necessitating secure programming practices to protect customers' financial information.

The Payment Card Industry Data Security Standard (PCI DSS) is a global framework that governs organizations handling payment card transactions. Compliance with PCI DSS requires secure coding practices to protect cardholder data, emphasizing encryption, secure coding guidelines, and vulnerability management. As the digital landscape evolves, legal frameworks such as the California Consumer Privacy Act (CCPA) and its successor, the California Privacy Rights Act (CPRA), set stringent requirements for protecting the privacy rights of California residents. These regulations reinforce the importance of secure programming in handling personal information, empowering users with control over their data. International standards contribute to the global landscape of secure programming by providing a common framework for organizations worldwide. ISO/IEC 27001, for instance, outlines the requirements for establishing, implementing, maintaining, and continually improving an information security management system. Adhering to ISO/IEC 27001 involves integrating security controls into the software development lifecycle, ensuring that security considerations are part of the organization's overall risk management strategy. The OWASP Top Ten, although not a legal framework per se, is a widely recognized industry standard that identifies the most critical web application security risks. Many legal frameworks implicitly or explicitly refer to industry standards like OWASP, making them essential guides for secure programming.

In the context of government-led initiatives, the National Institute of Standards and Technology (NIST) in the United States provides a comprehensive framework for managing information security. NIST Special Publication 800-53, known as the Security and Privacy Controls for Federal Information Systems and Organizations, offers a catalog of security controls applicable to federal information systems. These controls encompass secure coding practices, emphasizing the importance of developing and maintaining software with a focus on security. NIST's Cybersecurity Framework, a voluntary framework applicable to organizations of all sizes, encourages secure programming as an integral part of a broader risk management strategy.

In the European Union, the Network and Information Systems Directive (NIS Directive) establishes a legal framework for the security of network and information systems. It mandates that operators of essential services and digital service providers adopt appropriate security measures, including secure software development practices, to ensure the resilience of their systems. The directive reflects a recognition that secure programming is a fundamental element in safeguarding critical infrastructure and essential services from cyber threats.

The legal frameworks mentioned so far primarily focus on data protection, privacy, and industry-specific regulations. However, criminal law also plays a role in addressing malicious activities related to software development. Laws prohibiting hacking, unauthorized access, and the distribution of malicious software are crucial for deterring cybercrime. The Computer Fraud and Abuse Act (CFAA) in the United States, for instance, criminalizes unauthorized access to computer systems, including those involved in software development. These legal provisions underscore the importance of ethical behavior and adherence to security practices in the programming community.

Open-source software development, a prominent aspect of the modern software landscape, operates within a legal framework defined by various licenses. The GNU General Public License (GPL) and the Apache License, among others, establish the terms under which software can be used, modified, and distributed. These licenses often include clauses related to security, requiring contributors to maintain the security of the software and report vulnerabilities responsibly. The legal frameworks governing open-source projects contribute to the overall security of the software ecosystem by promoting transparency, collaboration, and responsible disclosure.

As the Internet of Things (IoT) expands, legal frameworks are adapting to address the unique security challenges posed by connected devices. The Cybersecurity Improvement Act in the United States, for example, mandates minimum security standards for federal government IoT devices, emphasizing secure development practices to mitigate vulnerabilities. Similar initiatives globally recognize the critical role of secure programming in ensuring the resilience and safety of IoT ecosystems.

In conclusion, legal frameworks related to secure programming span a diverse range of regulations, standards, and initiatives. These frameworks reflect a global effort to address cybersecurity challenges and protect individuals, organizations, and critical infrastructure from evolving cyber threats. Whether focused on data protection, industry-specific regulations, international standards, or criminal law, these legal instruments emphasize the importance of integrating security into every phase of the development process. Adherence to these frameworks not only ensures regulatory compliance but also contributes to the creation of a more secure, resilient, and trustworthy digital environment.

Introduction to industry standards (e.g., ISO 27001) and compliance requirements.

Industry standards and compliance requirements form the backbone of a robust and secure information security framework, providing organizations with guidelines, best practices, and benchmarks to safeguard their sensitive data and maintain the confidentiality, integrity, and availability of information. One of the pivotal standards in this domain is ISO/IEC 27001, an international standard that delineates the specifications for establishing, implementing, maintaining, and continually improving an information security management system (ISMS). ISO/IEC 27001 serves as a comprehensive framework, applicable to organizations of all sizes and industries, offering a systematic approach to managing and securing information assets. By adhering to ISO/IEC 27001, organizations demonstrate their commitment to information security, aligning their practices with globally recognized standards and providing stakeholders with confidence in the effectiveness of their security measures.

ISO/IEC 27001 is characterized by its risk-based approach, emphasizing the identification and assessment of information security risks and the implementation of controls to mitigate these risks to an acceptable level. The standard's structure, aligned with the Plan-Do-Check-Act (PDCA) model, underscores the importance of continual improvement, ensuring that the ISMS evolves in response to changing threats, technologies, and organizational contexts. The certification process for ISO/IEC 27001 involves an independent assessment by accredited certification bodies, providing external validation of an organization's adherence to the standard. Achieving and maintaining ISO/IEC 27001 certification not only enhances an organization's information security posture but also instills confidence in clients, partners, and regulatory bodies.

Beyond ISO/IEC 27001, industry-specific compliance requirements play a pivotal role in shaping information security practices. In the healthcare sector, the Health Insurance Portability and Accountability Act (HIPAA) in the United States establishes standards for protecting the privacy and security of individuals' health information. Covered entities and business associates in the healthcare ecosystem must comply with HIPAA's security rule, implementing safeguards to protect electronic protected health information (ePHI). HIPAA's focus on secure programming, access controls, and risk assessments reflects the critical role of information security in preserving the confidentiality and integrity of sensitive healthcare data.

The financial industry is subject to various compliance requirements, with the Gramm-Leach-Bliley Act (GLBA) being a key regulatory framework. GLBA mandates financial institutions to establish information security programs to protect the nonpublic personal information (NPI) of their customers. This includes implementing measures such as secure coding practices, encryption, and access controls to ensure the confidentiality and integrity of customer data. Failure to comply with GLBA can result in severe penalties, highlighting the importance of integrating security into every facet of financial operations.

Another crucial compliance framework is the Payment Card Industry Data Security Standard (PCI DSS), applicable to organizations that handle credit card transactions. PCI DSS encompasses a set of security requirements that aim to secure payment cardholder data, emphasizing secure programming practices, encryption, and network segmentation. Compliance with PCI DSS is mandatory for entities involved in processing, transmitting, or storing payment card information. Non-compliance can lead to financial penalties and reputational damage, underscoring the imperative for organizations to embed security into their payment processing systems.

In the European Union, the General Data Protection Regulation (GDPR) represents a landmark regulation that governs the processing of personal data and has significant implications for information security. GDPR mandates organizations to implement appropriate technical and organizational measures to ensure the security of personal data, including pseudonymization, encryption, and regular security assessments. The regulation's emphasis on data protection by design and by default aligns with the principles of secure programming, requiring organizations to integrate security into their data processing activities from the outset.

The financial and securities industry is subject to regulations such as the Sarbanes-Oxley Act (SOX) in the United States. SOX imposes requirements on public companies and their auditors to establish and maintain internal controls over financial reporting. While SOX is primarily focused on financial controls, its impact extends to information security practices, as the reliability and integrity of financial data depend on secure information systems and processes.

On a global scale, the International Electrotechnical Commission (IEC) and the International Organization for Standardization (ISO) collaboratively develop standards that address various aspects of information security. ISO/IEC 27002, a companion standard to ISO/IEC 27001, provides a code of practice for information security controls. It offers detailed guidance on the implementation of security controls, serving as a valuable resource for organizations seeking to align their practices with internationally recognized standards. ISO/IEC 27701, an extension of ISO/IEC 27001, focuses on privacy information management, providing guidelines for organizations to establish, implement, maintain, and continually improve a privacy information management system (PIMS).

Compliance with these industry standards and regulations is not solely driven by legal requirements but is increasingly becoming a business imperative. Adhering to recognized standards enhances an organization's credibility, fosters customer trust, and facilitates international business transactions. Additionally, the evolving threat landscape and the increasing frequency of data breaches underscore the necessity for organizations to prioritize information security. Standards and compliance frameworks serve as invaluable tools, offering a structured and systematic approach to addressing cybersecurity challenges and building a resilient defense against a myriad of threats.

In conclusion, industry standards and compliance requirements play a pivotal role in guiding organizations toward effective information security practices. ISO/IEC 27001 stands as a cornerstone, providing a holistic framework applicable across industries. Industry-specific regulations, such as HIPAA, GLBA, PCI DSS, GDPR, and SOX, address the unique challenges of different sectors, shaping information security practices to safeguard sensitive data and ensure the trust of stakeholders. As the digital landscape continues to evolve, adherence to these standards not only ensures regulatory compliance but also establishes a foundation for organizations to thrive in an era where information security is integral to business success and resilience.

Creating comprehensive documentation for security processes.

Creating comprehensive documentation for security processes is a fundamental and strategic undertaking that forms the bedrock of a robust information security program. Documentation serves as the blueprint for implementing, managing, and continuously improving security measures within an organization. It encompasses a wide range of artifacts, including policies, procedures, guidelines, standards, and incident response plans, all of which collectively contribute to establishing a structured and effective security framework.

The cornerstone of comprehensive security documentation is the development of a robust information security policy. This policy serves as the overarching document that articulates an organization's commitment to information security, delineates the scope and objectives of the security program, and establishes the foundational principles that guide security-related decisions and actions. An effective information security policy addresses key areas such as data classification, access controls, encryption, incident response, and employee responsibilities, providing a high-level view of the organization's security posture.

From the information security policy, organizations derive more granular documents such as security standards and guidelines. Security standards set specific requirements and expectations for the implementation of security controls, ensuring a consistent and uniform approach to security across the organization. These standards may cover areas such as password management, network security, and software development practices. Guidelines, on the other hand, offer detailed recommendations and best practices for implementing security controls, providing practical insights for those responsible for their execution.

Procedures represent another crucial component of comprehensive security documentation. While policies, standards, and guidelines set the overarching framework, procedures detail step-by-step instructions for specific security processes and activities. This includes procedures for user account management, data backup and recovery, vulnerability assessments, and incident response. Well-defined procedures ensure that security tasks are executed consistently, reducing the risk of errors and ensuring that security measures are implemented effectively across the organization.

Security documentation also extends to risk management processes. A comprehensive risk management framework includes risk assessment methodologies, risk treatment plans, and risk mitigation strategies. Risk assessment methodologies guide organizations in identifying, evaluating, and prioritizing risks to their information assets. Risk treatment plans outline the measures to be taken to mitigate identified risks, and mitigation strategies provide guidance on implementing controls to reduce risk to an acceptable level. This documentation not only helps organizations understand their risk landscape but also informs decision-making processes related to resource allocation and risk acceptance.

Incident response documentation is a critical aspect of a comprehensive security framework. Incident response plans outline the organization's approach to managing and mitigating security incidents, ensuring a coordinated and effective response in the event of a security breach. These plans include predefined roles and responsibilities, communication protocols, incident detection and reporting procedures, and steps for containing, eradicating, and recovering from incidents. A well-documented incident response plan contributes to a swift and efficient response, minimizing the impact of security incidents on the organization.

Change management documentation is integral to ensuring that security is considered throughout the lifecycle of systems and processes. Change management processes dictate how changes to the IT environment are evaluated, authorized, and implemented. Documentation in this area includes change control policies, procedures, and guidelines, detailing the steps involved in assessing the security impact of changes, obtaining approvals, and implementing changes in a controlled manner. Integrating security considerations into change management processes is vital for preventing unintended security consequences resulting from system modifications or updates.

Training and awareness documentation is essential to foster a security-conscious culture within the organization. Security awareness programs often include training materials, communication plans, and guidelines for educating employees about security risks, best practices, and organizational policies. By documenting these efforts, organizations ensure that employees receive consistent and relevant security training, empowering them to make informed decisions and contribute to the overall security posture.

Regular audits and assessments of security controls are critical for verifying and validating the effectiveness of security measures. Comprehensive documentation in this context includes audit plans, assessment methodologies, and reports detailing the findings and recommendations for improvement. Auditing and assessment documentation provide insights into the organization's compliance with internal policies and external regulations, enabling continuous improvement and demonstrating adherence to security best practices.

Comprehensive documentation also plays a pivotal role in regulatory compliance. Depending on the industry and geographical location, organizations may be subject to various legal and regulatory requirements related to information security. Documentation serves as evidence of compliance, demonstrating to regulatory authorities that the organization has implemented and adhered to security measures mandated by specific laws or industry regulations. This documentation often includes records of security assessments, policy reviews, and evidence of security controls in place.

Documentation is not a static artifact but rather a living and evolving resource that should be regularly reviewed, updated, and improved. Changes in technology, emerging threats, and organizational dynamics necessitate continuous refinement of security documentation. Regular reviews ensure that documentation remains current, aligns with organizational goals, and reflects the most recent best practices and industry standards.

In conclusion, creating comprehensive documentation for security processes is a multifaceted endeavor that encompasses policies, standards, guidelines, procedures, and plans across various aspects of information security. This documentation serves as the foundation for building a robust and resilient security framework within an organization. It provides guidance, consistency, and transparency, enabling stakeholders to understand, implement, and continuously improve security measures. From risk management and incident response to change management and compliance, comprehensive security documentation is a cornerstone of effective information security governance, contributing to the overall resilience and trustworthiness of an organization in an increasingly complex and dynamic digital landscape.

Establishing a culture of security through training programs.

Establishing a culture of security within an organization is a multifaceted and dynamic endeavor that requires a comprehensive approach, with training programs playing a central role. Cultivating a security-conscious culture involves instilling a collective awareness, understanding, and commitment to information security among all employees. Training programs serve as the linchpin for achieving this cultural transformation, equipping individuals at all levels with the knowledge, skills, and behaviors necessary to navigate the complex and evolving landscape of cybersecurity.

The foundation of any effective security training program lies in the clear articulation of organizational policies, procedures, and expectations related to information security. Employees need to understand the importance of protecting sensitive data, recognizing potential security threats, and adhering to established security protocols. Training materials should be developed with clarity and accessibility in mind, ensuring that employees from diverse backgrounds and levels of technical expertise can engage with and comprehend the content. By providing a solid foundation of knowledge, organizations lay the groundwork for a culture of security that is rooted in understanding and shared commitment.

Beyond mere awareness, security training programs should foster a sense of ownership and accountability among employees. This involves conveying the message that security is not solely the responsibility of the IT department but a collective effort that involves every individual within the organization. Training initiatives can emphasize the role of each employee as a steward of the organization's information assets, underscoring the idea that everyone has a part to play in maintaining a secure environment. Encouraging a sense of shared responsibility instills a proactive mindset, where employees are empowered to identify and report security incidents, adhere to best practices, and actively contribute to the overall security posture.

Interactive and engaging training methods are vital for capturing the attention and interest of employees. Traditional, lecture-style training sessions may not be as effective as interactive approaches that incorporate real-world scenarios, case studies, and practical exercises. Simulations of phishing attacks, for example, can provide employees with hands-on experience in recognizing and responding to potential threats. By making training programs dynamic and relevant to daily work scenarios, organizations increase the likelihood of knowledge retention and application in real-world situations.

Leadership commitment is pivotal for the success of security training programs. When organizational leaders actively endorse and participate in training initiatives, it sends a powerful message about the significance of security within the organizational culture. Leadership involvement not only reinforces the importance of security but also sets the tone for a culture where security is prioritized at all levels. Executives and managers who demonstrate a commitment to security create an environment where employees are more likely to embrace security principles and integrate them into their daily activities.

Tailoring training programs to specific roles and responsibilities within the organization enhances their relevance and effectiveness. Different departments and job functions may have distinct security considerations, and training content should address these nuances. For example, employees in the finance department may require specific training on financial fraud prevention, while software developers may benefit from secure coding practices. Customizing training content to align with job roles ensures that employees receive targeted information that directly relates to their responsibilities, fostering a more practical and applicable understanding of security.

Continuous learning and reinforcement are essential components of a sustainable security culture. One-time training sessions are insufficient to address the evolving nature of cybersecurity threats. Regularly scheduled refresher courses, updates on emerging threats, and ongoing communication about security best practices help to keep security at the forefront of employees' minds. Consistent reinforcement ensures that security remains a priority and is integrated into the day-to-day operations of the organization, preventing complacency and promoting a long-term commitment to security principles.

Organizations should leverage technology to enhance the accessibility and effectiveness of security training programs. Online training platforms, webinars, and e-learning modules offer flexibility for employees to engage with training content at their own pace and convenience. Gamification elements, such as quizzes and interactive scenarios, can make learning more enjoyable and encourage active participation. Additionally, incorporating multimedia elements, such as videos and simulations, can enhance the overall engagement and impact of the training.

Measuring the effectiveness of security training programs is crucial for evaluating their impact and identifying areas for improvement. Organizations can implement assessments, quizzes, and simulated exercises to gauge employees' understanding of security concepts. Monitoring key security metrics, such as incident response times and the frequency of security incidents, can provide insights into the overall effectiveness of the security culture. Feedback mechanisms, such as surveys and open forums, allow employees to share their perspectives on the training programs, enabling organizations to refine and tailor future initiatives.

Building a culture of security is an ongoing process that requires adaptability to changing threats and technologies. Training programs should evolve in response to emerging cybersecurity trends, regulatory changes, and organizational developments. Regularly updating training content ensures that employees stay informed about the latest security risks and best practices. It also demonstrates the organization's commitment to staying proactive in the face of an ever-changing threat landscape.

In conclusion, establishing a culture of security through training programs is a holistic and dynamic effort that goes beyond simply conveying information. It involves creating a shared understanding of the importance of security, fostering a sense of ownership and accountability, and continuously reinforcing security principles. By investing in comprehensive and tailored training initiatives, organizations can empower employees to become active contributors to the organization's security posture, creating a culture where security is not just a set of rules to follow but a collective mindset that permeates every aspect of the organizational fabric.

Developing effective incident response plans.

Developing effective incident response plans (IRPs) is a critical aspect of an organization's cybersecurity strategy, providing a structured and coordinated approach to managing and mitigating security incidents. An incident response plan serves as a proactive roadmap, outlining the steps and procedures to be followed when a security incident occurs. The goal is not only to minimize the impact of incidents but also to enable a swift and efficient response that safeguards the organization's data, systems, and reputation.

The foundation of an effective incident response plan lies in a thorough understanding of the organization's assets, risks, and potential threat landscape. Organizations must conduct a comprehensive risk assessment to identify and prioritize potential threats and vulnerabilities. This risk assessment serves as the basis for tailoring the incident response plan to address specific risks and scenarios relevant to the organization's operations. By aligning the plan with the organization's risk profile, it becomes more targeted and responsive to the unique challenges the organization may face.

Clear delineation of roles and responsibilities is a fundamental component of an incident response plan. Designating individuals or teams responsible for specific tasks, such as incident detection, analysis, containment, eradication, recovery, and communication, ensures a coordinated and efficient response. These roles may include members from the IT department, legal, public relations, and executive leadership. The incident response team should be well-trained and regularly participate in simulations and drills to ensure they are prepared to handle various types of incidents.

The incident response plan should establish a tiered and well-defined incident classification system. Incidents vary in severity, ranging from minor security events to major breaches, and having a clear classification system helps prioritize and allocate resources appropriately. The classification should consider the impact on confidentiality, integrity, and availability of data and systems. This tiered approach allows the incident response team to respond proportionally to the severity of the incident, ensuring a scalable and adaptive response.

Integration with other organizational processes is crucial for the effectiveness of an incident response plan. The plan should align with the organization's overall business continuity and disaster recovery strategies, ensuring a seamless transition between incident response and recovery efforts. Collaboration with legal and compliance teams is also essential to ensure that incident response activities adhere to relevant laws, regulations, and contractual obligations. By integrating incident response into the broader organizational framework, the plan becomes a cohesive part of the organization's resilience strategy.

Documentation is a key component of incident response planning. The plan should include detailed documentation of procedures, contact information, and technical details to guide responders during an incident. This documentation serves as a reference point, particularly during the chaotic and time-sensitive moments following the detection of an incident. Regularly reviewing and updating documentation ensures that the incident response plan remains current, reflecting changes in technology, personnel, and organizational processes.

Communication is a critical aspect of incident response, both internally and externally. The plan should outline clear communication protocols, including notification procedures for internal stakeholders, external partners, regulatory bodies, and, when necessary, the public. Effective communication helps manage the perception of the incident, maintains transparency, and aids in the preservation of the organization's reputation. Establishing communication channels and templates in advance streamlines the response process and facilitates timely and accurate information dissemination.

Continuous monitoring and detection capabilities are integral to incident response preparedness. The incident response plan should incorporate robust monitoring mechanisms to detect security events and incidents in their early stages. This includes the use of intrusion detection systems, security information and event management (SIEM) tools, and other monitoring solutions. Real-time alerts and automated responses can significantly reduce the time between incident occurrence and detection, allowing the incident response team to initiate timely action.

An effective incident response plan acknowledges the inevitability of incidents and embraces a "lessons learned" approach. After the resolution of an incident, a post-incident review should be conducted to analyze the response effectiveness, identify areas for improvement, and update the incident response plan accordingly. This continuous improvement cycle ensures that the organization learns from each incident, adapts its response strategies, and fortifies its defenses against future incidents.

Simulations and drills are indispensable components of incident response planning. Regularly conducting tabletop exercises and simulated incident scenarios allows the incident response team to practice and refine their response procedures. These simulations not only test the technical aspects of the plan but also assess the effectiveness of communication, coordination, and decision-making under simulated stress. Through repeated drills, the incident response team gains valuable experience and hones their ability to respond swiftly and effectively when faced with a real incident.

The incident response plan should include predefined metrics and key performance indicators (KPIs) to measure the success and efficiency of the response efforts. Metrics may include the time to detect an incident, the time to contain and eradicate the threat, and the overall impact on operations. Regularly analyzing these metrics provides insights into the organization's incident response capabilities, allowing for adjustments and improvements to be made based on performance data.

Technology plays a vital role in incident response, and the plan should leverage automation and response technologies to augment human efforts. Automated incident response tools can assist in rapidly identifying and containing threats, reducing manual intervention time. Integration with threat intelligence feeds enhances the organization's ability to detect and respond to emerging threats. However, it is crucial to strike a balance between automation and human decision-making, ensuring that human expertise is applied where nuanced judgment is required.

Legal considerations are paramount in incident response planning, especially in the context of data breaches and privacy regulations. The plan should address legal requirements for incident reporting, evidence preservation, and interactions with law enforcement. Organizations should work closely with legal counsel to ensure that their incident response activities align with legal obligations and are conducted in a manner that preserves the admissibility of evidence in potential legal proceedings.

In conclusion, developing effective incident response plans is an ongoing and collaborative effort that requires a combination of strategic planning, technical preparedness, and organizational coordination. An incident response plan serves as a proactive and adaptive framework for addressing security incidents, guiding organizations through the detection, analysis, containment, eradication, recovery, and communication phases. By integrating incident response

into the broader organizational context, aligning roles and responsibilities, fostering a culture of continuous improvement, and leveraging technology and automation, organizations can fortify their resilience against a diverse range of cybersecurity threats.

**Exploring emerging technologies and trends in cybersecuri-
ty.**

Exploring emerging technologies and trends in cybersecurity unveils a dynamic landscape shaped by rapid advancements, evolving
threat vectors, and the imperative to stay ahead of sophisticated adversaries. One of the prominent trends is the rise of artificial intelligence (AI) and machine learning (ML) in cybersecurity. AI and ML
algorithms are increasingly employed to analyze vast amounts of data, detect patterns, and identify anomalies indicative of potential security incidents. These technologies enhance the accuracy and speed
of threat detection, enabling organizations to respond proactively to
emerging cyber threats.

The integration of automation and orchestration is another notable trend in cybersecurity. Security orchestration, automation, and
response (SOAR) platforms streamline and coordinate incident response processes, allowing organizations to automate repetitive
tasks, accelerate response times, and improve overall efficiency. By integrating disparate security tools and automating incident response
workflows, SOAR platforms empower cybersecurity teams to focus
on higher-value tasks, such as threat analysis and strategy development.

Blockchain technology is gaining traction as a means to enhance
cybersecurity, particularly in the context of securing transactions and
sensitive data. The decentralized and tamper-resistant nature of
blockchain provides a foundation for creating secure and transparent
systems. Applications include securing financial transactions, supply
chain integrity, and decentralized identity management.
Blockchain's potential to reduce the risk of data tampering and en-

hance trust in digital transactions positions it as an emerging technology with significant implications for cybersecurity.

The advent of 5G technology introduces both opportunities and challenges for cybersecurity. The increased speed and connectivity promised by 5G networks expand the attack surface, requiring organizations to reevaluate their security postures. The proliferation of Internet of Things (IoT) devices on 5G networks introduces new vectors for cyber attacks, necessitating robust security measures to protect against IoT-related threats. As organizations embrace the benefits of 5G, cybersecurity strategies must adapt to the unique challenges posed by this transformative technology.

Cloud security remains a focal point as organizations migrate their infrastructure and services to cloud environments. The shared responsibility model in cloud computing necessitates a collaborative approach between cloud service providers and customers to ensure the security of data and applications. Security tools tailored for cloud environments, such as cloud access security brokers (CASBs) and container security solutions, are gaining prominence to address the evolving threat landscape in cloud computing.

The increasing prevalence of ransomware attacks has propelled the development of advanced threat intelligence and threat hunting capabilities. Organizations are investing in threat intelligence platforms that aggregate and analyze data from various sources to provide actionable insights into emerging threats. Threat hunting involves proactively searching for signs of malicious activity within an organization's network, enabling security teams to detect and respond to threats before they escalate. This proactive approach aligns with the evolving nature of cyber threats, emphasizing the importance of early detection and mitigation.

Quantum computing poses both opportunities and challenges for cybersecurity. While quantum computing holds the potential to break widely used encryption algorithms, it also offers the prospect of developing quantum-resistant cryptographic methods. As quantum computing research advances, organizations are exploring post-quantum cryptography to future-proof their encryption practices. Preparing for the quantum era requires a strategic and forward-looking approach to cryptographic agility and resilience against emerging threats.

Endpoint security is undergoing transformation with the adoption of zero trust architectures. Traditional perimeter-based security models are increasingly deemed insufficient in the face of sophisticated attacks and the prevalence of remote work. Zero trust architectures assume that threats may exist both outside and inside the network, requiring continuous verification of user identity and device integrity. This approach minimizes the attack surface, enhances visibility, and improves the overall security posture by adopting a least-privilege access model.

The human factor in cybersecurity is gaining recognition as a critical aspect of defense against cyber threats. Security awareness training and education programs are becoming integral components of cybersecurity strategies. Organizations recognize the need to educate employees about the risks of social engineering, phishing, and other cyber threats. Cultivating a security-aware culture helps empower employees to be vigilant and proactive in recognizing and reporting potential security incidents.

Biometric authentication technologies are advancing as organizations seek to enhance identity verification and access control. Facial recognition, fingerprint scanning, and other biometric modalities offer secure and convenient alternatives to traditional authentication methods. Biometric data, however, raises privacy concerns, necessitating careful consideration of ethical and legal implications in their implementation. As biometric technologies continue to evolve, they present opportunities for strengthening identity and access management in cybersecurity.

Collaborative security approaches are gaining prominence as organizations recognize the value of information sharing and collective defense. Information sharing platforms, such as Information Sharing and Analysis Centers (ISACs), enable organizations within specific industries to exchange threat intelligence and best practices. Public-private partnerships, threat intelligence sharing, and collaborative incident response efforts contribute to a more resilient cybersecurity ecosystem, where collective defense is paramount in addressing the scale and complexity of modern cyber threats.

As the attack surface expands with the proliferation of connected devices, the security of the Internet of Things (IoT) is a growing concern. IoT devices, ranging from smart appliances to industrial sensors, present unique security challenges due to their often limited computational resources and diverse deployment environments. Security standards and frameworks specific to IoT, along with the development of secure-by-design principles, are essential for mitigating the inherent risks associated with the increasing connectivity of IoT ecosystems.

Regulatory frameworks and compliance requirements continue to shape cybersecurity practices, with a growing emphasis on data privacy. Regulations such as the General Data Protection Regulation (GDPR) and the California Consumer Privacy Act (CCPA) mandate organizations to implement robust data protection measures and disclose data breaches promptly. The intersection of cybersecurity and privacy underscores the importance of a holistic and compliance-driven approach to safeguarding sensitive information.

In conclusion, the exploration of emerging technologies and trends in cybersecurity reveals a landscape characterized by innovation, complexity, and the ongoing evolution of both threats and defenses. From the integration of artificial intelligence and machine learning to the challenges posed by 5G and quantum computing, organizations must navigate a dynamic environment that demands adaptability and strategic foresight. By embracing these emerging technologies, adopting collaborative security approaches, and staying abreast of regulatory developments, organizations can fortify their cybersecurity postures and proactively address the intricacies of the modern threat landscape.

Chapter 2: Understanding Common Vulnerabilities

Defining vulnerabilities in the context of software development.
Vulnerabilities in the realm of software development encompass a wide array of weaknesses and susceptibilities that expose computer systems and applications to potential threats and compromise. These vulnerabilities arise from flaws in the design, implementation, or configuration of software, providing avenues for malicious actors to exploit and compromise the integrity, confidentiality, and availability of information and resources. One fundamental category of vulnerabilities lies in coding errors, where developers inadvertently introduce bugs, logical flaws, or insecure practices during the software development lifecycle. Such errors may include buffer overflows, input validation issues, and insecure data storage mechanisms, all of which can be exploited by attackers to execute arbitrary code, inject malicious payloads, or gain unauthorized access.

Additionally, architectural vulnerabilities contribute to the susceptibility of software systems, involving shortcomings in the overall design and structure of applications. Weaknesses in authentication and authorization mechanisms, for instance, can permit unauthorized access to sensitive data or functionalities, posing a significant risk to the security posture of the software. Insecure communication channels, such as the use of unencrypted protocols, also fall within this category, enabling eavesdropping and tampering by malicious entities. Furthermore, software systems may be vulnerable to external threats due to insufficient input validation, allowing attackers to inject malicious data and manipulate the behavior of the application.

Another critical aspect of vulnerabilities in software development relates to the dependencies and third-party components that applications rely on. These external components may contain their own vulnerabilities, and if not regularly updated or patched, they can serve as entry points for attackers seeking to exploit known weaknesses. Consequently, software developers must diligently manage and monitor the security of these dependencies to mitigate the risk of exploitation. Moreover, configuration vulnerabilities, stemming from misconfigurations of software components or underlying infrastructure, create opportunities for attackers to bypass security controls, escalate privileges, or launch denial-of-service attacks.

The web application domain introduces a distinct set of vulnerabilities, with common issues such as Cross-Site Scripting (XSS) and Cross-Site Request Forgery (CSRF) posing significant threats. XSS vulnerabilities, for instance, arise when an application fails to properly validate and sanitize user input, allowing attackers to inject malicious scripts that can be executed within the context of a user's browser. CSRF vulnerabilities, on the other hand, enable attackers to forge and submit unauthorized requests on behalf of a legitimate user, potentially leading to unauthorized actions or data manipulation.

In the context of software development, vulnerabilities are not solely limited to the code level but extend to the entire software supply chain. Supply chain vulnerabilities encompass risks associated with the acquisition, integration, and distribution of software components from external sources. Malicious actors may exploit the lack of visibility and control in the software supply chain to introduce backdoors, malware, or other forms of compromise, leading to widespread security incidents.

As the complexity of software ecosystems continues to grow, vulnerabilities also emerge in the form of human factors, encompassing errors, oversights, or intentional actions by individuals involved in the development process. Social engineering attacks, insider threats, and inadequate training on secure coding practices contribute to the human element of vulnerabilities. Developers, administrators, and other personnel involved in software development must be aware of security best practices and adhere to principles of least privilege to minimize the risk of human-induced vulnerabilities.

Addressing vulnerabilities in software development requires a holistic and proactive approach that spans the entire software development lifecycle. Secure coding practices, code reviews, and automated static analysis tools can help identify and remediate coding errors early in the development process. Robust authentication and authorization mechanisms, along with secure communication protocols, must be implemented to fortify the software architecture against external threats. Regular security assessments, including penetration testing and vulnerability scanning, are essential for identifying and mitigating vulnerabilities at various stages of the software lifecycle. Additionally, continuous monitoring and response mechanisms are critical to detect and address emerging threats and vulnerabilities in real-time.

In conclusion, vulnerabilities in software development encompass a multifaceted landscape of weaknesses that span coding errors, architectural flaws, external dependencies, configuration issues, and human factors. Recognizing and understanding these vulnerabilities is imperative for building resilient and secure software systems. By adopting a comprehensive and proactive approach to security throughout the software development lifecycle, organizations can mitigate the risk of exploitation and enhance the overall security posture of their software applications.

Understanding SQL injection and other common injection vulnerabilities.

SQL injection and other injection vulnerabilities represent a pervasive and critical class of security threats within the realm of web application development. SQL injection, in particular, is a technique where malicious actors exploit vulnerabilities in an application's handling of user-supplied input to inject arbitrary SQL code into the backend database queries. This can lead to unauthorized access, manipulation, or exfiltration of sensitive data stored in the database. The crux of SQL injection lies in inadequate input validation and sanitization, allowing attackers to craft malicious input that manipulates the structure and logic of SQL queries executed by the application. By injecting specially crafted SQL statements, attackers can bypass authentication mechanisms, retrieve or modify data, and even execute arbitrary commands on the underlying database server.

Beyond SQL injection, injection vulnerabilities manifest in various forms, including but not limited to command injection, LDAP injection, and XPath injection. Command injection occurs when untrusted input is directly concatenated with system commands, enabling attackers to execute arbitrary commands on the host operating system. This type of vulnerability is particularly prevalent in applications that utilize user input to construct command-line commands without proper validation. LDAP injection targets applications that interact with LDAP (Lightweight Directory Access Protocol) servers, where attackers manipulate input to alter the structure of LDAP queries, leading to unauthorized access or information disclosure. XPath injection exploits weaknesses in applications that use XPath (XML Path Language) to query XML data, allowing attackers to modify queries and potentially extract sensitive information.

The root cause of injection vulnerabilities often lies in the failure to properly separate data from executable code. When user input is not adequately validated, sanitized, or parameterized, it becomes susceptible to manipulation by malicious actors. In the context of SQL injection, for instance, input fields that directly incorporate user input into SQL queries without proper validation create opportunities for attackers to insert malicious SQL code. The use of prepared statements and parameterized queries, where user input is treated as data rather than executable code, represents a fundamental mitigation strategy against injection vulnerabilities. Additionally, input validation and sanitization mechanisms, such as white-listing acceptable input and escaping special characters, play a crucial role in preventing injection attacks.

The impact of injection vulnerabilities extends beyond unauthorized data access and manipulation to encompass broader security risks, including remote code execution, denial of service, and the potential compromise of the entire application or server. As web applications become more complex and interconnected, the exploitation of injection vulnerabilities can have cascading effects, affecting not only the confidentiality and integrity of data but also the availability and functionality of the entire system.

Mitigating injection vulnerabilities requires a comprehensive and layered approach to security. Secure coding practices, such as input validation, parameterized queries, and proper error handling, should be ingrained in the software development lifecycle. Developers must be vigilant in validating and sanitizing all user-supplied input, ensuring that it adheres to expected formats and values. Moreover, the principle of least privilege should be applied to database and system accounts, minimizing the potential impact of successful injection attacks. Regular security assessments, including penetration testing and code reviews, are essential for identifying and addressing injection vulnerabilities proactively.

Web application firewalls (WAFs) also play a vital role in mitigating injection attacks by inspecting and filtering incoming HTTP traffic for malicious patterns and payloads. However, reliance solely on WAFs is not a panacea, as they may have limitations and cannot substitute for robust coding practices. Organizations must prioritize the education and training of developers, administrators, and other personnel involved in web application development to foster a security-conscious culture and instill awareness of injection vulnerabilities and best practices.

In conclusion, injection vulnerabilities, including the notorious SQL injection, pose significant threats to the security of web applications. The consequences of successful exploitation can range from unauthorized data access to remote code execution, highlighting the need for robust mitigation strategies. Through secure coding practices, input validation, parameterized queries, and continuous security assessments, organizations can fortify their web applications against injection vulnerabilities and build a more resilient defense against evolving cyber threats.

Exploring the types of XSS attacks and their consequences.

Cross-Site Scripting (XSS) stands as a persistent and pervasive threat in the realm of web security, encompassing various types of attacks with distinct methods and consequences. One common form of XSS is reflected XSS, where malicious scripts are injected into a web application and then reflected back to users in the application's response. This type of attack typically relies on tricking users into clicking on a crafted link that contains the malicious payload. Once executed, the injected script runs within the context of the user's browser, enabling attackers to steal sensitive information, such as login credentials or session tokens, and manipulate the content presented to the user.

Stored XSS represents another variant, wherein the malicious script is permanently stored on the target server, awaiting execution when a user accesses the compromised page. This type of XSS attack is particularly potent as it can impact multiple users who visit the affected page. Attackers often exploit vulnerabilities in input validation and sanitization mechanisms, injecting malicious scripts that persistently alter the behavior of the application for subsequent users. Consequences of stored XSS attacks range from the theft of sensitive user data to the facilitation of more sophisticated attacks, such as session hijacking or defacement of web pages.

Dom-based XSS, on the other hand, involves the manipulation of the Document Object Model (DOM) within a user's browser. Instead of targeting the server-side code or response, attackers inject malicious scripts that directly manipulate the DOM, altering the behavior of the web page dynamically. This type of XSS can lead to a range of consequences, including the theft of user data, redirection to malicious websites, or the execution of unauthorized actions on behalf of the user. Dom-based XSS attacks often exploit client-side vulnerabilities and may be more challenging to detect through traditional server-side security measures.

XSS attacks also exhibit variations based on the context in which they occur. For example, in non-persistent or stored XSS attacks, the injected script is embedded in the web application and delivered to users who access a specific, compromised URL. In contrast, in DOM-based XSS attacks, the malicious payload manipulates the client-side behavior of the web page within the user's browser, making detection and prevention more complex. Consequences of these attacks can extend beyond individual user compromises to impact the overall security and trustworthiness of the web application.

The consequences of XSS attacks are far-reaching, affecting both users and organizations. One of the primary outcomes is the compromise of sensitive user information, including usernames, passwords, and session tokens. Attackers leverage XSS vulnerabilities to steal authentication credentials, leading to unauthorized access to user accounts. Session hijacking, where attackers take control of a user's active session, is a particularly severe consequence, as it allows malicious actors to impersonate legitimate users and perform actions on their behalf.

Financial repercussions also accompany XSS attacks, especially when attackers exploit the compromised web application to engage in fraudulent activities or conduct transactions on behalf of users. The trust and credibility of the affected organization may be undermined, leading to reputational damage and potential loss of business. Additionally, XSS vulnerabilities can be exploited to deliver secondary payloads, such as malware or ransomware, further amplifying the scope and severity of the impact.

Moreover, XSS attacks serve as a gateway for other malicious activities. Once an attacker establishes a foothold through XSS, they may escalate their privileges, pivot to other attack vectors, or engage in lateral movement within the network. The compromised web application can become a launchpad for broader attacks, including data breaches, network intrusions, or the compromise of additional web services.

Mitigating XSS attacks requires a multifaceted approach, combining secure coding practices, input validation, and the implementation of security controls at various layers of the application architecture. Developers must adhere to best practices such as output encoding, input validation, and the use of Content Security Policy (CSP) to restrict the execution of scripts to trusted sources. Web application firewalls (WAFs) play a crucial role in detecting and blocking malicious payloads, providing an additional layer of defense against XSS attacks.

Educating developers and organizations about the risks and consequences of XSS is paramount. Security training programs should emphasize secure coding practices and the importance of ongoing vulnerability assessments and penetration testing. Additionally, automated tools can assist in identifying and remediating XSS vulnerabilities during the development lifecycle, helping organizations address potential issues before they reach production environments.

In conclusion, XSS attacks, in their various forms, represent a formidable threat to the security of web applications. The consequences of these attacks extend from the compromise of user data and credentials to financial losses, reputational damage, and the facilitation of broader malicious activities. To effectively mitigate XSS vulnerabilities, a comprehensive strategy involving secure coding practices, input validation, security controls, and ongoing education is imperative. As the digital landscape evolves, the resilience of web applications against XSS attacks becomes a critical factor in safeguarding user trust and organizational integrity.

The mechanics of CSRF attacks and potential risks.

Cross-Site Request Forgery (CSRF) attacks represent a significant threat to the security of web applications, exploiting the trust a website has in a user's browser. The mechanics of a CSRF attack involve an attacker tricking a victim into unknowingly submitting a malicious request on a target website where the victim is authenticated. Unlike other types of attacks, CSRF does not require the attacker to directly interact with the victim's credentials; instead, it leverages the existing session established between the user and the target website. The attacker crafts a malicious HTML or script, often embedded in a webpage or email, which, when accessed by the victim, causes an unauthorized action to be executed on the target website on behalf of the authenticated user.

The potential risks associated with CSRF attacks are diverse and can have severe consequences for both users and the targeted web applications. One common outcome is unauthorized actions performed on behalf of the victim, leading to the manipulation of sensitive data, account settings, or financial transactions. For instance, an attacker could forge requests to change the victim's email address, password, or perform financial transactions without the victim's knowledge or consent. CSRF attacks are particularly potent when targeting functionalities that have high-impact consequences, such as password changes, fund transfers, or account deletions.

Financial implications accompany CSRF attacks, especially when attackers manipulate the victim's session to perform fraudulent transactions. By exploiting the trust established between the user and the targeted website, attackers can initiate financial operations, purchase items, or transfer funds without the victim's awareness. This not only poses a direct financial risk to the user but can also result in reputational damage for the targeted organization, as users may attribute the fraudulent actions to negligence on the part of the website.

Moreover, CSRF attacks can be leveraged for broader security breaches, especially when targeting privileged functionalities within the web application. If an authenticated user with administrative privileges is subject to a CSRF attack, the attacker can perform actions with elevated permissions, such as creating or deleting user accounts, modifying access controls, or altering the configuration of the application. This escalation of privileges can lead to more severe security incidents, impacting the overall integrity and confidentiality of the web application.

In addition to direct financial and operational risks, CSRF attacks can be exploited to manipulate user data and settings, leading to a degradation of user trust and confidence in the affected web application. For example, an attacker could forge requests to change profile information, post unauthorized content, or tamper with privacy settings, creating a sense of insecurity and discomfort among users. This erosion of trust can have long-lasting consequences, affecting user retention, engagement, and the reputation of the targeted organization.

Mitigating CSRF attacks requires a comprehensive understanding of the underlying mechanisms and the implementation of effective countermeasures. One fundamental defense mechanism is the use of anti-CSRF tokens. These tokens are unique, unpredictable values embedded in web forms or included in HTTP requests, serving as a validation mechanism to ensure that the request originates from the legitimate user and not from a malicious source. When a user accesses a form or initiates a request, the anti-CSRF token is included, and the web application verifies its authenticity before processing the action. This mitigates the risk of unauthorized requests initiated by malicious actors.

Implementing SameSite cookie attributes is another crucial mitigation strategy against CSRF attacks. By setting the SameSite attribute to 'Strict' or 'Lax' in HTTP cookies, web developers can control when cookies are sent with cross-origin requests. This helps prevent attackers from exploiting the user's active session to forge requests on behalf of the victim. Additionally, secure coding practices such as utilizing proper authentication mechanisms, session management, and input validation contribute to a more robust defense against CSRF attacks.

Web application firewalls (WAFs) also play a vital role in detecting and blocking CSRF attacks by monitoring and analyzing HTTP traffic for suspicious patterns and behaviors. However, relying solely on WAFs is not sufficient, and a defense-in-depth approach, combining multiple layers of protection, is recommended. Regular security assessments, including penetration testing and code reviews, help identify and remediate potential CSRF vulnerabilities during the development lifecycle, reducing the likelihood of successful attacks in production environments.

Educating developers, administrators, and users about CSRF risks and prevention measures is essential for building a security-conscious culture. Developers must be aware of secure coding practices and incorporate anti-CSRF mechanisms into their applications. Administrators should configure web servers and applications securely, and users should be cautious about clicking on unfamiliar links and accessing content from untrusted sources. A collaborative and informed approach is crucial for effectively mitigating the risks associated with CSRF attacks and enhancing the overall security posture of web applications.

Identifying and avoiding common security misconfigurations.

Identifying and avoiding common security misconfigurations is a paramount aspect of establishing a robust defense against cyber threats. Security misconfigurations occur when systems, applications, or network devices are not set up or maintained securely, leaving vulnerabilities that attackers can exploit. One prevalent area of concern is the misconfiguration of web servers, where default settings or unnecessary features may be left enabled, exposing potential attack vectors. For example, leaving directory listing enabled or using default credentials for administrative interfaces can provide unauthorized access to sensitive information. Identifying and mitigating these misconfigurations requires a thorough review of server configurations, regular audits, and adherence to security best practices.

Similarly, misconfigurations in cloud environments pose significant risks as organizations increasingly migrate to cloud-based infrastructures. The complexity of cloud services and the shared responsibility model necessitate careful configuration to prevent unintended exposure of data or services. Inadequate access controls, overly permissive permissions, and misconfigured storage buckets are common pitfalls that can lead to data breaches or unauthorized access. Cloud misconfigurations highlight the importance of understanding the specific security implications of the chosen cloud platform and utilizing tools and services that assist in the detection and remediation of misconfigurations.

Database misconfigurations are another prevalent area of concern, with consequences ranging from data leaks to unauthorized access and manipulation. Open and unprotected database ports, weak authentication mechanisms, and overly permissive user privileges are common misconfigurations that attackers exploit. Regular security assessments, including penetration testing and vulnerability scanning, are crucial for identifying and addressing database misconfigurations. Additionally, organizations should adopt the principle of least privilege, ensuring that users and applications have only the necessary access to databases and associated resources.

Web application misconfigurations can have severe implications for security, as they often expose vulnerabilities that attackers can leverage to compromise sensitive data or execute arbitrary code. Misconfigured security headers, inadequate session management, and improper error handling are common issues that developers must address. Regular security testing, including dynamic analysis and static code reviews, aids in identifying and remediating web application misconfigurations. Employing automated tools and frameworks that assess the security posture of web applications can help organizations stay vigilant against evolving threats.

Network misconfigurations, including insecure firewall rules, open ports, and unencrypted communication, present opportunities for attackers to gain unauthorized access or eavesdrop on sensitive information. A comprehensive network security strategy involves regular audits of firewall configurations, adherence to the principle of least privilege, and the use of encryption protocols to protect data in transit. Network misconfigurations can be mitigated by employing intrusion detection and prevention systems, conducting regular security assessments, and staying informed about emerging threats and best practices in network security.

Operating system misconfigurations introduce vulnerabilities that attackers can exploit to compromise the overall security of a system. Default configurations, unnecessary services, and weak password policies are common misconfigurations that should be addressed during system setup and maintenance. Organizations must follow industry best practices for hardening operating systems, regularly apply security patches, and leverage configuration management tools to ensure consistency across multiple systems. Continuous monitoring and auditing of system configurations are essential for detecting and rectifying misconfigurations promptly.

Containerization and orchestration platforms, such as Docker and Kubernetes, have become integral components of modern application deployment. However, misconfigurations in these environments can lead to significant security risks. Insecure container images, overly permissive permissions, and misconfigured network policies are areas of concern. Organizations must adopt secure container development practices, regularly scan container images for vulnerabilities, and follow best practices for configuring container orchestration platforms. Additionally, ongoing monitoring and auditing of containerized environments help identify and remediate misconfigurations in real-time.

To avoid common security misconfigurations, organizations should implement a proactive and comprehensive security posture. This involves conducting regular security assessments, staying informed about the latest security vulnerabilities and best practices, and fostering a culture of security awareness among developers, administrators, and other personnel. Security misconfigurations are not static; they evolve with changes in technology, software, and threat landscapes. Therefore, organizations must embrace a continuous improvement mindset, incorporating security into their development and operational processes to reduce the risk of misconfigurations and enhance overall cybersecurity resilience.

Risks associated with weak authentication and session management.

Weak authentication and session management represent critical vulnerabilities that can have far-reaching consequences for the security of systems and applications. Authentication is the process of verifying the identity of users, ensuring that they are who they claim to be, while session management involves maintaining a secure connection between the user and the application throughout their interaction. Risks associated with weak authentication mechanisms are multifaceted and can lead to unauthorized access, identity theft, and a compromise of sensitive information. Weak or easily guessable passwords, the absence of multi-factor authentication (MFA), and inadequate account lockout policies contribute to the vulnerability of authentication processes. Attackers can exploit these weaknesses through methods such as brute-force attacks, password spraying, or credential stuffing, gaining unauthorized access to user accounts and potentially escalating their privileges within the system.

Moreover, weak authentication mechanisms can result in the compromise of entire systems or networks, especially when privileged accounts, such as administrator credentials, are inadequately protected. The use of default passwords or shared credentials across multiple accounts increases the risk of unauthorized access, enabling attackers to manipulate configurations, install malicious software, or exfiltrate sensitive data. Credential compromise is a common vector for various cyber threats, including ransomware attacks and data breaches, as attackers leverage weak authentication to infiltrate and maneuver within targeted environments.

In addition to the risks associated with weak authentication, inadequate session management introduces vulnerabilities that can be equally detrimental to the security of applications and user data. Session management involves the creation, maintenance, and termination of user sessions, typically facilitated through session tokens or cookies. When session management is weak, attackers can exploit session-related vulnerabilities to hijack active sessions, impersonate users, or gain unauthorized access to sensitive areas of an application. Insufficiently randomized session tokens, long session timeouts, and the absence of secure session termination mechanisms contribute to these vulnerabilities.

One significant risk associated with weak session management is session hijacking, where attackers intercept or steal session tokens to gain unauthorized access to a user's account. This can occur through various means, such as man-in-the-middle attacks, session sidejacking, or the compromise of session tokens stored on the client side. Once an attacker successfully hijacks a session, they can impersonate the legitimate user, perform actions on their behalf, and potentially access sensitive information or functionalities within the application. The impact of session hijacking extends beyond individual accounts, affecting the overall trust and integrity of the application.

Furthermore, weak session management can lead to session fixation attacks, where attackers set or manipulate session identifiers to control a user's session. This type of attack allows malicious actors to force users to authenticate with predetermined session identifiers, potentially leading to unauthorized access or session hijacking. Developers must implement secure session management practices, including the use of strong, random session tokens, short session timeouts, and secure session termination mechanisms to mitigate these risks.

Additionally, insufficient protection against session replay attacks poses another threat associated with weak session management. In a session replay attack, attackers intercept and later replay legitimate session data to gain unauthorized access. This can occur when session data is not adequately protected during transmission or when predictable patterns in session tokens allow attackers to predict or reuse valid session information. Implementing secure communication protocols, such as HTTPS, and incorporating anti-replay mechanisms are essential measures to prevent session replay attacks and enhance the overall security of session management.

Mitigating the risks associated with weak authentication and session management requires a holistic approach that combines technical measures, best practices, and user education. Strong authentication mechanisms, including the use of complex passwords, MFA, and secure account lockout policies, are fundamental to thwarting credential-based attacks. Organizations should enforce password policies that encourage the use of unique, non-trivial passwords and regularly educate users about the importance of strong authentication practices.

Effective session management involves the implementation of secure session token generation, transmission, and storage practices. Developers must ensure that session tokens are sufficiently random, securely transmitted over encrypted channels, and stored securely on the client side. Regular security assessments, including penetration testing and code reviews, aid in identifying and addressing authentication and session management vulnerabilities during the development lifecycle. Additionally, organizations should adopt security frameworks and standards, such as OAuth and OpenID Connect, to enhance the security of authentication and session management in their applications.

Continuous monitoring and auditing of authentication and session management processes are crucial for detecting and responding to potential threats in real-time. Security information and event management (SIEM) systems can help organizations track and analyze authentication and session-related events, enabling timely identification of suspicious activities and proactive response to potential security incidents.

In conclusion, the risks associated with weak authentication and session management are multifaceted and pose significant threats to the security of systems and user data. From unauthorized access and identity theft to the compromise of sensitive information, the consequences of these vulnerabilities are severe. By implementing strong authentication mechanisms, secure session management practices, and a culture of security awareness, organizations can mitigate these risks and build a more resilient defense against evolving cyber threats.

Understanding the dangers of insecure direct object references.

Insecure Direct Object References (IDOR) constitute a pervasive and potentially severe security vulnerability that exposes sensitive information and functionality within web applications. This vulnerability arises when an application provides improper or insufficient authorization checks, allowing attackers to directly access and manipulate objects or resources without proper authentication. The danger lies in the unauthorized access to sensitive data, files, or functionalities that are not intended to be accessible to the user. Unlike other security vulnerabilities that involve exploiting weaknesses in authentication or session management, IDOR attacks allow adversaries to bypass these controls entirely, posing a significant risk to the confidentiality and integrity of the application and its data.

One common manifestation of IDOR vulnerabilities occurs in web applications with inadequate access controls on resources such as files, databases, or user accounts. For instance, a web application may use predictable or easily guessable identifiers for objects, such as sequential numbers or simple strings, making it straightforward for attackers to manipulate these identifiers and access unauthorized resources. Attackers can exploit such weaknesses to view or modify sensitive information, such as other users' private data, confidential documents, or administrative functionalities, leading to unauthorized disclosure or manipulation of critical resources.

File upload functionalities within web applications are particularly susceptible to IDOR vulnerabilities, presenting a significant danger when not adequately secured. Insecure file uploads may allow attackers to upload malicious files or overwrite existing files, potentially leading to the execution of arbitrary code on the server or the dissemination of malicious content. Moreover, attackers may leverage IDOR vulnerabilities in file upload functionalities to access restricted files, including configuration files, credentials, or sensitive documents, thereby escalating the impact of the attack.

Furthermore, IDOR vulnerabilities can have cascading effects when integrated with business logic flaws, enabling attackers to perform actions that were not intended or authorized. For instance, in an online shopping application, an attacker might manipulate object references to view or modify the contents of other users' shopping carts, leading to unauthorized access or manipulation of purchase orders. Similarly, in a healthcare application, an attacker exploiting IDOR could access medical records of other patients, breaching privacy and violating regulatory requirements.

The dangers associated with IDOR vulnerabilities extend beyond the compromise of sensitive data to encompass potential financial losses, reputational damage, and regulatory non-compliance. In industries where compliance with privacy regulations such as GDPR or HIPAA is imperative, the unauthorized access and disclosure of personal or healthcare information through IDOR vulnerabilities can result in severe legal consequences and financial penalties. Additionally, the loss of customer trust and confidence in the security of an application can lead to reputational damage, impacting an organization's brand and market position.

Mitigating the dangers of IDOR vulnerabilities requires a multifaceted approach that encompasses secure coding practices, robust access controls, and thorough security testing. Developers must implement proper authorization checks to ensure that users can only access the resources and functionalities that they are authorized to use. This involves employing proper session management, validating user permissions, and adopting the principle of least privilege, granting users only the minimum level of access necessary for their roles. Security awareness training for developers is crucial to instill an understanding of the risks associated with IDOR and foster a security-conscious mindset throughout the development lifecycle.

Securely implementing unique and unpredictable identifiers for objects is a fundamental practice to mitigate IDOR vulnerabilities.

By using random and unguessable references, developers can prevent attackers from predicting or manipulating identifiers to access unauthorized resources. File upload functionalities should enforce strict validation and sanitization of file types, implement secure file naming conventions, and utilize appropriate storage mechanisms to prevent unauthorized access or execution of uploaded files.

Incorporating automated security testing, such as static analysis tools and dynamic application security testing (DAST), into the development process aids in identifying and addressing IDOR vulnerabilities. Regular security assessments, including penetration testing, are essential to simulate real-world attack scenarios and identify potential weaknesses in access controls and object references. Additionally, organizations should implement web application firewalls (WAFs) to detect and block anomalous or malicious activities related to IDOR, providing an additional layer of defense against potential attacks.

Continuous monitoring and logging of application activities help in detecting and responding to potential IDOR attacks in real-time. Anomalies in user behavior or unexpected access patterns can be indicative of unauthorized object references, triggering alerts for further investigation. Incorporating threat modeling during the design phase of the application enables developers to proactively identify and address potential IDOR vulnerabilities by considering the interaction between various components and user roles.

In conclusion, the dangers of Insecure Direct Object References are profound, posing a significant risk to the confidentiality, integrity, and availability of web applications and their data. The potential for unauthorized access, data manipulation, and business logic abuse underscores the importance of addressing IDOR vulnerabilities proactively. Through secure coding practices, robust access controls, thorough testing, and a security-aware development culture, organizations can mitigate the dangers associated with IDOR and build more resilient and secure web applications in an ever-evolving threat landscape.

Debunking the myth of security through obscurity.

Debunking the myth of security through obscurity requires a critical examination of the concept and a recognition of its limitations within the broader context of cybersecurity. The notion of security through obscurity suggests that a system's security is enhanced by keeping its inner workings, algorithms, or implementation details hidden from potential attackers. Proponents of this concept argue that if the design and implementation of a system are obscure or not widely known, it becomes more challenging for attackers to identify vulnerabilities and exploit them. However, this approach fundamentally rests on a flawed assumption and has been widely discredited within the field of cybersecurity.

One of the primary criticisms of security through obscurity is that it does not align with the principles of transparency and openness that underpin effective security practices. In a truly secure system, the security mechanisms should be robust and capable of withstanding scrutiny, even when the inner workings are known to the public. Relying on secrecy as a primary defense measure introduces a false sense of security, as it assumes that attackers will never discover or understand the concealed aspects of the system. History has shown that determined attackers can reverse engineer, analyze, or discover hidden elements through various means, rendering the supposed protection offered by obscurity ineffective in the long run.

Furthermore, security through obscurity tends to discourage transparency and collaboration, hindering the ability of the broader cybersecurity community to contribute to the improvement and fortification of security measures. In an open and collaborative environment, security researchers, developers, and experts can collectively assess, analyze, and improve the security of systems by identifying vulnerabilities, proposing solutions, and sharing best practices. Obscuring details about a system impedes this collaborative effort, limiting the pool of expertise that can contribute to its security and increasing the likelihood of undiscovered vulnerabilities persisting.

Another critical flaw in the security through obscurity mindset is its vulnerability to the inevitability of information disclosure. Over time, as systems evolve, personnel change, or circumstances shift, the details of a system's implementation are likely to become known to a wider audience. This may occur through accidental leaks, reverse engineering efforts, or insider threats. Once the obscurity is compromised, the security of the system is left exposed, and the lack of foundational security measures becomes glaringly evident. Relying solely on secrecy as a protective measure neglects the dynamic and evolving nature of cybersecurity threats, leaving systems vulnerable to exploitation.

The myth of security through obscurity also fails to account for the reality of targeted attacks and advanced persistent threats (APTs). Determined adversaries with sophisticated capabilities and resources are unlikely to be deterred by the lack of visibility into a system's internals. APTs are known for their patience, adaptability, and persistence, and they often invest significant resources in understanding and overcoming security measures. Obscuring details about a system may momentarily slow down less sophisticated attackers, but it provides little resistance against persistent, well-funded adversaries who are motivated to breach security barriers.

A notable example that underscores the shortcomings of security through obscurity is the field of cryptography. Cryptographic algorithms are designed to be secure based on their mathematical properties rather than relying on secrecy. The security of widely-used cryptographic algorithms, such as those employed in encryption standards, is rooted in their ability to withstand intense scrutiny and analysis by the cryptographic community. Obscuring the details of cryptographic algorithms would not enhance their security; instead, it is their openness to scrutiny and continuous evaluation that instills confidence in their reliability.

In contrast, a more effective approach to cybersecurity embraces the principles of defense in depth, resilience, and proactive threat mitigation. This involves implementing multiple layers of security controls, regularly patching and updating systems, conducting security audits and assessments, and fostering a culture of security awareness and continuous improvement. These measures are based on the understanding that security is a dynamic and evolving discipline, requiring adaptability and a commitment to addressing vulnerabilities as they arise, rather than relying on secrecy to maintain an illusion of invulnerability.

Moreover, the security community widely recognizes that disclosing vulnerabilities responsibly, often referred to as responsible disclosure, is a crucial aspect of improving security. Responsible disclosure allows security researchers to report vulnerabilities to the affected organizations, giving them an opportunity to patch or mitigate the issues before public disclosure. This collaborative approach acknowledges that the discovery of vulnerabilities is inevitable and seeks to address them constructively, rather than perpetuating the illusion that security can be maintained through the concealment of weaknesses.

In conclusion, the myth of security through obscurity rests on an outdated and misguided approach to cybersecurity. It fails to withstand scrutiny in the face of determined attackers, discourages collaboration and transparency, and does not align with the principles of openness and adaptability that underpin effective security practices. A more robust and realistic approach to cybersecurity involves implementing a combination of well-designed security controls, proactive threat mitigation, responsible disclosure practices, and a commitment to continuous improvement. As the cybersecurity landscape evolves, organizations and security professionals must embrace these principles to build resilient and effective security postures.

Risks associated with file uploads and potential exploits.

The risks associated with file uploads in web applications are multifaceted, encompassing a range of potential exploits that can lead to severe security vulnerabilities. File upload functionalities, while essential for user interactions and data sharing, introduce challenges related to validation, security controls, and the potential for abuse by malicious actors. One of the primary risks is the possibility of uploading malicious files that can compromise the integrity and security of the hosting environment. Malicious files may include various forms of malware, such as viruses, worms, or trojans, capable of exploiting vulnerabilities in the server or client-side systems. Attackers often attempt to disguise malicious files as benign content, leveraging the trust established by file upload features to introduce threats into the application and compromise user data or the underlying infrastructure.

Beyond the direct threat of uploading malicious files, file upload functionalities can be exploited to conduct attacks such as remote code execution (RCE). In cases where the application does not adequately validate and sanitize file inputs, attackers can upload files containing executable code. Once uploaded, these files may be executed by the server, leading to arbitrary code execution and potentially granting attackers unauthorized access to the system. RCE exploits are particularly dangerous as they can enable attackers to take full control of the server, manipulate data, and execute arbitrary commands with the privileges of the compromised application.

File upload vulnerabilities also expose the risk of server-side request forgery (SSRF) attacks. By uploading files that trigger SSRF, attackers can manipulate the application to make unauthorized requests to internal resources or external systems. This can lead to information disclosure, unauthorized access to internal services, or exploitation of vulnerabilities in other components of the infrastructure. SSRF exploits can be used to bypass network restrictions, access sensitive data, or perform reconnaissance activities within the target environment.

Moreover, insufficient file type validation poses a significant risk, allowing attackers to upload files with disguised or unexpected extensions. By manipulating the file type information, attackers can upload files that the application incorrectly processes or interprets. For example, an attacker might upload a file with a ".jpg" extension that is actually an executable script. This type of exploit, known as content spoofing or content type confusion, can result in the execution of unintended actions, disclosure of sensitive information, or the injection of malicious content into the application.

Insecure file storage practices contribute to additional risks associated with file uploads. If uploaded files are stored in directories with inadequate access controls, attackers may exploit directory traversal vulnerabilities to access or manipulate files outside the intended storage location. This can lead to unauthorized access to sensitive files, data disclosure, or the compromise of other critical system components. In cases where uploaded files contain sensitive information, such as user credentials or proprietary data, insecure storage practices can have severe consequences for the confidentiality and integrity of the application and its users.

Furthermore, denial of service (DoS) attacks can be facilitated through file upload functionalities, particularly if the application lacks proper size and content type restrictions. Attackers may attempt to overwhelm the system by uploading large or numerous files, consuming server resources and degrading the application's performance. DoS attacks not only disrupt the availability of the application for legitimate users but can also be used as a distraction tactic to divert attention from other malicious activities occurring within the compromised environment.

To mitigate the risks associated with file uploads, web applications must implement robust security controls throughout the entire lifecycle of the upload process. One crucial measure is enforcing strict file type validation, ensuring that only files with legitimate and expected extensions are accepted. Additionally, implementing content-type validation based on file signatures and utilizing file analysis tools can enhance the accuracy of file type identification, reducing the risk of content spoofing or type confusion.

Implementing file size restrictions is essential to prevent resource exhaustion and DoS attacks. By defining reasonable limits on file sizes, applications can thwart attempts to overwhelm the system with excessively large uploads. Furthermore, enforcing proper access controls on file storage directories helps prevent unauthorized access and manipulation of uploaded files. Developers should adhere to the principle of least privilege, ensuring that uploaded files are stored in directories with minimal permissions required for legitimate application functionality.

Security headers, such as Content Security Policy (CSP) and X-Content-Type-Options, can be leveraged to enhance the security of file upload functionalities. CSP allows web developers to specify which domains are considered valid sources for content, helping to mitigate the risk of malicious file inclusion or execution. X-Content-Type-Options is used to prevent browsers from interpreting files in ways that could lead to security vulnerabilities, particularly in cases of content type confusion.

Utilizing anti-virus and malware scanning tools during the file upload process adds an additional layer of defense against malicious content. These tools can identify and block files containing known malware signatures, reducing the likelihood of uploading malicious files that may compromise the security of the application and its users.

Conducting thorough security assessments, including penetration testing and code reviews, is imperative for identifying and addressing file upload vulnerabilities during the development lifecycle. Automated tools designed to detect vulnerabilities related to file uploads can assist in identifying potential weaknesses and ensuring that security controls are effectively implemented. Regular security audits and updates are essential to address emerging threats, vulnerabilities, and evolving attack techniques that could impact the security of file upload functionalities.

In conclusion, the risks associated with file uploads in web applications are diverse and require comprehensive mitigation strategies. From the potential upload of malicious files to the exploitation of vulnerabilities leading to RCE, SSRF, and content spoofing, the consequences of insecure file upload practices can be severe. By implementing robust security controls, conducting thorough assessments, and fostering a security-aware development culture, organizations can reduce the risks associated with file uploads and enhance the overall security posture of their web applications in an ever-evolving threat landscape.

Securing APIs against common vulnerabilities.

Securing APIs against common vulnerabilities is a critical aspect of building robust and trustworthy applications in the interconnected digital landscape. APIs (Application Programming Interfaces) play a central role in facilitating communication and data exchange between different software systems. However, the openness and accessibility of APIs also expose them to various security threats that, if left unaddressed, can lead to severe consequences such as unauthorized access, data breaches, and service disruptions.

One of the fundamental security considerations for APIs is proper authentication and authorization mechanisms. Inadequate or flawed authentication can result in unauthorized access to sensitive data and functionalities. API developers must implement strong authentication mechanisms, such as OAuth 2.0 or API keys, to ensure that only authorized users or applications can access the API resources. Additionally, enforcing granular authorization controls is crucial to restrict access based on the principle of least privilege, ensuring that users or systems have only the necessary permissions to perform specific actions.

Beyond authentication and authorization, API security demands the implementation of secure communication channels. Employing HTTPS (Hypertext Transfer Protocol Secure) with strong encryption protocols is essential to protect data transmitted between clients and APIs from eavesdropping and man-in-the-middle attacks. It also helps in preventing attackers from intercepting sensitive information, such as access tokens or user credentials, during transit. Regularly updating and patching cryptographic libraries is imperative to address vulnerabilities and ensure the continued effectiveness of encryption measures.

API developers should prioritize input validation to mitigate the risk of injection attacks, a prevalent and potentially devastating vulnerability. By validating and sanitizing input data, developers can prevent malicious actors from injecting malicious code or manipulating API requests to exploit vulnerabilities in the underlying systems. This is particularly important for APIs that process user-generated content or accept data from external sources, as injection attacks can lead to unauthorized access, data manipulation, or even the execution of arbitrary code.

Protection against SQL injection attacks is of paramount importance when dealing with APIs that interact with databases. Developers must employ parameterized queries or prepared statements to ensure that user input is properly sanitized before being included in SQL queries. Failure to address SQL injection vulnerabilities can result in unauthorized access to databases, data exfiltration, or the manipulation of sensitive information stored within the backend systems.

Similarly, protection against NoSQL injection is crucial for APIs interacting with NoSQL databases. Developers should validate and sanitize input data, utilize parameterized queries, and employ access controls to prevent attackers from exploiting vulnerabilities in the NoSQL database systems. Implementing proper error handling and logging practices assists in identifying and responding to injection attempts, providing valuable insights into potential security incidents.

Cross-Site Scripting (XSS) poses a significant threat to API security, especially when APIs deliver content to web browsers. To mitigate XSS vulnerabilities, developers must validate and sanitize user input, encode output to prevent script execution, and implement secure coding practices to avoid inadvertently introducing XSS vulnerabilities. Content Security Policy (CSP) headers can be leveraged to define and enforce a policy that mitigates the impact of XSS attacks by specifying valid sources for scripts and mitigating the risk of unauthorized code execution.

Securing APIs against Cross-Site Request Forgery (CSRF) attacks is crucial for preventing attackers from performing unauthorized actions on behalf of authenticated users. Developers should implement anti-CSRF tokens, validate the origin of incoming requests, and ensure that sensitive actions, such as state-changing operations, require explicit user consent. By incorporating anti-CSRF measures, APIs can protect against attackers tricking authenticated users into unintentionally performing actions on the API without their knowledge or consent.

Rate limiting and throttling mechanisms are effective defenses against brute-force and denial-of-service attacks targeting APIs. By imposing restrictions on the number of requests a user or IP address can make within a specified time frame, API providers can mitigate the risk of abuse and ensure the availability and performance of their services. Implementing these mechanisms requires careful consideration of user experience to avoid unintentional disruption of legitimate access.

Securing sensitive information in transit and at rest is a critical component of API security. Developers must utilize appropriate encryption techniques to protect data stored in databases or transmitted between systems. This includes encrypting API keys, access tokens, and any other sensitive information to prevent unauthorized access in case of data breaches. Regularly rotating encryption keys and credentials enhances security by limiting the impact of compromised or leaked credentials.

Security testing is an integral part of securing APIs against vulnerabilities. Regularly conducting penetration testing, code reviews, and security assessments helps identify and remediate potential weaknesses in the API implementation. Automated tools designed for API security testing can assist in scanning for common vulnerabilities and ensuring that security controls are effectively implemented. Continuous monitoring of API traffic and logs allows organizations to detect and respond to suspicious activities or potential security incidents in real-time.

The adoption of industry standards and best practices contributes to the overall security posture of APIs. Following the principles outlined in the OWASP API Security Top Ten, API developers can address common vulnerabilities systematically and proactively. Staying informed about emerging threats, security updates, and changes in the threat landscape is essential for adapting security measures to evolving risks.

API security is a shared responsibility that extends beyond the development phase. API providers and consumers must collaborate to ensure the secure integration of APIs into applications and services. API documentation should include clear and concise security guidelines, best practices, and recommendations for developers integrating with the API. Educating API consumers about secure coding practices, the importance of authentication, and the potential risks associated with certain API functionalities fosters a culture of security awareness throughout the development community.

In conclusion, securing APIs against common vulnerabilities requires a comprehensive and proactive approach that addresses authentication, authorization, secure communication, input validation, and protection against injection attacks. By implementing best practices, leveraging industry standards, conducting regular security testing, and fostering collaboration between API providers and consumers, organizations can build resilient and trustworthy APIs that withstand the evolving challenges of the cybersecurity landscape.

Chapter 3: Coding Defensively: Best Practices

Establishing and adhering to a set of secure coding guidelines.

Establishing and adhering to a set of secure coding guidelines is a fundamental pillar in building robust, resilient, and secure software applications. These guidelines serve as a blueprint for developers, outlining best practices and principles to follow during the software development lifecycle. A crucial aspect of secure coding is the proactive identification and mitigation of potential vulnerabilities and security risks from the early stages of development. Secure coding guidelines encompass a wide array of principles, covering areas such as authentication, authorization, input validation, secure communication, error handling, and more.

One cornerstone of secure coding guidelines is the principle of input validation. Validating and sanitizing user inputs is paramount in preventing common vulnerabilities such as injection attacks, where malicious code is injected into an application. By rigorously validating input data, developers can ensure that only expected and legitimate values are accepted, mitigating the risk of SQL injection, NoSQL injection, and other injection-based exploits. Additionally, input validation helps thwart Cross-Site Scripting (XSS) attacks by preventing the injection of malicious scripts into web applications, enhancing the overall security posture of the software.

Authentication and authorization mechanisms represent another critical area covered by secure coding guidelines. Effective authentication ensures that users are who they claim to be, preventing unauthorized access to sensitive data and functionalities. Secure coding guidelines guide developers in implementing robust authentication practices, including the use of strong password policies, multi-factor authentication (MFA), secure storage of credentials, and session management. Authorization guidelines complement authentication measures by defining and enforcing access controls, ensuring that users or systems have the appropriate permissions to perform specific actions based on their roles.

Secure communication practices play a pivotal role in protecting data in transit. Secure coding guidelines advocate for the use of secure communication protocols, such as HTTPS, to encrypt data exchanged between clients and servers. This helps prevent eavesdropping, man-in-the-middle attacks, and the unauthorized interception of sensitive information. Adherence to secure communication guidelines extends to the careful management of cryptographic keys, secure configuration of encryption algorithms, and periodic updates to address emerging vulnerabilities in cryptographic libraries.

Error handling is a crucial aspect of secure coding that is often overlooked. Secure coding guidelines emphasize the importance of providing meaningful error messages to developers and users without disclosing sensitive information that could aid attackers. Proper error handling helps prevent information leakage and assists in identifying and addressing issues during development and testing phases. By implementing secure error handling practices, developers can contribute to a more resilient and secure application that withstands potential attacks.

Secure coding guidelines also address the significance of secure file handling and storage practices. Developers are advised to avoid storing sensitive information, such as passwords or encryption keys, in plaintext. Instead, secure coding practices advocate for the use of secure storage mechanisms, such as hashing and encryption, to protect sensitive data. Additionally, guidelines provide recommendations for secure file uploads, preventing potential exploits related to file type validation, storage location, and access controls.

Concurrency and thread safety considerations are essential elements of secure coding guidelines, particularly in applications with multithreading or parallel processing. Guidelines provide insights into to avoiding race conditions, deadlocks, and other concurrency-related vulnerabilities. By adopting secure coding practices related to concurrency, developers contribute to the stability and reliability of the application under varying load conditions.

In the context of web applications, secure coding guidelines address common web vulnerabilities such as Cross-Site Scripting (XSS), Cross-Site Request Forgery (CSRF), and security misconfigurations. Developers are guided on implementing proper input validation to prevent XSS attacks, employing anti-CSRF tokens to protect against request forgery, and conducting regular security assessments to identify and remediate misconfigurations that could expose vulnerabilities. The goal is to establish a strong defense against common web-based exploits and create a more resilient web application environment.

Code reviews are an integral component of secure coding guidelines, emphasizing the importance of peer reviews to identify security vulnerabilities, coding errors, and deviations from established guidelines. Code reviews provide an opportunity for developers to share knowledge, learn from each other, and collectively enhance the security posture of the codebase. By integrating code reviews into the development process, organizations foster a collaborative environment that prioritizes security and continuous improvement.

Static code analysis and automated security testing tools complement secure coding guidelines by enabling developers to identify and address potential vulnerabilities in the codebase efficiently. These tools analyze source code or compiled binaries for security flaws, adherence to coding standards, and potential weaknesses. Integrating static code analysis into the development pipeline allows organizations to catch security issues early in the development process, reducing the likelihood of vulnerabilities making their way into the production environment.

Regular security training and awareness programs are advocated in secure coding guidelines to ensure that developers stay informed about evolving security threats, attack vectors, and best practices. By fostering a culture of security awareness, organizations empower developers to make security-conscious decisions throughout the development lifecycle. Security training programs cover topics such as secure coding practices, threat modeling, and the principles of least privilege, equipping developers with the knowledge and skills needed to create more secure software.

Continuous integration and continuous deployment (CI/CD) pipelines are incorporated into secure coding guidelines to automate the testing and validation of code changes before deployment. Automated testing ensures that security checks are consistently applied, and vulnerabilities are promptly identified and remediated. By integrating security checks into the CI/CD pipeline, organizations streamline the development process while maintaining a high level of security assurance.

In summary, establishing and adhering to secure coding guidelines is a comprehensive and ongoing effort that spans various aspects of software development. From input validation and authentication to secure communication, error handling, and beyond, these guidelines provide a framework for developers to build secure, resilient, and trustworthy applications. By incorporating secure coding practices into the development culture, leveraging automated testing tools, and fostering a commitment to continuous improvement, organizations can mitigate security risks and deliver software that meets the highest standards of security in an ever-evolving threat landscape.

The importance of validating and sanitizing user input.

The importance of validating and sanitizing user input in software development cannot be overstated, as it constitutes a foundational element of building secure and robust applications. User input, any data provided by users through various interfaces such as forms or API requests, is a potential vector for a wide range of security vulnerabilities and attacks. Effective validation and sanitization practices are paramount for preventing malicious exploitation of these vulnerabilities and ensuring the integrity, confidentiality, and reliability of the application.

One of the primary security risks associated with inadequate input validation is injection attacks, where malicious code is inserted into input fields with the intent of altering the behavior of the application. SQL injection (SQLi) is a well-known example, where attackers manipulate input to execute arbitrary SQL queries against a database. By validating and sanitizing user input, developers can thwart injection attacks, ensuring that input data adheres to expected formats and structures, and eliminating the possibility of injecting malicious code that could compromise the application's database or execute unauthorized operations.

In the context of web applications, Cross-Site Scripting (XSS) represents a pervasive threat that can be mitigated through effective input validation. XSS occurs when attackers inject malicious scripts into web pages that are later executed by unsuspecting users. Input validation helps prevent the injection of script tags or other malicious code into input fields, protecting users from potential attacks that could lead to the theft of sensitive information, session hijacking, or unauthorized actions on behalf of the user.

Furthermore, input validation is crucial for safeguarding against Cross-Site Request Forgery (CSRF) attacks. CSRF exploits the trust that a web application has in a user's browser by tricking it into making unintended and potentially harmful requests. By validating and verifying the integrity of input data, developers can implement measures such as anti-CSRF tokens, ensuring that requests originated from legitimate sources and preventing attackers from forging requests on behalf of authenticated users.

Insecure direct object references (IDOR) are another class of vulnerabilities that can be addressed through robust input validation. IDOR occurs when attackers manipulate input, such as URLs or form parameters, to gain unauthorized access to resources or data. By validating and sanitizing user input, developers can ensure that users are only able to access the data and resources for which they have proper authorization, mitigating the risk of unauthorized data exposure or manipulation.

Beyond security concerns, proper input validation is essential for maintaining data integrity and preventing unintended consequences within an application. Inadequate validation may lead to the acceptance of malformed or unexpected input, potentially causing data corruption, system errors, or erratic behavior. For instance, if an application expects numeric input for a calculation but receives non-numeric characters, the results may be unpredictable and compromise the application's functionality.

Effective input validation also contributes to the overall user experience by ensuring that users provide correct and expected input. By guiding users toward the correct format and structure of input data through validation messages and constraints, developers can enhance the usability of the application, reduce user errors, and minimize frustration. This not only improves the overall quality of the user interface but also promotes a positive user experience, which is integral to the success and adoption of any software application.

Moreover, input validation is an essential defense against unintentional vulnerabilities introduced by developers themselves. As developers build and update code, the risk of inadvertently introducing bugs or security weaknesses rises. Comprehensive input validation acts as a safety net, catching and preventing unintended vulnerabilities that may arise during the development process. It acts as a proactive measure to identify and address potential issues before they

can be exploited by malicious actors, saving developers time and resources in the long run.

The significance of input validation extends to the realm of compliance and regulatory requirements, especially in industries dealing
with sensitive data such as healthcare, finance, or personal information. Adherence to industry standards and regulations often mandates robust input validation practices to ensure the protection of
sensitive data, maintain privacy, and comply with legal requirements.
Failure to implement proper input validation may result in regulatory penalties, legal consequences, and damage to an organization's
reputation.

In the era of dynamic and interactive web applications, where
user input plays a central role in shaping the user experience, the importance of input validation becomes even more pronounced. Asynchronous JavaScript technologies, single-page applications, and rich
client-side interactions underscore the need for client-side and server-side input validation to prevent a range of security issues. By validating input on both the client and server sides, developers create
a layered defense mechanism that enhances security and reduces the
risk of exploitation.

While client-side validation provides immediate feedback to
users and improves responsiveness, it is imperative to recognize that
it can be bypassed by malicious actors. Therefore, server-side validation remains the primary line of defense against manipulation attempts and ensures that only valid and sanitized data reaches the
backend systems. The combination of client-side and server-side input validation represents a comprehensive approach that enhances
security while delivering a seamless and interactive user experience.

In conclusion, the importance of validating and sanitizing user
input is integral to the security, functionality, and user experience
of software applications. Robust input validation practices protect
against a wide array of security vulnerabilities, from injection attacks

to Cross-Site Scripting and beyond. Beyond security, proper input validation contributes to data integrity, user experience, and regulatory compliance. By incorporating thorough input validation into the development process, organizations can build software that not only meets security standards but also delivers a reliable, user-friendly, and compliant solution in an increasingly interconnected and dynamic digital landscape.

Developing effective error handling mechanisms.

Developing effective error handling mechanisms is a critical aspect of building robust and reliable software applications. Errors are an inevitable part of software development, arising from a variety of sources such as invalid inputs, unexpected conditions, system failures, or external dependencies. How an application handles errors directly impacts its resilience, user experience, and the ability to diagnose and rectify issues promptly. Effective error handling goes beyond simply reporting errors to users; it involves anticipating potential issues, providing meaningful feedback, logging relevant information, and maintaining a graceful degradation of functionality to ensure the application remains responsive and secure even in the face of unexpected events.

A foundational principle in effective error handling is providing clear and user-friendly error messages. When errors occur, users should be presented with messages that are comprehensible, concise, and guide them toward understanding the nature of the problem. Meaningful error messages not only contribute to a positive user experience but also assist users in reporting issues accurately, facilitating the troubleshooting process. Developers should avoid exposing technical details in user-facing error messages, as this information can be exploited by malicious actors. Instead, error messages should strike a balance between transparency and user-friendliness, conveying information without compromising security.

Beyond user-facing messages, effective error handling involves logging detailed information about errors for internal use. Logging is a crucial tool for developers and system administrators to diagnose issues, trace the root causes of errors, and monitor the health of the application. Logs should include relevant contextual information, such as the user involved, the specific operation being performed, timestamps, and any relevant environmental details. By incorporating this information into logs, developers gain valuable insights into the conditions leading to errors, enabling them to identify patterns, troubleshoot effectively, and iteratively improve the application's robustness.

Implementing a structured and consistent error-handling strategy throughout the application is vital for maintaining code readability, maintainability, and efficiency. Adopting a standardized approach allows developers to easily understand and navigate error-handling code, reducing the likelihood of overlooking critical details during the development process. Consistency in error handling extends to the use of appropriate error codes, status codes, and error classes, enabling developers to categorize and respond to errors systematically. This standardization facilitates collaboration among development teams, ensures a coherent approach to error handling across the application, and streamlines the debugging and maintenance processes.

A proactive approach to error handling involves anticipating potential issues and implementing mechanisms to prevent or mitigate them. Developers should incorporate input validation routines to check the validity of user inputs and prevent common vulnerabilities, such as injection attacks or data format issues. By validating inputs at the earliest possible stage, applications can avoid propagating invalid data throughout the system, reducing the likelihood of errors and enhancing overall security. Moreover, developers should anticipate potential failure points, such as network outages or external service disruptions, and implement appropriate fallback mechanisms or graceful degradation of functionality to maintain the application's usability during adverse conditions.

Effective error handling is closely tied to the concept of fault tolerance, which is the application's ability to continue operating in the presence of errors or failures. Implementing fault tolerance mechanisms involves designing the application to gracefully handle unexpected situations without crashing or compromising the overall user experience. Techniques such as retrying operations, implementing circuit breakers, and providing fallback mechanisms contribute to the fault tolerance of an application. These mechanisms are particularly crucial in distributed systems where dependencies on external services or components introduce additional points of failure.

In the context of web applications, the importance of client-side error handling cannot be understated. Client-side errors, such as those arising from JavaScript code execution, network issues, or user interactions, can significantly impact the user experience. Implementing effective client-side error handling involves capturing and logging errors, providing users with relevant feedback, and ensuring that errors do not result in the application entering an inconsistent or unusable state. Additionally, client-side error handling should encompass proper validation of user inputs to prevent common web vulnerabilities, such as Cross-Site Scripting (XSS) or Cross-Site Request Forgery (CSRF), and ensure a secure browsing experience for users.

A well-designed error handling strategy also involves considering the needs of different stakeholders, including developers, system administrators, and end-users. For developers, error messages and logs should convey actionable information, guiding them toward identifying and fixing the root causes of issues. System administrators benefit from logs that provide insights into the health and performance of the application, aiding in proactive monitoring, incident response, and infrastructure management. End-users, on the other hand, require user-friendly and informative error messages that assist them in understanding and resolving issues without unnecessary frustration.

Security considerations are integral to effective error handling, especially in scenarios where inadequate error handling can inadvertently expose sensitive information or contribute to security vulnerabilities. Error messages should avoid disclosing sensitive details about the internal workings of the application, as such information can be leveraged by attackers to exploit vulnerabilities. Instead, error messages should provide enough information for developers to diagnose issues while protecting sensitive data. Regular security assessments, code reviews, and penetration testing help identify and address potential security risks associated with error handling mechanisms, ensuring that the application remains resilient to malicious exploits.

Implementing effective error handling mechanisms requires ongoing testing and validation to ensure that the system behaves as expected under various conditions. Comprehensive testing includes unit testing, integration testing, and end-to-end testing to validate error-handling logic at different levels of the application stack. Additionally, incorporating stress testing and failure injection scenarios allows developers to evaluate the resilience of error handling mechanisms under adverse

conditions, preparing the application for real-world scenarios where errors and failures are inevitable.

In conclusion, developing effective error handling mechanisms is a multifaceted endeavor that spans user experience, system stability, security, and maintainability. Clear and user-friendly error messages, comprehensive logging practices, standardized approaches, proactive fault tolerance mechanisms, and consideration for different stakeholders are all essential elements of an effective error handling strategy. By integrating these practices into the development lifecycle and fostering a culture of continuous improvement, developers can create applications that not only handle errors gracefully but also provide a resilient and reliable user experience in the dynamic and complex landscape of modern software development.

Securing user sessions through encryption and tokenization. Securing user sessions through encryption and tokenization is a fundamental practice in safeguarding sensitive data and maintaining the integrity of user interactions within software applications. User sessions, which encompass the duration of a user's interaction with an application from login to logout, often involve the exchange of sensitive information such as authentication credentials, personal data, and session tokens. The implementation of robust security measures during these sessions is paramount to prevent unauthorized access, data breaches, and various forms of cyber threats.

Encryption plays a central role in securing user sessions by transforming data into an unreadable format that can only be deciphered by authorized entities possessing the appropriate cryptographic keys. For user sessions, the use of Transport Layer Security (TLS) or its predecessor, Secure Sockets Layer (SSL), is a common encryption mechanism employed to establish a secure and encrypted communication channel between the user's device and the application server. This ensures that data transmitted during the session, including login credentials and sensitive personal information, is protected from eavesdropping and man-in-the-middle attacks. The strength of encryption algorithms and the security of cryptographic key management directly influence the effectiveness of session encryption, requiring continuous attention to evolving security standards and practices.

Tokenization, another critical aspect of securing user sessions, involves replacing sensitive data with unique tokens that serve as references to the actual data stored in a secure location. In the context of user sessions, tokenization is often applied to handle authentication and authorization processes. Authentication tokens, commonly generated during the login process, serve as proof of a user's identity without exposing the actual credentials. Authorization tokens, on the other hand, convey the user's permissions and entitlements within the application, guiding access to specific resources or functionalities. By tokenizing sensitive data, applications reduce the risk of exposing valuable information even if the tokens themselves were intercepted.

Session tokens, a subset of tokens in the realm of user sessions, are pivotal in maintaining secure and authenticated interactions between users and applications. These tokens act as digital keys that validate a user's identity throughout the duration of their session. It is essential to implement secure practices for session token generation, storage, transmission, and expiration to prevent unauthorized access and session hijacking. Secure randomization techniques, cryptographic hashing, and periodic regeneration of session tokens contribute to the resilience of the session management system against various attack vectors.

To enhance the security of session tokens, the adoption of industry best practices such as JSON Web Tokens (JWT) and OAuth 2.0 becomes increasingly prevalent. JWT provides a standardized format for encoding claims between parties in a compact and self-contained manner, making it a popular choice for representing session tokens. OAuth 2.0, on the other hand, is an authorization framework that enables secure delegation of access, allowing applications to obtain limited access to user resources without exposing sensitive credentials. Integrating these standards into the session management process helps ensure interoperability, scalability, and adherence to security principles across diverse software ecosystems.

The implementation of secure session management extends beyond encryption and tokenization to encompass proper session lifecycle management. This involves the establishment of secure session initiation, where users are authenticated through robust mechanisms, such as multi-factor authentication, to fortify the initial phase of the session. Session persistence mechanisms, such as cookies or URL parameters, play a role in maintaining user state across multiple requests, requiring careful configuration to prevent security risks such as session fixation or session hijacking.

Periodic validation and reauthentication during a user session add an extra layer of security by ensuring that a session remains valid only as long as necessary and is not prone to long-term exploitation. Implementing session timeouts, whereby sessions are automatically terminated after a specified period of inactivity, mitigates the risk of unauthorized access due to abandoned or forgotten sessions. Furthermore, incorporating secure logout mechanisms helps users terminate their sessions explicitly, rendering stolen or compromised session tokens ineffective for unauthorized access.

In distributed and microservices architectures, where applications are composed of multiple independent services, securing user sessions demands additional attention to interoperability and communication between these services. Implementing secure protocols for inter-service communication, such as mutual TLS, ensures that session tokens and sensitive information exchanged between services are protected from interception or tampering. Additionally, centralized identity and access management systems, often built on standards like OpenID Connect, contribute to the secure propagation of identity and session information across distributed environments.

The secure handling of user sessions becomes particularly critical in scenarios involving Single Sign-On (SSO) and federated identity management. SSO enables users to authenticate once and gain access to multiple connected systems or applications without repeated logins. Federated identity management extends this concept across different domains or organizations, necessitating secure protocols and standards for exchanging authentication and session information. Security Assertion Markup Language (SAML) and OpenID Connect are widely adopted standards in federated identity scenarios, ensuring secure authentication and authorization across diverse environments.

However, despite the robust security measures in place, it is imperative to acknowledge and prepare for potential threats to user sessions. Session hijacking, where attackers gain unauthorized access to a user's active session, remains a persistent risk. Implementing secure practices such as regularly rotating session tokens, monitoring user activity for anomalies, and employing intrusion detection systems contribute to detecting and mitigating session hijacking attempts. Regular security audits and penetration testing help identify vulnerabilities and weaknesses in the session management system, enabling organizations to proactively address potential threats.

In conclusion, securing user sessions through encryption and tokenization is a multifaceted endeavor that involves a combination of technologies, standards, and best practices. Encryption safeguards the confidentiality of data in transit, while tokenization protects sensitive information and facilitates secure authentication and authorization processes. The secure management of session tokens, adherence to industry standards, proper session lifecycle management, and preparation for potential threats collectively contribute to building a robust and trustworthy session management system. As applications continue to evolve in complexity and interconnectedness, prioritizing the security of user sessions remains paramount in the ever-changing landscape of digital interactions.

Overview of HTTP security headers and their significance.

An overview of HTTP security headers and their significance reveals a crucial aspect of web application security, where the implementation of these headers plays a pivotal role in protecting against various vulnerabilities and enhancing the overall resilience of websites. HTTP security headers are additional pieces of information sent by a web server along with a web page to a browser, instructing the browser on how to behave and imposing security-related policies. These headers address a range of threats, from cross-site scripting (XSS) and clickjacking to content sniffing and man-in-the-middle attacks. Understanding the significance of these headers is integral to building a robust defense mechanism against common web application security risks.

One of the foundational HTTP security headers is the Content Security Policy (CSP). CSP allows website owners to define a set of rules that govern the types of content that a browser should execute or load on a web page. By mitigating the risks associated with XSS attacks, CSP helps prevent attackers from injecting and executing malicious scripts in the context of a trusted website. The significance of CSP lies in its ability to create a strong barrier against one of the most prevalent and damaging web application vulnerabilities, safeguarding both the website and its users from the potential exploitation of script injection vulnerabilities.

Another critical security header is the Strict-Transport-Security (HSTS) header. HSTS instructs the browser to communicate with the server only over secure, encrypted connections, mitigating the risk of man-in-the-middle attacks and eavesdropping. The significance of HSTS is evident in its role in enforcing HTTPS (HTTP Secure), ensuring that communication between the browser and the server is encrypted, and reducing the likelihood of attackers intercepting sensitive information, such as login credentials or session tokens, during transit. HSTS provides an additional layer of security by preventing the downgrade of connections from HTTPS to the less secure HTTP.

X-Content-Type-Options is another HTTP security header designed to enhance security by preventing browsers from interpreting files as a different MIME type than declared by the server. This header mitigates content sniffing attacks, where attackers attempt to manipulate the interpretation of files to execute malicious code. The significance of X-Content-Type-Options lies in its ability to reinforce the intended content type, ensuring that browsers do not deviate from the server's declaration and mitigating potential vulnerabilities associated with content-type mismatches.

Referrer-Policy is a security header that controls how much information is included in the HTTP Referer header when a user navigates from one page to another. This header helps protect user privacy and mitigate the risk of information leakage. The significance of Referrer-Policy is evident in scenarios where sensitive information, such as user-specific tokens or identifiers, should not be exposed in the Referer header. By configuring the appropriate referrer policy, developers can strike a balance between security and functionality, tailoring the level of information disclosed in the Referer header based on the specific requirements of the application.

Cross-Origin Resource Sharing (CORS) is addressed through the use of the Access-Control-Allow-Origin header, which controls which domains are permitted to access resources on a web page. The significance of CORS and the associated header lies in its role in preventing unauthorized cross-origin requests that could lead to data theft or unauthorized actions on behalf of authenticated users. By specifying which origins are allowed to access resources, developers can establish a secure and controlled environment, reducing the risk of Cross-Site Request Forgery (CSRF) and other cross-origin threats.

HTTP security headers also contribute to protecting against clickjacking attacks, where attackers attempt to trick users into interacting with hidden or disguised elements on a web page. The X-Frame-Options header addresses this threat by controlling whether a browser should allow a web page to be displayed within a frame or iframe. By preventing unauthorized framing of web pages, X-Frame-Options mitigates the risk of clickjacking and ensures that users interact with web content in the intended context. The significance of this header lies in its role in preserving the integrity of the user interface and preventing deceptive attacks that manipulate user interactions.

Cache-related security headers, such as Cache-Control and Pragma, contribute to mitigating the risk of sensitive information exposure through cached responses. These headers allow web developers to control how browsers cache content and whether caching is allowed. By configuring these headers appropriately, developers can prevent the caching of sensitive information, such as user-specific data or authentication tokens, and reduce the risk of attackers gaining unauthorized access to cached content. The significance of cache-related security headers is evident in their role in maintaining the confidentiality of information and preventing unintended data exposure.

The Expect-CT header addresses security concerns related to Certificate Transparency (CT), a system designed to detect and mitigate vulnerabilities in the SSL/TLS certificate issuance process. By enforcing certificate transparency, Expect-CT helps ensure that browsers only accept certificates that are logged in public, append-only CT logs. The significance of Expect-CT lies in its role in enhancing the security of SSL/TLS connections, preventing attackers from using misissued certificates and protecting users from potential man-in-the-middle attacks.

Feature Policy headers, such as Permissions-Policy and Feature-Policy, offer granular control over browser features and permissions, reducing the attack surface and limiting the potential impact of security vulnerabilities. These headers allow developers to specify which features are allowed or disallowed on a web page, providing a defense against abuse and exploitation of certain functionalities. The significance of Feature Policy headers lies in their role in fine-tuning the permissions granted to web features, enhancing security by restricting the capabilities that could be leveraged by attackers to execute malicious actions.

In conclusion, the significance of HTTP security headers in web application security is profound, as these headers collectively form a defense-in-depth strategy against a wide range of threats and vulnerabilities. From mitigating the risks of cross-site scripting and content sniffing to enforcing secure connections and preventing unauthorized framing, each security header plays a crucial role in fortifying the security posture of web applications. By understanding and implementing these headers appropriately, developers can create resilient, secure, and privacy-aware web applications that withstand the challenges posed by the dynamic and ever-evolving landscape of online threats.

Incorporating security aspects into code review processes.

Ensuring robust security measures within the code review process is imperative for safeguarding software applications against potential vulnerabilities and cyber threats. Integrating security aspects into code reviews demands a multifaceted approach that spans various stages of the software development lifecycle. One fundamental aspect involves instilling a security-first mindset among developers, emphasizing the importance of writing secure code from the outset. This cultural shift sets the foundation for a proactive approach to security rather than a reactive one, fostering a collective responsibility for identifying and addressing security concerns. Furthermore, incorporating security considerations into the code review process necessitates the adoption of established coding standards and best practices that are aligned with security frameworks and guidelines. This includes adherence to principles such as the Principle of Least Privilege, input validation, and proper error handling.

A critical element of integrating security into code reviews involves conducting thorough static code analysis to identify potential vulnerabilities before the code even reaches the testing phase. Static analysis tools can automatically scan code for security issues, offering a proactive means of detecting vulnerabilities, such as injection flaws, cross-site scripting, and insecure configurations. This preemptive approach enables developers to rectify security issues early in the development cycle, reducing the likelihood of these vulnerabilities making their way into the final product. Additionally, static analysis tools can be customized to align with specific security requirements and compliance standards, ensuring that code adheres to industry-specific security protocols.

In parallel, dynamic code analysis during the code review process is essential for assessing how the software behaves in real-world scenarios. This involves executing the code and analyzing its runtime behavior to uncover vulnerabilities that may not be apparent through static analysis alone. Dynamic analysis tools can simulate various attack scenarios, enabling developers to identify weaknesses related to authentication, authorization, and data protection. By combining static and dynamic analysis, organizations can establish a comprehensive security posture within their code review processes, addressing both inherent code vulnerabilities and runtime-related security concerns.

Moreover, a robust code review process that incorporates security aspects necessitates the involvement of security experts who possess a deep understanding of potential threats and attack vectors. These experts can contribute valuable insights during code reviews, offering guidance on secure coding practices and identifying potential security gaps that may elude the untrained eye. Collaborative efforts between developers and security experts foster knowledge sharing and contribute to a holistic understanding of security considerations throughout the development team.

As the software development landscape evolves, the integration of automated security testing tools and technologies becomes increasingly pivotal. Continuous integration (CI) and continuous delivery (CD) pipelines can be augmented with security-focused plug-ins and scripts that automatically trigger security scans as part of the build and deployment processes. This ensures that every code change undergoes a comprehensive security assessment, minimizing the risk of introducing new vulnerabilities during the development lifecycle. Automation not only enhances the efficiency of the code review process but also promotes consistency in applying security checks across all codebases.

Additionally, the incorporation of threat modeling into the code review process enhances the proactive identification of potential security threats and weaknesses. By systematically analyzing the system architecture and identifying potential points of vulnerability, developers can design and implement mitigations early in the development process. Threat modeling enables the development team to prioritize security measures based on potential risks, ensuring that resources are allocated to address the most critical threats first.

Furthermore, the establishment of secure coding guidelines and checklists serves as a foundational component of integrating security into code reviews. These guidelines can encompass a wide array of security principles, including data encryption, secure communication protocols, and secure coding patterns. By providing developers with a comprehensive set of guidelines, organizations can standardize secure coding practices and facilitate a consistent approach to security across development teams.

In conclusion, integrating security aspects into the code review process is an essential practice for organizations committed to developing secure and resilient software. This multifaceted approach encompasses cultural changes, the adoption of coding standards and best practices, static and dynamic code analysis, collaboration with security experts, automation through continuous integration and delivery pipelines, threat modeling, and the establishment of secure coding guidelines. By embedding security into the fabric of the development lifecycle, organizations can fortify their applications against potential vulnerabilities and cyber threats, ultimately enhancing the overall security posture of their software products.

Risks associated with outdated dependencies.

The utilization of outdated dependencies within software development introduces a myriad of risks that extend across various dimensions, encompassing security, functionality, and overall system stability. One of the primary concerns associated with outdated dependencies lies in the realm of security vulnerabilities. As technologies and programming languages evolve, developers continually discover and patch security flaws within libraries and frameworks. Consequently, failing to update dependencies regularly exposes software to known vulnerabilities that malicious actors can exploit. This can lead to severe consequences, ranging from unauthorized access to sensitive data and system manipulation to the compromise of the entire software ecosystem. Cybercriminals often target applications with outdated dependencies, as they represent low-hanging fruit with known weaknesses.

Beyond security, the functionality of a software application can be compromised when reliant on outdated dependencies. As the software landscape evolves, new features, optimizations, and bug fixes are introduced into libraries and frameworks. Outdated dependencies may lack these critical updates, hindering the software's ability to leverage advancements in technology and potentially causing compatibility issues with other components of the system. This can result in decreased performance, diminished user experience, and an inability to integrate seamlessly with emerging technologies. Software that falls behind in terms of functionality may struggle to meet user expectations and industry standards, putting the organization at a competitive disadvantage.

Furthermore, the risk associated with outdated dependencies extends to the realm of regulatory compliance. Many industries are subject to stringent regulations and standards governing data protection, privacy, and security. Utilizing outdated dependencies may lead to non-compliance with these regulations, exposing organizations to legal ramifications, fines, and damage to their reputation. Compliance requirements often mandate the use of up-to-date software components to ensure that security patches and privacy safeguards are promptly implemented. Neglecting these updates can result in a failure to meet regulatory standards and jeopardize the organization's standing within its respective industry.

Another significant risk stems from the lack of support and maintenance for outdated dependencies. As libraries and frameworks evolve, developers typically discontinue support for older versions to focus on more recent releases. This means that organizations relying on outdated dependencies may encounter challenges when seeking assistance, troubleshooting issues, or accessing relevant documentation. The absence of support can lead to prolonged downtime during critical incidents, hampering the organization's ability to respond swiftly to emerging challenges. Additionally, the lack of maintenance may result in a dwindling community of developers actively addressing issues and providing solutions, exacerbating the risk of unresolved problems and diminishing the overall resilience of the software.

Moreover, the financial implications of using outdated dependencies should not be overlooked. While the upfront costs of updating dependencies may seem burdensome, the long-term financial consequences of neglecting updates can be significantly more detrimental. Security breaches, loss of customer trust, and reputational damage can lead to substantial financial losses. The cost of remediating a security incident, addressing compliance violations, and recovering from the impact of a compromised software system far outweighs the investment required to keep dependencies current. Thus, organizations must recognize the economic value of maintaining a proactive and strategic approach to dependency management.

In the context of collaboration and open-source development, the risks associated with outdated dependencies also extend to the broader ecosystem. When developers contribute to open-source projects or utilize shared libraries, their actions impact not only their own software but also the larger community relying on those dependencies. Failure to update and contribute back to the ecosystem hinders the collective progress of software development, potentially perpetuating the propagation of vulnerabilities and suboptimal practices. Therefore, a commitment to maintaining and updating dependencies is not only an organizational responsibility but also a contribution to the health and sustainability of the wider software development community.

In conclusion, the risks associated with outdated dependencies in software development are multifaceted and encompass security vulnerabilities, compromised functionality, regulatory non-compliance, lack of support, financial implications, and implications for the broader development ecosystem. Proactive dependency management is crucial for mitigating these risks, ensuring that software remains resilient, secure, and capable of meeting evolving user expectations and industry standards. As organizations navigate the dynamic landscape of software development, prioritizing the timely update of dependencies is an essential practice for fostering a secure, efficient, and sustainable software ecosystem.

Best practices for reading, writing, and storing files securely.

Securing the processes of reading, writing, and storing files is paramount in software development to safeguard sensitive data, maintain data integrity, and prevent unauthorized access. When it comes to reading files securely, developers should adopt the principle of least privilege, ensuring that applications only have the necessary permissions to access specific files. Implementing proper input validation is essential to thwart common attacks such as directory traversal, where malicious actors attempt to access files outside the intended scope. Additionally, developers should utilize secure APIs for file operations to mitigate the risk of exploitation through low-level file system calls. Employing encryption for sensitive files during transmission and storage adds an extra layer of protection, rendering the data unreadable to unauthorized entities.

Writing files securely demands similar precautions. Developers must validate user input rigorously to prevent injection attacks that may lead to the creation or overwriting of files. File permissions should be set judiciously to restrict access and modification rights, adhering to the principle of least privilege. Employing unique file names and avoiding predictable patterns can thwart potential attackers attempting to exploit known file paths. Furthermore, implementing proper error handling mechanisms during file write operations is crucial to detect and address issues promptly, preventing unintended consequences.

Securely storing files involves considerations throughout the entire lifecycle, from creation to deletion. Employing strong encryption algorithms for data at rest ensures that even if unauthorized access occurs, the data remains indecipherable. Utilizing secure storage solutions and practices, such as encrypted file systems or secure cloud storage with robust access controls, adds an additional layer of protection. Regularly updating and patching software components involved in file storage, such as databases and file servers, is imperative to address known vulnerabilities and maintain a secure environment. Organizations should implement secure backup strategies to prevent data loss due to accidents, system failures, or cyberattacks, and ensure that backups themselves are appropriately protected.

Implementing proper access controls is fundamental in securing file operations. Role-based access control (RBAC) mechanisms should be employed to restrict access to files based on the principle of least privilege, ensuring that users only have the permissions necessary for their roles. Additionally, auditing and monitoring file access activities can help organizations detect and respond to unauthorized or suspicious behavior promptly. Regularly reviewing and updating access controls in response to changes in personnel, roles, or security requirements is crucial for maintaining the integrity of the access management system.

Securely handling file uploads is a critical aspect of web application security. Implementing size restrictions, content-type verification, and malware scanning for uploaded files helps prevent common vulnerabilities like denial-of-service attacks and malicious file execution. Storing uploaded files outside the web root directory mitigates the risk of attackers exploiting vulnerabilities to gain access to sensitive files. Renaming uploaded files to prevent overwriting and employing secure file naming conventions adds an extra layer of protection against potential attacks.

Secure file deletion is often an overlooked aspect of file management. Simply removing a file from the file system does not guarantee its complete elimination; residual data may still be recoverable. Employing secure deletion methods, such as overwriting the file with random data or utilizing file shredding tools, ensures that sensitive information is irreversibly erased. Additionally, incorporating proper access controls to prevent unauthorized users from deleting critical files is essential in maintaining data integrity.

In distributed systems, securely transmitting files between different components or services requires the implementation of secure communication protocols. Utilizing secure file transfer protocols such as SFTP (Secure File Transfer Protocol) or HTTPS ensures the confidentiality and integrity of the transmitted data. Employing encryption during file transmission protects against eavesdropping and man-in-the-middle attacks. Implementing proper authentication mechanisms for file transfers, such as the use of secure credentials and keys, ensures that only authorized entities can send or receive files.

Security awareness and education play a pivotal role in ensuring that development teams and system administrators understand and adhere to best practices for file handling. Regular training programs can empower personnel to recognize potential security risks, understand the importance of secure coding practices, and stay informed about the latest developments in file security. Emphasizing the significance of continuous learning and staying updated on security standards and best practices contributes to a proactive security culture within the organization.

In conclusion, securing the processes of reading, writing, and storing files is a multifaceted endeavor that requires a combination of secure coding practices, robust access controls, encryption, and continuous monitoring. Adhering to the principle of least privilege, implementing proper input validation, employing strong encryption algorithms, and ensuring secure transmission and storage are essential elements in fortifying file operations. Additionally, integrating secure practices for access controls, file uploads, and deletion, as well as fostering a security-aware culture within the organization, collectively contribute to a comprehensive and resilient approach to file security in software development.

Techniques for obscuring code to deter reverse engineering.
Obfuscating code is a practice employed by software developers to deter reverse engineering attempts and protect intellectual property. This technique involves intentionally making the source code difficult to understand while preserving its functionality. One common method of code obfuscation is through renaming variables, functions, and classes to obscure their purpose. By using non-descriptive or randomized names, the readability of the code is significantly reduced, making it challenging for reverse engineers to discern the original intent of the code. This approach hinders the un-

derstanding of the program's logic and structure, serving as an initial deterrent against reverse engineering.

Control flow obfuscation is another technique used to complicate the analysis of code. This involves altering the order and structure of the code without changing its ultimate functionality. Techniques such as code flattening, where nested structures are flattened into a single level, and opaque predicate insertion, where irrelevant or always true/false conditions are added, introduce complexity and confusion for reverse engineers. The resulting convoluted control flow can impede the automated analysis tools commonly used in reverse engineering, requiring a significant investment of time and effort to unravel the obscured code.

String encryption is a widely adopted method to protect hard-coded strings within the code. In reverse engineering, extracting meaningful strings such as API keys, URLs, or encryption keys can facilitate the understanding of the code's purpose. By encrypting these strings and dynamically decrypting them during runtime, developers make it more difficult for reverse engineers to identify and comprehend the embedded information. This adds an extra layer of complexity to the reverse engineering process and obstructs attempts to extract critical information from the code.

Code splitting and merging techniques contribute to the obfuscation arsenal by breaking down the code into smaller units or combining multiple functions into one. This makes it challenging for reverse engineers to follow the program's logic and identify specific functionalities. Additionally, inserting dead code – code that does not affect the program's output – can further confuse reverse engineers by leading them down unproductive paths during analysis. Code that appears to be functional but serves no actual purpose introduces noise, diverting attention away from the core functionality of the software.

Furthermore, incorporating anti-debugging techniques within the code hampers reverse engineering attempts by preventing or complicating the use of debugging tools. These techniques include checks for the presence of a debugger, introducing intentional errors, or utilizing anti-debugging APIs. By actively detecting and resisting debugging attempts, the obfuscated code can frustrate reverse engineers and slow down the process of uncovering the software's inner workings.

Metamorphic and polymorphic transformations are advanced obfuscation techniques that alter the code's structure and appearance dynamically. In metamorphic transformations, the code is transformed into semantically equivalent but structurally different representations each time it is executed. Polymorphic transformations involve changing the code's appearance while preserving its functionality. These techniques aim to create a moving target for reverse engineers, making it extremely challenging to develop static analysis tools that can reliably understand and deobfuscate the code.

In addition to these techniques, utilizing code obfuscation tools and frameworks simplifies the process of implementing various obfuscation strategies. These tools often automate the application of obfuscation techniques, allowing developers to integrate obfuscation into the build process seamlessly. However, it is essential to note that while code obfuscation adds a layer of protection, it does not make the code immune to reverse engineering. Skilled and determined attackers may still overcome obfuscation barriers, emphasizing the importance of employing multiple layers of security measures.

It is crucial to consider the potential trade-offs associated with code obfuscation. While obfuscation enhances the difficulty of reverse engineering, it may also introduce challenges for legitimate software maintenance and debugging. Developers need to strike a balance between securing their code and maintaining a level of readability and maintainability that facilitates collaboration and future development. Additionally, reliance solely on code obfuscation should not be considered a comprehensive security strategy, and it is recommended to complement obfuscation with other security measures, such as strong encryption, secure coding practices, and robust access controls.

In conclusion, code obfuscation comprises a range of techniques aimed at making source code challenging to understand and reverse engineer. From variable and function renaming to control flow obfuscation, string encryption, code splitting, anti-debugging measures, and advanced metamorphic and polymorphic transformations, these methods collectively contribute to creating a formidable barrier against reverse engineering attempts. While code obfuscation serves as a valuable tool in protecting intellectual property and deterring casual reverse engineers, it is essential to recognize its limitations and integrate it as part of a broader security strategy to fortify software against determined adversaries.

Evaluating and selecting secure third-party libraries.

The evaluation and selection of third-party libraries are critical components of building secure and resilient software applications. Third-party libraries offer a myriad of functionalities, saving developers time and effort, but they also introduce potential security risks that must be carefully assessed. One primary consideration in the evaluation process is the reputation and track record of the library's developers. Choosing libraries maintained by reputable and actively engaged developers or organizations enhances the likelihood of timely security updates and ongoing support. Online communities and forums can provide insights into the developer's responsiveness to security concerns, helping organizations gauge the level of commitment to maintaining a secure codebase.

Conducting a thorough security review of the third-party library is paramount. Analyzing the library's source code for potential vulnerabilities, adhering to secure coding practices, and following industry standards can unveil hidden risks. Tools and services that automate static code analysis and vulnerability scanning can assist in identifying common security issues within the library. Additionally, consulting vulnerability databases and security advisories specific to the library can offer valuable information regarding its historical security posture.

Compatibility with the organization's security policies and compliance requirements is a crucial aspect of the evaluation process. Ensuring that the third-party library aligns with industry standards and regulatory frameworks is essential for maintaining a secure and compliant software environment. Compatibility considerations extend beyond security and may include licensing agreements, data privacy regulations, and other legal aspects that may impact the organization's ability to use the library in a compliant manner.

Assessing the community support surrounding a third-party library is instrumental in evaluating its long-term viability and security. Robust community engagement indicates an active user base and a higher likelihood of discovering and addressing security issues promptly. Active communities often contribute to a library's continuous improvement, with developers sharing insights, solutions, and best practices. On the contrary, libraries with limited community support may pose a higher risk, as the lack of collective vigilance can result in delayed detection and resolution of security vulnerabilities.

Understanding the dependencies of the third-party library is a critical consideration in evaluating its security implications. Dependencies introduce additional layers of complexity and potential vulnerabilities. Evaluating the security practices of these dependencies, their update frequency, and their alignment with the organization's security standards is essential. Regularly checking for updates and security patches for both the primary library and its dependencies is crucial for maintaining a secure and up-to-date software ecosystem.

Performance considerations should not be overlooked in the evaluation process, as they can indirectly impact security. A poorly designed or inefficient library may introduce vulnerabilities or degrade the overall performance of the application. Assessing the library's impact on the application's performance under various conditions ensures that security is not compromised in pursuit of functionality. Striking a balance between security and performance is essential for delivering a software solution that meets both functional and operational requirements.

Transparent and accessible documentation is a key factor in the evaluation and selection of third-party libraries. Well-documented libraries provide clear instructions on usage, configuration, security considerations, and best practices. Comprehensive documentation aids developers in understanding how to integrate the library securely into their applications, reducing the likelihood of misconfigurations or insecure usage. In contrast, poorly documented libraries may lead to implementation errors that could introduce security vulnerabilities.

Consideration of the update and maintenance practices of the third-party library is crucial for ongoing security. Regularly updated libraries are more likely to receive timely security patches and improvements. Understanding the library's versioning strategy, release cycle, and the developer's commitment to maintaining backward compatibility is essential for making informed decisions regarding its long-term use. Libraries with infrequent updates or those that have been deprecated may pose a security risk due to the lack of ongoing support.

Integration with the organization's software development lifecycle (SDLC) is a vital aspect of evaluating third-party libraries. Ensuring that the library aligns with the organization's development processes, testing methodologies, and deployment pipelines facilitates seamless integration without compromising security. Evaluating how the library fits into the organization's SDLC allows for the establishment of robust practices for testing, updating, and monitoring the library throughout its lifecycle.

Security certifications and compliance with industry standards can serve as indicators of a third-party library's commitment to security. Libraries that undergo security assessments, adhere to recognized security standards, and obtain certifications demonstrate a proactive approach to security. These certifications can provide organizations with confidence in the library's security posture and may be especially important in regulated industries where compliance with specific standards is mandatory.

In conclusion, the evaluation and selection of third-party libraries demand a comprehensive and meticulous approach to ensure the security, reliability, and long-term sustainability of software applications. Assessing factors such as the reputation of developers, security reviews, community support, compatibility with security policies, understanding dependencies, considering performance implications, documentation quality, update and maintenance practices, integration with SDLC, and security certifications collectively contribute to a holistic evaluation process. By incorporating these considerations, organizations can make informed decisions that not only enhance the security of their software but also contribute to the overall resilience and success of their development initiatives.

Chapter 4: Encryption and Data Protection

Basics of encryption algorithms and their applications.

Encryption algorithms form the backbone of modern information security, providing a crucial layer of protection for sensitive data in various applications. At its core, encryption involves the transformation of plaintext information into ciphertext using a specific algorithm and a cryptographic key. This process ensures that even if unauthorized individuals gain access to the encrypted data, they cannot decipher it without the corresponding key. The two main types of encryption algorithms are symmetric-key and public-key (asymmetric) encryption.

Symmetric-key encryption relies on a single secret key for both the encryption and decryption processes. The key is shared between the communicating parties, necessitating a high level of trust. A well-known symmetric-key algorithm is the Advanced Encryption Standard (AES), widely used for securing sensitive information in various applications such as file and disk encryption, network communications, and secure messaging. AES operates on fixed-size blocks of data and supports key lengths of 128, 192, or 256 bits, providing a balance between security and computational efficiency.

Public-key or asymmetric encryption employs a pair of keys: a public key for encryption and a private key for decryption. The public key can be freely distributed, allowing anyone to encrypt data, while only the possessor of the corresponding private key can decrypt and access the original information. The security of asymmetric encryption relies on the mathematical complexity of certain problems, such as factoring large numbers. One widely used asymmetric algorithm is RSA (Rivest-Shamir-Adleman), which is instrumental in securing online communications, digital signatures, and key exchange protocols.

Hash functions are another cryptographic tool with applications in data integrity verification and digital signatures. A hash function takes input data and produces a fixed-size output, known as the hash or digest. A key characteristic of a secure hash function is its one-way nature, making it computationally infeasible to reverse the process and obtain the original input from the hash. Commonly used hash functions include SHA-256 (Secure Hash Algorithm 256-bit), which generates a 256-bit hash, and MD5 (Message Digest Algorithm 5), though MD5 is considered insecure for cryptographic purposes due to vulnerabilities.

Digital signatures leverage asymmetric encryption and hash functions to provide authentication, integrity, and non-repudiation in communication. When a sender signs a message using their private key, recipients can use the sender's public key to verify the signature and confirm the message's origin. This process ensures that the message has not been tampered with during transit and that it indeed originated from the claimed sender. Digital signatures find applications in securing email communications, online transactions, and ensuring the authenticity of software updates.

Transport Layer Security (TLS) and its predecessor, Secure Sockets Layer (SSL), are cryptographic protocols that provide secure communication over a computer network. TLS and SSL use a combination of symmetric and asymmetric encryption to secure data exchanged between clients and servers. They establish a secure session by negotiating encryption algorithms, exchanging keys, and verifying the authenticity of the parties involved. TLS is widely employed to secure web communication through HTTPS (Hypertext Transfer Protocol Secure), ensuring the confidentiality and integrity of sensitive information transmitted over the internet.

Virtual Private Networks (VPNs) utilize encryption algorithms to create secure and private communication channels over public networks. By encrypting data traffic between the user's device and the VPN server, VPNs safeguard information from potential eavesdropping or interception. Common encryption protocols used in VPNs include the Point-to-Point Tunneling Protocol (PPTP), Layer 2 Tunneling Protocol (L2TP), and Internet Protocol Security (IPsec). The choice of protocol depends on factors such as security requirements, compatibility, and the balance between performance and encryption strength.

End-to-End Encryption (E2EE) is a privacy-enhancing technique that ensures only the communicating users can read the messages. Even service providers facilitating the communication cannot access the encrypted content. E2EE is commonly employed in messaging applications like Signal and WhatsApp, where only the intended recipients possess the necessary decryption keys. This approach significantly enhances the privacy and security of user communications, mitigating the risks associated with data interception or unauthorized access.

Homomorphic encryption represents an advanced cryptographic concept with applications in secure data processing. Unlike traditional encryption methods that require decryption for data manipulation, homomorphic encryption allows computations to be performed directly on encrypted data. This enables secure outsourcing of data processing tasks to external entities while maintaining the confidentiality of the information. Homomorphic encryption finds applications in secure cloud computing, privacy-preserving data analytics, and collaborative computation scenarios.

Blockchain technology, the foundation of cryptocurrencies like Bitcoin and Ethereum, relies on cryptographic principles to ensure the integrity and security of transactions. Cryptographic hash functions are extensively used in creating blocks of data, each linked to the previous one, forming an immutable chain. Public-key cryptography is employed to facilitate secure transactions, where users have a pair of cryptographic keys for digital wallets – a public key for receiving funds and a private key for authorizing transactions. The decentralized and tamper-resistant nature of blockchain relies on robust cryptographic techniques to maintain trust in the integrity and security of the shared ledger.

In conclusion, encryption algorithms are fundamental to the field of cryptography, providing essential tools for securing data, communications, and transactions in various applications. Whether through symmetric-key encryption like AES, asymmetric encryption like RSA, hash functions for data integrity, or advanced concepts like homomorphic encryption, cryptographic techniques underpin the security infrastructure of modern digital systems. From securing web communications through TLS to enhancing privacy with end-to-end encryption in messaging applications, these algorithms play a pivotal role in safeguarding sensitive information in our interconnected and digitalized world.

Securing data stored on devices and databases.

Securing data stored on devices and databases is a critical aspect of information security, considering the ever-growing volume of sensitive information being stored and processed in various digital environments. On the device level, encrypting data is a fundamental practice to protect it from unauthorized access. Full Disk Encryption (FDE) ensures that all data on a device's storage is automatically encrypted, mitigating the risk of data exposure in the event of device theft or unauthorized access. File-level encryption is another approach that allows users to selectively encrypt specific files or folders, providing a granular level of control over data security on the device. By encrypting data at rest on devices, organizations can safeguard confidential information and maintain the privacy and integrity of stored data.

In addition to encryption, implementing strong access controls is paramount for securing data on devices. User authentication mechanisms, such as passwords, biometrics, or multi-factor authentication, restrict access to authorized individuals. Role-based access control (RBAC) ensures that users have only the necessary permissions to access and manipulate specific data, adhering to the principle of least privilege. These measures prevent unauthorized users from gaining access to sensitive information on devices, forming a foundational layer of defense against data breaches and unauthorized data manipulation.

Securing data stored in databases is equally crucial, as databases often house vast amounts of sensitive information. Database Encryption is a key strategy to protect data at rest in database systems. This involves encrypting the entire database or specific columns containing sensitive information. Transparent Data Encryption (TDE) is a common technique that encrypts the entire database file, ensuring that even if the physical storage is compromised, the data remains unreadable without the appropriate decryption keys. Application-layer encryption, where sensitive data is encrypted within the application before being stored in the database, adds an extra layer of protection against potential vulnerabilities in the database management system.

Database Access Controls are essential for restricting access to databases and ensuring that only authorized users can query or modify data. Database management systems offer robust access control mechanisms, allowing administrators to define user roles, permissions, and access restrictions. Regularly reviewing and auditing database access logs helps identify and respond to any anomalous or unauthorized activities, contributing to the overall security posture of the stored data. Additionally, implementing Database Activity Monitoring (DAM) solutions enables real-time monitoring of database activities, enhancing the ability to detect and respond to potential security incidents promptly.

Data Masking or Anonymization is a technique employed to protect sensitive information in non-production environments or when sharing data for testing or analytics. By replacing, encrypting, or scrambling sensitive data, organizations can ensure that the data retains its usability for non-production purposes while minimizing the risk of exposing confidential information. Data masking techniques are especially crucial when working with personally identifiable information (PII) or other sensitive data categories, helping organizations comply with privacy regulations and protect the privacy of individuals.

Regularly Patching and Updating Database Systems is a fundamental practice for addressing known vulnerabilities and strengthening the security of stored data. Database vendors release patches and updates to address security flaws and improve system resilience. Timely application of these updates helps mitigate the risk of exploitation by malicious actors seeking to compromise the integrity and confidentiality of the data. Establishing a systematic approach to patch management, including testing updates in a controlled environment before deployment, is essential for maintaining a secure database infrastructure.

Backup and Disaster Recovery Planning are integral components of securing data stored in databases. Regularly backing up data ensures that organizations can recover critical information in the event of data loss, corruption, or a security incident. Off-site backups provide an additional layer of protection against physical disasters or catastrophic events. Implementing a robust disaster recovery plan involves defining recovery objectives, establishing backup schedules, and conducting regular drills to validate the effectiveness of the recovery process. A well-designed backup and recovery strategy contributes to data availability, minimizing the impact of potential disruptions on business operations.

Database Encryption Key Management is a critical consideration to ensure the secure generation, storage, and distribution of encryption keys used to protect data. Proper key management practices include securely storing encryption keys separate from the encrypted data, regularly rotating keys to mitigate the impact of key compromise, and establishing strong controls for key distribution and access. Key management is a foundational element of database encryption, and its proper implementation contributes to the overall effectiveness of the encryption strategy in safeguarding stored data.

Database Auditing and Monitoring play a pivotal role in maintaining the security of stored data by providing insights into user activities, system events, and potential security incidents. Database audit trails record actions such as login attempts, data modifications, and privilege changes, enabling organizations to trace and investigate suspicious activities. Real-time monitoring solutions can detect anomalies or deviations from normal behavior, triggering alerts and facilitating a swift response to potential security threats. The combination of auditing and monitoring enhances the visibility and accountability of database activities, contributing to a proactive security posture.

Data Retention and Disposal Policies are essential for managing the lifecycle of stored data and minimizing the risk of data exposure. Organizations should define clear policies for how long data should be retained based on business and regulatory requirements. Securely disposing of data that is no longer needed involves using methods such as secure deletion or shredding to prevent unauthorized recovery. Implementing data retention and disposal policies not only enhances data security but also supports compliance with privacy regulations governing the responsible handling of sensitive information.

Database Security Assessments and Penetration Testing are proactive measures to identify and address vulnerabilities in database systems before malicious actors can exploit them. Regular security assessments, conducted internally or by third-party experts, involve evaluating the configuration, access controls, and overall security posture of the database environment. Penetration testing simulates real-world attacks to identify potential weaknesses and assess the effectiveness of security measures. By proactively addressing vulnerabilities through assessments and testing, organizations can fortify their database security and reduce the likelihood of successful attacks.

In conclusion, securing data stored on devices and databases requires a multifaceted approach encompassing encryption, access controls, regular updates, backup and recovery planning, key management, auditing, and proactive assessments. Whether at rest on devices or within databases, sensitive data demands robust protection to safeguard confidentiality, integrity, and availability. By implementing comprehensive security measures, organizations can navigate the evolving threat landscape and ensure that their stored data remains resilient against potential breaches, unauthorized access, or data loss incidents.

The importance of securing data during transmission.

The importance of securing data during transmission is paramount in the modern digital landscape, where vast amounts of information traverse networks and communication channels daily. The transmission phase, whether across the internet, internal networks, or wireless connections, represents a vulnerable point where data is susceptible to interception, eavesdropping, and manipulation by malicious actors. Without adequate security measures, sensitive information such as personal data, financial transactions, and proprietary business data becomes exposed to the risk of unauthorized access, leading to potential breaches, identity theft, financial fraud, or the compromise of critical business operations.

One of the primary reasons for emphasizing data security during transmission is the pervasive use of open networks, such as the internet, for data exchange. In an interconnected world, organizations, individuals, and systems rely heavily on transmitting data over public networks. However, the open nature of these networks means that data packets can be intercepted by unauthorized entities. Secure data transmission mitigates the risks associated with data interception, ensuring that information remains confidential and retains its integrity from the sender to the intended recipient.

Encryption plays a central role in securing data during transmission. By employing encryption algorithms, organizations can transform plaintext data into ciphertext, rendering it unreadable to anyone without the appropriate decryption key. This cryptographic technique is instrumental in preventing eavesdroppers from understanding the content of transmitted data, even if they manage to intercept it. Transport Layer Security (TLS) and its predecessor, Secure Sockets Layer (SSL), are widely adopted protocols that provide a secure communication channel over the internet. They use a combination of symmetric and asymmetric encryption to establish a secure connection between the communicating parties, ensuring the confidentiality and integrity of the transmitted data.

Securing data during transmission is especially critical in the context of financial transactions and online commerce. With the rise of e-commerce platforms and digital payment systems, sensitive financial information, including credit card details and banking credentials, is transmitted over networks regularly. The compromise of such data during transmission could have severe consequences, leading to financial losses, identity theft, and compromised user trust. Implementing secure transmission protocols, coupled with encryption, safeguards financial transactions and reinforces the trustworthiness of online transactions, fostering a secure digital economy.

For organizations, protecting proprietary and confidential business information during transmission is imperative to maintaining a competitive edge and safeguarding intellectual property. The exchange of sensitive business data, strategic plans, and trade secrets often occurs over networks, and any interception or compromise during transmission can result in severe consequences, including financial losses and damage to the organization's reputation. Secure data transmission protocols, coupled with encryption and access controls, provide a robust defense against industrial espionage and unauthorized access to critical business information, preserving the confidentiality and competitiveness of organizations.

In the realm of healthcare, securing data during transmission is a fundamental requirement to comply with privacy regulations and protect patient information. Electronic Health Records (EHRs) and health-related data are frequently transmitted between healthcare providers, insurers, and other stakeholders. The Health Insurance Portability and Accountability Act (HIPAA) in the United States, and similar regulations worldwide, mandate the secure transmission of sensitive health information to ensure patient privacy and prevent unauthorized access. Implementing secure communication protocols and encryption mechanisms is essential for healthcare organizations to uphold legal and ethical standards, instilling confidence in patients regarding the confidentiality of their medical data.

The proliferation of mobile devices and wireless communication further underscores the significance of securing data during transmission. Mobile devices, including smartphones and tablets, have become ubiquitous in both personal and professional settings. As these devices communicate wirelessly over various networks, they introduce additional vulnerabilities to data interception and unauthorized access. Implementing secure communication protocols, such as

Virtual Private Networks (VPNs) or secure Wi-Fi protocols, helps protect data transmitted to and from mobile devices, safeguarding personal information, business communications, and sensitive data accessed on the go.

In collaborative work environments and cloud computing scenarios, securing data during transmission is vital to protect shared information and maintain the privacy of collaborative efforts. As organizations increasingly adopt cloud-based services and collaborate across geographically dispersed teams, data is transmitted between users and cloud servers or among users within the cloud environment. Secure data transmission protocols, coupled with end-to-end encryption, ensure that sensitive information shared among collaborators remains confidential and immune to interception, whether in transit or stored within the cloud.

The proliferation of Internet of Things (IoT) devices further amplifies the importance of securing data during transmission. IoT devices, ranging from smart home devices to industrial sensors, constantly exchange data over networks. The nature of IoT communication introduces diverse data types, including sensor readings, environmental data, and control commands. Securing these transmissions is critical to prevent unauthorized access to sensitive data, manipulation of device functionalities, and potential disruptions to critical IoT-enabled systems. Implementing secure communication protocols and encryption mechanisms safeguards the integrity and reliability of data exchanged within IoT ecosystems.

Beyond confidentiality, securing data during transmission is crucial for preserving data integrity. The risk of data tampering or manipulation during transit can lead to misinformation, compromised decision-making processes, and potential harm. Integrity checks, such as cryptographic hash functions, are employed to verify that transmitted data has not been altered maliciously. By ensuring the integrity of data during transmission, organizations can trust the accuracy and reliability of the information exchanged, fostering confidence in decision-making processes and preventing the propagation of erroneous or manipulated data.

In conclusion, the importance of securing data during transmission cannot be overstated in today's interconnected and digitalized world. From financial transactions and online commerce to healthcare, collaborative work environments, mobile communications, and IoT ecosystems, the secure transmission of data is foundational to protecting confidentiality, maintaining data integrity, and fostering trust. Encryption, secure communication protocols, access controls, and integrity verification mechanisms collectively form a robust defense against the myriad threats posed by malicious actors seeking to exploit vulnerabilities in data transmission. As technology continues to advance, ensuring the security of data in transit remains a constant and critical imperative for organizations, individuals, and the overall stability of the digital ecosystem.

Best practices for secure key generation, storage, and distribution.

Secure key generation, storage, and distribution are fundamental components of cryptographic systems, playing a pivotal role in ensuring the confidentiality and integrity of sensitive information. Key generation marks the inception of cryptographic processes, where robust randomization techniques are employed to create cryptographic keys that resist predictability and ensure the security of encrypted data. Pseudorandom number generators (PRNGs) or true random number generators (TRNGs) are commonly used for key generation, with TRNGs leveraging physical processes like electronic noise for entropy. The unpredictability and entropy of the generated keys are crucial factors in their resistance to cryptographic attacks, emphasizing the need for high-quality key generation mechanisms.

Once cryptographic keys are generated, secure storage is essential to prevent unauthorized access and potential compromises.

Physical security measures, such as secure hardware modules (Hardware Security Modules or HSMs), provide a dedicated and tamper-resistant environment for key storage. HSMs are designed to protect cryptographic keys and perform cryptographic operations, safeguarding them from physical attacks and unauthorized extraction. In software-based environments, secure key storage involves encrypting the keys themselves and implementing access controls to restrict the individuals or processes that can retrieve or utilize the keys. Secure key storage mechanisms ensure that cryptographic keys remain confidential and are only accessible to authorized entities.

Effective key distribution is critical for establishing secure communication channels and facilitating cryptographic operations across different entities. Public-key cryptography relies on the secure distribution of public keys, while symmetric-key cryptography necessitates a secure mechanism for sharing secret keys among communicating parties. Public Key Infrastructure (PKI) is a widely adopted framework for secure key distribution in public-key cryptography. Certificate Authorities (CAs) validate and vouch for the authenticity of public keys through digital certificates, establishing a trust hierarchy. In symmetric-key scenarios, secure key distribution involves protocols like the Diffie-Hellman key exchange or the use of key distribution centers. The challenge lies in ensuring that keys are exchanged securely without being intercepted or compromised during the distribution process.

Secure key generation, storage, and distribution are particularly critical in the context of cryptographic protocols such as Transport Layer Security (TLS). TLS relies on both symmetric and asymmetric keys to establish secure communication between clients and servers. During the TLS handshake, cryptographic keys are generated, exchanged, and verified to establish a secure channel for data transmission. The compromise of keys at any stage of this process could lead to the exposure of sensitive information, unauthorized access, or

Man-in-the-Middle (MitM) attacks. Consequently, adhering to best practices in key generation, secure storage, and distribution is imperative to the overall security of TLS and similar cryptographic protocols.

In the realm of cloud computing, where data is often distributed across various servers and services, the secure generation, storage, and distribution of cryptographic keys become even more challenging. Cloud environments introduce additional complexities related to multi-tenancy, shared resources, and dynamic scaling. Cloud service providers often offer Key Management Services (KMS) or Hardware Security Modules as a service, providing centralized and secure key management capabilities. Leveraging these services ensures that cryptographic keys are generated and stored securely, with access controls to manage key distribution among authorized entities within the cloud environment.

Blockchain technology, the foundation of cryptocurrencies like Bitcoin and Ethereum, relies heavily on secure key generation, storage, and distribution for the creation and protection of digital wallets. Users are assigned a pair of cryptographic keys: a public key for receiving funds and a private key for authorizing transactions. The secure generation of these keys is crucial to prevent the compromise of funds. Wallets may be software-based, relying on secure key storage practices, or hardware wallets, which physically isolate and secure the private keys. The secure distribution of public keys allows for the verification of transactions, while the secure storage of private keys prevents unauthorized access to the user's cryptocurrency holdings.

In the context of Internet of Things (IoT) devices, secure key management becomes a challenging yet crucial aspect of ensuring the integrity and confidentiality of data exchanged between devices. IoT devices often have limited computational resources, making secure key generation a delicate balance between efficiency and cryptographic strength. Secure storage mechanisms, such as Trusted Platform Modules (TPMs) or embedded Secure Elements, help protect keys from physical tampering. Distributing keys securely to IoT devices, especially during the initial setup phase, requires robust protocols and mechanisms to prevent potential attacks on the transmission of keys.

In secure communications and messaging applications, end-to-end encryption relies on secure key generation, storage, and distribution for ensuring the privacy of user conversations. End-to-end encryption ensures that only the communicating users can read the messages, preventing intermediaries or service providers from accessing the plaintext content. Secure key exchange protocols, such as the Signal Protocol, facilitate the secure distribution of encryption keys between users. Secure storage practices on devices involve encrypting the keys and implementing access controls to prevent unauthorized access, ensuring that the confidentiality of user messages is maintained.

One of the key challenges in secure key management is the balance between usability and security. Cryptographic keys, especially long and complex ones, can be challenging for users to remember or manage manually. Key Derivation Functions (KDFs) play a role in transforming user-friendly passwords into cryptographic keys, striking a balance between memorability and cryptographic strength. Securely storing derived keys on devices involves employing secure key storage mechanisms such as key vaults or secure key containers. Usability considerations are crucial to encouraging users to adopt secure key management practices, preventing insecure practices like key reuse or choosing weak passwords.

Periodic Key Rotation is a best practice employed to enhance the security of cryptographic systems by regularly updating cryptographic keys. Key rotation minimizes the impact of potential key compromises, limiting the window of opportunity for adversaries. In scenarios where keys are compromised or suspected to be compromised, immediate key rotation is imperative to mitigate the risk of unauthorized access. Implementing automated key rotation processes ensures that cryptographic keys are regularly updated without disrupting the overall functionality of cryptographic systems. Regularly rotating keys is a proactive security measure that aligns with the principle of continuous improvement and adaptation to emerging security threats.

Audit and Monitoring mechanisms are essential components of secure key management practices. Auditing key-related activities, such as key generation, usage, and distribution, provides a trail of events that can be analyzed to detect and respond to potential security incidents. Real-time monitoring of key-related activities, especially access to sensitive key material, helps identify and respond to unauthorized or anomalous behavior promptly. Integrating key management with security information and event management (SIEM) systems enhances visibility into key-related events, contributing to a comprehensive security posture.

Compliance with industry standards and best practices is integral to secure key management. Various standards, such as the Federal Information Processing Standards (FIPS) for cryptographic modules, provide guidelines and requirements for secure key generation, storage, and distribution. Adhering to these standards ensures that cryptographic systems meet recognized benchmarks for security and interoperability. Compliance with standards also helps organizations demonstrate their commitment to security to customers, partners, and regulatory authorities.

In conclusion, secure key generation, storage, and distribution are foundational elements of cryptographic systems, influencing the overall security and integrity of sensitive information in diverse contexts. Whether applied to secure communication protocols, cloud environments, blockchain technology, IoT devices, or end-to-end encryption in messaging applications, the principles of secure key management remain consistent. Striking a balance between cryptographic strength, usability, and compliance with industry standards is essential to building resilient and trustworthy cryptographic systems that protect against evolving security threats. As technology continues to advance, the importance of robust key management practices remains central to ensuring the confidentiality, integrity, and security of digital information.

Understanding the role of hashing in data integrity and password storage.

Hashing plays a fundamental role in ensuring data integrity and securing password storage, providing cryptographic mechanisms that are central to modern information security practices. In the context of data integrity, hashing functions serve as powerful tools to verify the integrity of transmitted or stored data. A hash function takes input data, regardless of its size, and produces a fixed-size string of characters, commonly known as the hash or digest. This one-way process ensures that any slight modification to the input data results in a drastically different hash value. By comparing the computed hash of the received or stored data with the original hash value, organizations can quickly detect any alterations, corruption, or tampering of the data. Hashing functions, such as those based on the SHA-256 (Secure Hash Algorithm 256-bit) standard, are widely employed for data integrity verification in various applications, including file integrity checks, digital signatures, and data transmission.

In the realm of password storage, hashing serves as a crucial mechanism to protect user credentials and enhance overall security. Traditional practices of storing passwords in plaintext or using weak encryption mechanisms are susceptible to various security risks, including unauthorized access, data breaches, and the compromise of user accounts. Hashing addresses these vulnerabilities by transforming user passwords into irreversible hash values before storing them.

When a user attempts to log in, the entered password undergoes the same hashing process, and the computed hash is compared to the stored hash value. Since the hashing process is one-way, even if the stored hashes are exposed, attackers face significant challenges in reverse-engineering the original passwords.

However, the security of password storage through hashing introduces the concept of salting to mitigate the risks associated with hash-based attacks, particularly rainbow table attacks. A salt is a randomly generated value unique to each user that is combined with their password before hashing. This means that even if two users have the same password, the addition of unique salts ensures that their resulting hash values will be distinct. Salting significantly increases the complexity of password attacks and hinders the effectiveness of precomputed rainbow tables, where attackers precompute hashes for commonly used passwords.

The choice of a robust hashing algorithm is critical in both data integrity verification and password storage. Commonly used hash functions, such as those from the SHA-2 family, are designed to be collision-resistant, meaning it is computationally infeasible for two different inputs to produce the same hash value. The collision resistance property ensures the reliability of hash functions in both scenarios. However, the landscape of cryptography evolves, and it is essential to stay abreast of developments, transitioning to newer and more secure hashing algorithms as needed. The emergence of SHA-3, for example, demonstrates the ongoing efforts to enhance cryptographic standards and algorithms to withstand emerging threats.

Understanding the role of hashing in data integrity and password storage also involves recognizing its limitations. While hashing provides a robust mechanism for verifying data integrity and protecting passwords, it is susceptible to attacks such as brute-force and dictionary attacks. Brute-force attacks involve systematically trying all possible inputs to find the one that produces a matching hash. To counter this threat, organizations often incorporate key stretching techniques, such as iterating the hash function multiple times or using computationally intensive algorithms, to slow down the hashing process and increase the time required for brute-force attacks.

In addition to key stretching, the concept of adaptive hashing further enhances password security. Adaptive hashing algorithms, like bcrypt and Argon2, introduce the notion of work factors, which dynamically adjust the computational effort required for hashing based on evolving hardware capabilities. This adaptive nature serves as a defense against the increasing computational power available to attackers over time. Adaptive hashing algorithms contribute to the resilience of password storage mechanisms, making it more challenging for attackers to mount successful password cracking attempts.

The role of hashing in data integrity extends beyond individual files or pieces of information to include the secure storage and verification of digital signatures. Digital signatures are cryptographic mechanisms that provide a way to verify the authenticity and integrity of digital messages or documents. Hash functions are an integral component of digital signatures, as they produce a fixed-size digest of the message, which is then encrypted with the sender's private key to create the digital signature. The recipient can use the sender's public key to decrypt the signature and verify both the sender's identity and the integrity of the message by comparing the computed hash with the decrypted hash value. This application of hashing in digital signatures ensures the non-repudiation and integrity of digitally signed documents, bolstering trust in electronic communications and transactions.

Understanding the role of hashing in data integrity and password storage also involves considering the evolving landscape of cybersecurity threats. As computing power increases and new attack vectors emerge, cryptographic standards must adapt to maintain their effectiveness. The prevalence of hardware-based attacks, such as side-channel attacks and the emergence of quantum computing, introduces additional considerations for the future of hashing. Post-quantum cryptography research aims to develop hash functions and cryptographic algorithms that remain secure even in the presence of quantum computers, highlighting the importance of ongoing research and development in the field of hashing.

In conclusion, hashing is a foundational element in ensuring data integrity and securing password storage, playing a crucial role in various aspects of information security. Its one-way nature makes it a powerful tool for data integrity verification, digital signatures, and protecting user credentials. The integration of salting, key stretching, and adaptive hashing techniques enhances the resilience of hashing mechanisms against evolving threats and attack vectors. As organizations strive to protect sensitive information and user identities, a comprehensive understanding of hashing principles and best practices is essential. By staying informed about emerging cryptographic standards, advancements in hashing algorithms, and adapting to the evolving threat landscape, organizations can strengthen their overall security posture and maintain the trust of users and stakeholders in an increasingly interconnected and digitalized world.

The concept and applications of digital signatures.

Digital signatures represent a cryptographic concept that plays a pivotal role in ensuring the authenticity, integrity, and non-repudiation of digital messages, documents, and transactions. At its core, a digital signature is a cryptographic mechanism that involves the use of public-key cryptography. It relies on a pair of cryptographic keys: a private key, known only to the signer, and a public key, distributed widely. The process begins with the signer generating a hash value of the message or document using a hash function, creating a unique fingerprint of the content. The signer then encrypts this hash value with their private key, producing the digital signature. The resulting digital signature is appended to the original message or document, creating a signed entity.

One fundamental concept in digital signatures is the concept of asymmetric cryptography. In an asymmetric key pair, the public key is used for verification, allowing anyone with access to the public key to verify the signature's authenticity. Meanwhile, the private key is kept confidential and is used exclusively by the signer to generate the digital signature. The security of digital signatures hinges on the mathematical relationship between the public and private keys, ensuring that it is computationally infeasible to derive the private key from the public key or the digital signature.

Digital signatures find widespread applications across various domains, contributing to the security and reliability of digital communications and transactions. In the realm of electronic documents, digital signatures serve as a means to ensure the integrity of the document and authenticate the identity of the signer. For instance, in the context of legal documents, contracts, or official records, digital signatures provide a secure way to verify that the document has not been altered since it was signed and that it indeed originated from the claimed signer.

In the arena of email communication, digital signatures play a crucial role in securing messages and verifying the identity of the sender. By digitally signing an email, the sender provides recipients with assurance that the message has not been tampered with during transit and that it was genuinely sent by the claimed sender. This enhances trust in email communication, particularly in scenarios where sensitive information or critical instructions are conveyed electronically.

Digital signatures are integral to the concept of Public Key Infrastructure (PKI), a framework that facilitates the secure management of digital keys and certificates. Certificates, issued by trusted entities known as Certificate Authorities (CAs), bind individuals or entities to their public keys, forming the basis for verifying digital signatures. The use of digital signatures in PKI extends beyond document and message authentication to include secure website communication through the implementation of protocols such as Transport Layer Security (TLS) and its predecessor, Secure Sockets Layer (SSL). In these scenarios, digital signatures ensure the confidentiality and integrity of data exchanged between clients and servers.

In the context of software distribution and updates, digital signatures serve as a mechanism to verify the authenticity and integrity of software packages. Software developers sign their code with a digital signature, and users can verify the signature using the developer's public key. This ensures that the software has not been altered or tampered with by malicious actors during distribution. Digital signatures in software distribution are crucial for preventing the installation of compromised or unauthorized versions of software, safeguarding users from potential security threats.

One of the critical attributes of digital signatures is non-repudiation, which refers to the inability of the signer to deny their involvement in generating the signature. Non-repudiation is particularly essential in legal and contractual scenarios where proof of origin and agreement is crucial. Digital signatures provide a robust mechanism for establishing non-repudiation, as the private key used for signing is known only to the signer. In the event of a dispute, the digital signature serves as irrefutable evidence that the claimed signer indeed authenticated the associated message or document.

Digital signatures are also instrumental in securing online financial transactions and electronic payments. In the realm of e-commerce and online banking, digital signatures ensure the integrity of transaction data and authenticate the parties involved. Secure communication protocols, such as the use of digital signatures within the EMV (Europay, MasterCard, and Visa) standard for chip-based payment cards, contribute to the overall security of financial transactions. Digital signatures play a role in protecting against unauthorized modifications to transaction data and mitigating the risk of fraudulent activities.

The adoption of blockchain technology, the decentralized and distributed ledger underlying cryptocurrencies like Bitcoin and Ethereum, further underscores the significance of digital signatures. Cryptocurrencies rely on digital signatures for transaction authentication and ensuring that only the legitimate owner of a cryptocurrency wallet can authorize transfers. Each transaction in a blockchain is digitally signed by the wallet's private key, providing a secure and tamper-evident record of financial activities. The use of digital signatures in blockchain technology aligns with the broader principles of decentralization, transparency, and cryptographic security.

In the context of legal frameworks and regulations, digital signatures are recognized as valid equivalents to handwritten signatures in many jurisdictions worldwide. Various countries have enacted laws and regulations, such as the Electronic Signatures in Global and National Commerce (ESIGN) Act in the United States and the eIDAS (Electronic Identification and Trust Services) Regulation in the European Union, acknowledging the legal validity and enforceability of digital signatures. This legal recognition has propelled the widespread adoption of digital signatures across industries and has contributed to the broader acceptance of electronic documents and transactions.

Despite their numerous advantages, the effectiveness of digital signatures relies on secure key management practices. Safeguarding the private key is paramount, as its compromise could lead to unauthorized digital signatures and undermine the trustworthiness of the signed content. Hardware Security Modules (HSMs) and secure key storage mechanisms play a crucial role in protecting private keys from unauthorized access and tampering. Organizations implementing digital signatures must adhere to best practices in key generation, storage, and distribution to maintain the security and reliability of their digital signatures.

In conclusion, the concept and applications of digital signatures are foundational to the modern landscape of secure digital communications, transactions, and document management. From ensuring the integrity and authenticity of electronic documents to enhancing the security of online financial transactions and providing a mechanism for non-repudiation, digital signatures contribute significantly to the trustworthiness of the digital ecosystem. As technology continues to advance and the reliance on digital interactions grows, the role of digital signatures in establishing security, authenticity, and non-repudiation will remain central to shaping the future of secure and trustworthy digital communication and transactions.

Implementing end-to-end encryption for secure communication.

Implementing end-to-end encryption for secure communication is a comprehensive and fundamental approach to safeguarding the confidentiality and integrity of digital communications in an era characterized by pervasive digital interactions. End-to-end encryption (E2EE) ensures that the content of messages or data is encrypted on the sender's device and only decrypted on the recipient's device, minimizing the exposure of sensitive information to potential eavesdroppers or intermediaries. This cryptographic technique hinges on the use of asymmetric key pairs, typically public and private keys, to secure the communication channel. The public key is used for encryption, while the private key, known only to the recipient, is employed for decryption.

The process of implementing end-to-end encryption begins with the generation of cryptographic keys on the devices of the communicating parties. These keys form the basis of the security architecture, and their secure generation and management are paramount to the overall effectiveness of E2EE. Asymmetric key pairs are created, typically involving long and complex cryptographic keys to enhance security. Users may have a pair of keys for each device they use, ensuring that each device can participate in secure communications independently. The challenge lies in securely distributing public keys to potential communication partners without compromising their integrity. Public Key Infrastructure (PKI) frameworks or decentralized key distribution mechanisms contribute to this aspect of key management, enabling users to validate and trust the authenticity of public keys.

Once keys are established, the actual process of end-to-end encryption involves the encryption of the data or messages before transmission. When a user sends a message, the content is transformed into ciphertext using the recipient's public key, ensuring that only the recipient with the corresponding private key can decrypt and access the original content. This encryption process occurs on the sender's device, guaranteeing that the data is secure even during transit across potentially untrusted networks or services. The encrypted data is then transmitted to the recipient's device, where it is decrypted using the recipient's private key, completing the end-to-end encryption cycle.

One of the essential applications of end-to-end encryption is in secure messaging platforms. Messaging apps that prioritize user privacy, such as Signal, WhatsApp, and Telegram, have embraced end-to-end encryption to provide users with a high level of assurance that their messages are private and secure. In these platforms, the encryption process is seamless and transparent to the users, who are not required to perform any manual cryptographic operations. The underlying encryption algorithms and key management processes are abstracted, simplifying the user experience while ensuring robust security.

Email communication, a cornerstone of digital communication, has also witnessed the integration of end-to-end encryption to address the longstanding challenge of email security. Pioneering solutions like Pretty Good Privacy (PGP) and its open-source counterpart GNU Privacy Guard (GPG) enable users to encrypt their email messages end-to-end. In this context, users generate their key pairs and share their public keys with email correspondents. Email messages are then encrypted using the recipient's public key, and only the recipient, possessing the corresponding private key, can decrypt and read the content. The adoption of end-to-end encryption in email provides a layer of defense against unauthorized access, surveillance, and potential interception of sensitive communication.

Beyond messaging and email, end-to-end encryption is increasingly becoming a standard feature in various cloud-based services. Cloud storage providers, recognizing the growing concerns about data privacy and security, implement end-to-end encryption to protect user files and documents stored in the cloud. This approach ensures that the stored data remains confidential, even if the cloud service provider is compromised or subjected to external threats. Users often have control over the encryption keys, and the encryption and decryption processes occur on the client side, reinforcing the principle of end-to-end security.

Collaboration and file-sharing platforms have also embraced end-to-end encryption to enhance the privacy and security of shared documents and communication. Services like Tresorit and CryptPad offer end-to-end encrypted collaboration tools, allowing users to work on documents, spreadsheets, or presentations without compromising the confidentiality of the shared content. The encryption occurs on the client side, ensuring that the service provider does not have access to the unencrypted data. This approach aligns with the increasing emphasis on user-controlled encryption and privacy-centric collaboration tools.

Video conferencing applications, especially in the wake of the global shift to remote work, have recognized the importance of end-to-end encryption in securing virtual meetings. Platforms like Zoom and Microsoft Teams have introduced or enhanced end-to-end encryption features to protect the confidentiality of audio and video communication. End-to-end encryption in video conferencing ensures that only the intended participants can access the content of the communication, preventing unauthorized interception or surveillance.

The deployment of end-to-end encryption faces challenges related to key management, user experience, and interoperability. Key management, specifically the secure distribution and verification of public keys, requires careful consideration to prevent man-in-the-middle attacks or other forms of key compromise. Usability is a critical factor influencing the success of end-to-end encryption implementations, as overly complex cryptographic workflows may deter users from adopting secure communication practices. Striking a balance between strong security and user-friendly experiences remains a design challenge for developers and service providers. Interoperability, especially in cross-platform communication, demands standardized approaches to ensure that end-to-end encrypted communication can occur seamlessly among different devices and applications.

The debate around the balance between privacy and law enforcement interests has also impacted the adoption and implementation of end-to-end encryption. While privacy advocates argue that strong encryption is essential for protecting individual rights and preventing unauthorized surveillance, law enforcement agencies express concerns about the potential hindrance to criminal investigations when access to encrypted communications is restricted. This tension has led to discussions about "backdoors" or exceptional access mechanisms, where authorities could access encrypted content under certain circumstances. However, the implementation of such mechanisms raises significant security and privacy concerns, as any intentional vulnerability in the encryption system poses a risk of exploitation by malicious actors.

In recent years, advancements in cryptographic research have led to the development of post-quantum cryptography, which aims to address the potential threat posed by quantum computers to existing encryption algorithms, including those used in end-to-end encryption. As quantum computers advance, they could potentially break current encryption schemes, emphasizing the need for quantum-resistant algorithms to ensure the continued security of end-to-end encryption in the quantum computing era.

In conclusion, implementing end-to-end encryption for secure communication represents a critical step in addressing the evolving landscape of digital threats and privacy concerns. The widespread adoption of E2EE in messaging, email, cloud services, collaboration tools, and video conferencing underscores its importance in preserving the confidentiality and integrity of digital communication. As technology continues to advance, the ongoing challenges related to key management, usability, interoperability, and the broader societal debate on privacy versus law enforcement interests will shape the future of end-to-end encryption. Striking the right balance between robust security and user-friendly experiences remains a focal point for developers, service providers, and policymakers seeking to establish a secure and privacy-respecting digital communication ecosystem.

Exploring the impact of quantum computing on encryption.

Exploring the impact of quantum computing on encryption delves into the potential paradigm shift that quantum computers could bring to the field of cryptography. Traditional encryption methods, such as those based on factorization and discrete logarithm problems, underpin the security of widely used cryptographic algorithms like RSA and ECC. The security of these algorithms relies on the computational infeasibility of solving certain mathematical problems within a reasonable timeframe. However, the unique computational capabilities of quantum computers, particularly their ability to perform parallel computations using quantum bits or qubits, pose a potential threat to the security foundations of classical encryption.

One of the most notable algorithms vulnerable to quantum attacks is Shor's algorithm, developed by mathematician Peter Shor. Shor's algorithm has the capability to efficiently factorize large composite numbers and compute discrete logarithms exponentially faster than the best-known classical algorithms. Since the security of widely deployed public-key cryptosystems, including RSA and ECC, relies on the difficulty of factoring large numbers and computing discrete logarithms, the advent of scalable quantum computers could compromise the security assurances provided by these classical encryption schemes. The potential ability of quantum computers to break widely used cryptographic protocols raises concerns about the confidentiality of sensitive information, including financial transactions, personal communications, and secure data storage.

The impact of quantum computing on encryption is not limited to public-key cryptography; it also extends to symmetric-key cryptography. Grover's algorithm, another quantum algorithm developed by Lov Grover, introduces the concept of quantum parallelism to search unsorted databases quadratically faster than classical algorithms. While this poses a lesser threat to symmetric-key encryption, where the key length can be increased to maintain security, it introduces the concept of "quantum speedup" that can significantly reduce the effective key strength of symmetric-key algorithms. As a result, symmetric-key cryptographic systems may need to adapt by using longer key lengths to counteract the potential quantum advantage, impacting computational efficiency.

The timeline for the realization of large-scale, fault-tolerant quantum computers capable of executing algorithms like Shor's and

Grover's remains uncertain. Quantum computers are inherently susceptible to errors due to environmental noise and decoherence, necessitating the development of error-correction techniques. Researchers are actively working on developing fault-tolerant quantum computers, and while progress is being made, practical and scalable quantum computing remains an ongoing challenge. Consequently, the impact of quantum computing on encryption is a future scenario that depends on the advancement of quantum technology and the successful mitigation of current technical challenges.

Quantum-safe or post-quantum cryptography emerges as a critical response to the potential threat posed by quantum computing to classical encryption algorithms. Post-quantum cryptography focuses on developing cryptographic algorithms that resist attacks from both classical and quantum computers. These algorithms are designed to maintain security even in the presence of a quantum computer capable of running Shor's or Grover's algorithms. The exploration of quantum-resistant algorithms involves embracing mathematical structures that are believed to be hard for both classical and quantum computers to solve efficiently. Popular approaches include lattice-based cryptography, hash-based cryptography, code-based cryptography, and multivariate polynomial cryptography. The NIST Post-Quantum Cryptography Standardization project, initiated by the National Institute of Standards and Technology (NIST), plays a central role in evaluating and standardizing post-quantum cryptographic algorithms to ensure their reliability and adoption.

Lattice-based cryptography stands out as a promising approach in the realm of post-quantum cryptography. Lattice problems, which involve the study of mathematical lattices, form the basis for cryptographic primitives that are believed to be resistant to quantum attacks. Lattice-based cryptography offers a range of primitives, including public-key encryption, digital signatures, and key exchange protocols. These primitives are being actively researched and evaluated for their suitability in providing robust security against quantum threats. The lattice-based paradigm leverages the hardness of lattice problems to ensure the security of cryptographic constructions, offering a potential avenue for building quantum-resistant cryptographic systems.

Hash-based cryptography represents another category of post-quantum cryptographic solutions. Hash-based cryptographic algorithms rely on the properties of cryptographic hash functions to achieve security. The Merkle-Damgård construction, widely used in hash functions like SHA-2, forms the basis for hash-based digital signatures and hash-based key exchange protocols. Hash-based cryptography is considered quantum-resistant due to the inherent structure of hash functions, which are believed to resist the types of attacks enabled by quantum computers. Research and standardization efforts are ongoing to explore the practicality and efficiency of hash-based cryptographic algorithms as viable post-quantum alternatives.

Code-based cryptography, drawing inspiration from error-correcting codes, is another avenue of research in the quest for post-quantum security. Code-based cryptographic primitives rely on the hardness of decoding specific linear codes to resist attacks from both classical and quantum computers. The McEliece cryptosystem, an early and well-studied example of code-based cryptography, forms the foundation for public-key encryption and digital signatures in this paradigm. Code-based cryptography offers the advantage of leveraging existing mathematical structures with proven resilience against certain types of attacks, making it an attractive candidate for post-quantum cryptographic solutions.

Multivariate polynomial cryptography is a further approach in the post-quantum cryptographic landscape. This paradigm exploits the complexity of solving systems of multivariate polynomial equations to provide security. The security of multivariate polynomial cryptographic schemes hinges on the difficulty of solving systems of polynomial equations, even when subjected to quantum attacks. The Rainbow and Unbalanced Oil and Vinegar (UOV) schemes exemplify multivariate polynomial cryptographic constructions, offering alternatives for public-key encryption and digital signatures that are believed to withstand quantum threats.

The transition to post-quantum cryptography involves not only the development of new cryptographic algorithms but also the integration of these algorithms into existing communication protocols and security infrastructures. Industry and standardization bodies are actively engaged in this transition, seeking to ensure a smooth and secure migration path from classical to post-quantum cryptographic systems. Protocols such as the Internet Key Exchange (IKE) and the Transport Layer Security (TLS) protocol, which underpins secure web communication, are being scrutinized for potential vulnerabilities to quantum attacks. As part of the ongoing efforts to enhance the security of communication systems, the exploration of quantum-resistant alternatives and the development of quantum-safe standards are essential components of the broader strategy to address the impact of quantum computing on encryption.

The impact of quantum computing on encryption extends beyond the technical realm, raising ethical, legal, and policy considerations. The prospect of a quantum-powered ability to break widely deployed encryption protocols has sparked discussions on the need for quantum-safe communication standards and the potential risks associated with the widespread deployment of quantum computers. Policymakers and legal experts are contemplating strategies for managing the transition to post-quantum cryptography, ensuring that critical infrastructure, sensitive data, and communication systems remain secure in the face of evolving technological landscapes.

In conclusion, exploring the impact of quantum computing on encryption is a multifaceted journey that encompasses the potential vulnerabilities of classical encryption algorithms, the ongoing efforts to develop post-quantum cryptographic solutions, and the broader implications for communication protocols and security infrastructures. The transition to post-quantum cryptography reflects a proactive and forward-looking approach to address the challenges posed by the advent of quantum computers. As the field of quantum computing progresses, the collaboration between researchers, industry stakeholders, and policymakers remains crucial to navigating the complexities of quantum-resistant cryptography and securing the foundations of digital communication in a quantum-enabled future.

The role of random numbers in encryption and security.

The role of random numbers in encryption and security is paramount, underpinning the robustness of cryptographic systems and serving as a foundational element in the protection of sensitive information. Randomness is a crucial factor in cryptography because predictable patterns or sequences can render encryption vulnerable to various attacks. In the context of cryptographic algorithms, the generation of random numbers is not arbitrary but is rather a carefully orchestrated process governed by deterministic algorithms called pseudo-random number generators (PRNGs). These algorithms aim to simulate true randomness by producing sequences of numbers that exhibit statistical properties resembling those of truly random sequences. PRNGs are extensively used in cryptographic applications, including key generation, initialization vector (IV) generation, and nonce creation.

Key generation is a fundamental aspect of cryptographic systems, and the security of cryptographic keys relies on their unpredictability. Random numbers play a pivotal role in generating cryptographic keys that resist brute-force and other attacks. The process involves selecting a sufficiently long random sequence of bits to serve as the key. The randomness ensures that each key is unique and not easily guessable, contributing to the overall security of encryption algorithms. In scenarios where cryptographic keys are derived from passwords, the introduction of randomness in the password generation process becomes crucial to thwarting dictionary attacks and enhancing the strength of derived keys.

Initialization vectors (IVs) are essential components in many encryption algorithms, particularly in block cipher modes of operation. An IV introduces an element of randomness into the encryption process, ensuring that the same plaintext does not produce the same ciphertext when encrypted multiple times with the same key. This property is crucial for preventing patterns and repetitions in encrypted data, making it more resistant to cryptanalysis. The use of a random IV adds an additional layer of complexity and security to encryption processes, particularly in scenarios where the same data might be encrypted multiple times.

Nonces, or "number used once," are random or unique values employed in cryptographic protocols to prevent replay attacks and ensure the freshness of data. In protocols like the Transport Layer Security (TLS) and Internet Protocol Security (IPsec), nonces play a crucial role in key exchange mechanisms, session resumption, and secure communication. The randomness of nonces is vital to prevent adversaries from predicting or reusing them, thereby safeguarding the integrity and security of cryptographic sessions. The unpredictable nature of nonces contributes to the resistance against various attacks, including man-in-the-middle attacks and replay attacks.

True randomness, as opposed to pseudo-randomness, is another dimension of the role of random numbers in encryption and security. True randomness is challenging to achieve in deterministic computing systems, but it is essential for certain cryptographic applications, such as the generation of cryptographic seeds or entropy sources. Hardware random number generators (HRNGs) leverage physical processes, such as electronic noise or radioactive decay, to generate truly random numbers. These sources of entropy are crucial for applications where a high degree of unpredictability is required, such as in the generation of cryptographic keys with sufficient entropy.

The security of cryptographic protocols also relies on the use of random numbers in the context of challenge-response mechanisms. Challenges, which are random values generated by one party, are presented to another party for a response. The unpredictable nature of these challenges and responses forms the basis for authentication and key agreement protocols. In scenarios like password-based authentication, challenges ensure that each authentication attempt involves a unique combination of parameters, preventing attackers from precomputing and reusing authentication attempts.

Random numbers are integral to the security of cryptographic algorithms beyond traditional encryption. In digital signatures, for instance, random numbers are used in the generation of ephemeral keys or nonces during the signing process. The unpredictability of these values is crucial for preventing the reuse of signatures and protecting against certain types of attacks, such as the Bleichenbacher attack on RSA signatures. The role of random numbers in digital signatures extends to the generation of random parameters in signature schemes like the Digital Signature Algorithm (DSA) and the Elliptic Curve Digital Signature Algorithm (ECDSA).

Cryptographic applications extend to secure communication and the establishment of secure channels between parties. The random numbers used in key exchange protocols, such as the Diffie-Hellman key exchange, contribute to the establishment of a shared secret key between communicating parties. The secrecy and unpredictability of the generated values are essential for thwarting eavesdroppers and man-in-the-middle attackers attempting to deduce the exchanged key. The Diffie-Hellman key exchange, when combined with randomness, forms the basis for establishing secure communication channels in various security protocols, including SSL/TLS for secure web communication.

Random numbers are also fundamental to the security of password-based encryption and key derivation functions. In scenarios where passwords are used to derive cryptographic keys, the introduction of randomness, often in the form of a salt, is crucial for preventing precomputation attacks, such as rainbow table attacks. A salt is a random value unique to each user or password, combined with the password before hashing or key derivation. The use of randomness in the salt ensures that even users with the same password will have distinct hashed or derived keys, enhancing the security of password-based cryptographic systems.

The role of random numbers in encryption and security extends to the realm of secure multi-party computation and privacy-preserving protocols. In scenarios where multiple parties wish to jointly compute a function without revealing their inputs, protocols like secure multi-party computation use random numbers to introduce uncertainty and prevent collusion attacks. The introduction of randomness ensures that individual parties cannot predict the outcomes of joint computations, preserving the privacy and security of participants.

While the role of random numbers is crucial in enhancing the security of cryptographic systems, it is not without challenges. The quality and entropy of random number sources, especially in the case of pseudo-random number generators, need careful consideration. Insufficient entropy or predictability in random number generation can lead to cryptographic vulnerabilities. Secure key management practices, including the secure storage of cryptographic seeds and the periodic reseeding of pseudo-random number generators, are essential to maintaining the integrity and unpredictability of random numbers over time.

In conclusion, the role of random numbers in encryption and security is multifaceted and foundational to the effectiveness of cryptographic systems. From key generation and initialization vectors to nonces, challenges, and secure communication protocols, randomness adds a layer of unpredictability crucial for thwarting various cryptographic attacks. The ongoing evolution of cryptographic standards, the development of true random number generation techniques, and the integration of random numbers into emerging privacy-preserving technologies underscore the continued significance of randomness in shaping the security landscape. As the field of cryptography evolves, the thoughtful integration and management of random numbers will remain central to the development and deployment of secure and resilient cryptographic systems.

Overview of data protection laws and regulations.

The landscape of data protection laws and regulations has undergone significant transformation in response to the digital era's challenges and the increasing reliance on technology to process vast amounts of personal information. This overview encompasses a global perspective, highlighting key principles and regulatory frameworks that govern the collection, processing, and handling of personal data.

The European Union's General Data Protection Regulation (GDPR) stands out as a cornerstone in global data protection. Enforced in May 2018, the GDPR introduces a harmonized set of rules aimed at safeguarding the privacy and rights of individuals within the EU. Its extraterritorial reach extends its applicability to organizations outside the EU that process the personal data of EU residents. The GDPR emphasizes transparency, consent, and the rights of data subjects, granting them control over their personal information. Organizations are required to implement measures ensuring data protection by design and default, conduct data protection impact assessments for high-risk processing activities, and appoint Data Protection Officers (DPOs) in certain cases. The GDPR imposes stringent penalties for non-compliance, emphasizing the growing importance of prioritizing data protection in the global digital economy.

In the United States, the regulatory landscape for data protection is characterized by sectoral laws and a state-by-state approach. The Health Insurance Portability and Accountability Act (HIPAA) regulates the protection of health information, while the Gramm-Leach-Bliley Act (GLBA) focuses on the financial sector. The absence of a comprehensive federal data protection law has led to a patchwork of state laws, with California's Consumer Privacy Act (CCPA) being a prominent example. The CCPA grants California residents certain rights over their personal information, including the right to know, delete, and opt-out of the sale of their data. The California Privacy Rights Act (CPRA), an extension of the CCPA, enhances consumer privacy rights and establishes the California Privacy Protection Agency for enforcement.

In Asia, data protection laws vary, reflecting diverse cultural, legal, and regulatory environments. Singapore's Personal Data Protection Act (PDPA) adopts a principles-based approach, emphasizing the fair and reasonable collection, use, and disclosure of personal data. Japan's Act on the Protection of Personal Information (APPI) regulates the handling of personal data by both the public and private sectors. China's Personal Information Protection Law (PIPL), enacted in 2021, establishes a comprehensive framework for the processing of personal information, imposing obligations on entities processing such data and introducing concepts such as "critical information infrastructure operators." India is in the process of formulating its data protection framework, with the Personal Data Protection Bill pending approval. These developments underscore the increasing recognition of data protection as a fundamental right and the need for comprehensive legislation across the Asia-Pacific region.

Latin America has witnessed a growing emphasis on data protection, with several countries enacting or updating their laws to align with global standards. Brazil's General Data Protection Law (LGPD), inspired by the GDPR, came into force in 2020, establishing principles for the processing of personal data and granting rights to data subjects. Mexico, with its Federal Law on the Protection of Personal Data Held by Private Parties, and Argentina, with its Personal Data Protection Law, have also taken steps to regulate the handling of personal information. The diversity of legal frameworks in the region reflects a shared commitment to protecting individuals' privacy rights while accommodating unique cultural and legal contexts.

Africa, while still in the early stages of formulating comprehensive data protection laws, has seen notable developments. South Africa's Protection of Personal Information Act (POPIA), implemented in 2020, aligns with international data protection standards and introduces obligations for responsible parties processing personal information. Nigeria, Kenya, and other countries are considering or drafting data protection legislation to address the challenges posed by the digital economy and protect the privacy rights of their citizens. The emerging focus on data protection in Africa reflects a recognition of the need to balance innovation and economic development with the protection of individuals' privacy.

International organizations, recognizing the global nature of data flows, have also contributed to the development of data protection standards. The Organisation for Economic Co-operation and Development (OECD) established privacy guidelines in 1980, forming the foundation for many subsequent data protection laws. The Asia-Pacific Economic Cooperation (APEC) Privacy Framework promotes a consistent approach to privacy protection in the region. Additionally, cross-border data transfer mechanisms, such as the EU-U.S. Privacy Shield (recently invalidated) and Standard Contractual Clauses (SCCs), provide frameworks for transferring personal data across jurisdictions while ensuring an adequate level of protection.

The role of supervisory authorities is pivotal in enforcing data protection laws and ensuring compliance. In the EU, each member state has a Data Protection Authority (DPA) responsible for enforcing the GDPR. Similarly, the U.S. Federal Trade Commission (FTC) oversees privacy and data security matters, while state attorneys general play a role in enforcing state-specific laws. In Asia, regulatory bodies such as the Personal Data Protection Commission (PDPC) in Singapore, the Personal Information Protection Commission (PPC) in Japan, and the China Cyberspace Administration (CAC) are entrusted with overseeing data protection enforcement. Supervisory authorities act as guardians of individuals' privacy rights, investigating complaints, imposing fines, and providing guidance to organizations on best practices for data protection.

The convergence of data protection laws worldwide has led to increased cooperation among regulators. For example, the GDPR's one-stop-shop mechanism allows organizations to deal with a single lead supervisory authority for cross-border data processing activities. The APEC Cross-Border Privacy Rules (CBPR) system facilitates the exchange of information and cooperation among participating economies. These mechanisms aim to streamline compliance for multinational organizations and foster a collaborative approach to addressing global privacy challenges.

Emerging technologies, such as artificial intelligence (AI) and the Internet of Things (IoT), pose new challenges to data protection. The ethical and responsible use of AI requires considerations of transparency, accountability, and fairness in automated decision-making processes. The GDPR includes provisions addressing automated decision-making and profiling, emphasizing the importance of human oversight and the right to meaningful information about the logic, significance, and consequences of such processing. The rise of IoT devices, collecting and processing vast amounts of personal data, necessitates robust security measures and privacy-by-design principles to ensure the protection of individuals' information.

Data breaches and cybersecurity incidents have heightened the focus on the security aspect of data protection. Many data protection laws include provisions requiring organizations to implement appropriate security measures to safeguard personal data from unauthorized access, disclosure, alteration, and destruction. Breach notification requirements mandate organizations to promptly inform supervisory authorities and affected individuals in the event of a data breach, allowing for timely response and mitigation efforts.

The interplay between privacy and innovation is a dynamic aspect of the data protection landscape. Organizations are increasingly adopting privacy-by-design principles, embedding privacy considerations into the development of products and services. Privacy impact assessments (PIAs) and data protection impact assessments (DPIAs) are becoming standard practices to identify and mitigate privacy risks associated with new projects or data processing activities. The integration of privacy into the innovation lifecycle reflects a shift toward a more ethical and sustainable approach to data processing.

While data protection laws aim to strike a balance between individual privacy rights and the legitimate interests of organizations, challenges persist. Global disparities in data protection standards, varying levels of enforcement, and differing cultural attitudes toward privacy contribute to a complex regulatory environment. Ongoing debates on the appropriate scope of data protection laws, the definition of personal data, and the balance between innovation and privacy underscore the evolving nature of this field.

In conclusion, the landscape of data protection laws and regulations reflects a global recognition of the importance of safeguarding individuals' privacy rights in the digital age. From the comprehensive and extraterritorial reach of the GDPR to the diverse approaches in the U.S., Asia, Latin America, and Africa, a common thread emerges – the acknowledgment of data protection as a fundamental right. As technology continues to advance and data becomes an increasingly valuable asset, the evolution of data protection laws will remain a dynamic and critical aspect of the broader societal discourse on privacy, ethics, and responsible innovation.

Chapter 5: Secure Communication Protocols

Overview of common communication protocols in software development.

The landscape of software development is intricately woven with a multitude of communication protocols that facilitate the exchange of data and information between different systems, applications, and devices. These protocols serve as the underpinning infrastructure, ensuring seamless and standardized communication in diverse computing environments. One of the foundational communication protocols is HTTP, the Hypertext Transfer Protocol, which forms the backbone of the World Wide Web. HTTP governs the transfer of hypertext, enabling the retrieval of resources such as HTML documents, images, and multimedia files. Its stateless nature and reliance on a request-response paradigm make it well-suited for web-based interactions, and its secure counterpart, HTTPS, employs encryption through protocols like TLS to ensure the confidentiality and integrity of data exchanged between clients and servers.

Beyond the web, the Simple Mail Transfer Protocol (SMTP) plays a pivotal role in email communication. SMTP facilitates the transmission of electronic mail, defining how messages are sent and received across networks. This text-based protocol relies on the client-server model, with email clients initiating communication with SMTP servers to send messages. To retrieve emails, the Post Office Protocol (POP) and Internet Message Access Protocol (IMAP) come into play. POP allows for the download of emails to a local device, typically removing them from the server, while IMAP synchronizes emails across multiple devices, providing a centralized and consistent view of the mailbox.

For real-time communication, the Extensible Messaging and Presence Protocol (XMPP) emerges as a widely used open standard. XMPP facilitates instant messaging and presence information, enabling users to exchange messages in near real-time. Its decentralized nature, extensibility, and support for a wide range of features make it a preferred choice for various chat applications. In contrast, the Session Initiation Protocol (SIP) is central to voice and video communication. SIP governs the initiation, modification, and termination of communication sessions, playing a crucial role in voice over IP (VoIP) systems and other real-time multimedia applications.

Within enterprise settings, the Simple Object Access Protocol (SOAP) and Representational State Transfer (REST) are prevalent communication protocols for web services. SOAP, based on XML, defines a standardized structure for messages exchanged between web services, ensuring interoperability across diverse platforms. REST, on the other hand, leverages the principles of statelessness and resource-based interactions. It relies on standard HTTP methods, such as GET, POST, PUT, and DELETE, making it lightweight and well-suited for scalable and loosely coupled systems. RESTful APIs have become ubiquitous in modern software development, powering a myriad of web and mobile applications.

In the realm of distributed computing, the Remote Procedure Call (RPC) protocol facilitates communication between processes on different machines. RPC allows a program to execute procedures or functions on a remote server, abstracting the complexities of network communication. Technologies like XML-RPC and JSON-RPC utilize XML and JSON, respectively, as data interchange formats to facilitate remote procedure calls over HTTP. Another widely adopted RPC protocol is gRPC, which employs the Protocol Buffers serialization format and supports multiple programming languages. Its use of HTTP/2 for transport and features like bidirectional streaming make gRPC well-suited for high-performance and efficient communication in microservices architectures.

Message-oriented middleware (MOM) systems often rely on the Advanced Message Queuing Protocol (AMQP) for asynchronous communication. AMQP defines a standard for message-oriented communication, enabling the exchange of messages between applications or services. It ensures reliability, supports various messaging patterns, and fosters interoperability among different messaging systems. RabbitMQ and Apache Kafka are prominent examples of messaging systems that implement the AMQP protocol, providing scalable and resilient infrastructures for handling messages in distributed environments.

WebSockets emerge as a vital protocol for achieving full-duplex communication over a single, long-lived connection. Unlike traditional request-response models, WebSockets enable bidirectional communication between clients and servers in real-time. This makes WebSockets well-suited for applications requiring low-latency updates, such as online gaming, live chat, and collaborative editing platforms. The WebSocket protocol leverages the same ports as HTTP and HTTPS (ports 80 and 443), simplifying firewall traversal and making it a pragmatic choice for modern web applications.

In the Internet of Things (IoT) landscape, the Message Queuing Telemetry Transport (MQTT) protocol has gained widespread adoption. Designed for resource-constrained devices and unreliable networks, MQTT follows a publish-subscribe model, allowing devices to subscribe to topics and receive messages from other devices or servers. Its lightweight nature, minimal overhead, and support for Quality of Service (QoS) levels make MQTT a preferred choice for IoT communication, enabling efficient data exchange among connected devices.

Security in communication protocols is of paramount importance, and the Transport Layer Security (TLS) protocol serves as the bedrock for ensuring secure connections. Formerly known as Secure Sockets Layer (SSL), TLS provides a secure layer for data transmission, encrypting communication channels and verifying the authenticity of parties involved. TLS is integral to securing various protocols, including HTTPS for secure web browsing, SMTP for secure email communication, and many other application-layer protocols. Its continual evolution, with successive versions addressing vulnerabilities and enhancing cryptographic algorithms, underscores its critical role in preserving the confidentiality and integrity of transmitted data.

As the software development landscape continues to evolve, emerging protocols like QUIC (Quick UDP Internet Connections) are gaining prominence. Developed by Google, QUIC is designed to optimize web traffic by reducing latency and enhancing security. It operates over UDP rather than TCP, offering faster connection establishment and improved congestion control. QUIC's integration with TLS ensures end-to-end encryption, addressing concerns related to data privacy and security in transit. Its adoption is particularly notable in the context of web applications and services striving to deliver enhanced performance and a more responsive user experience.

In conclusion, the fabric of software development is intricately woven with a diverse array of communication protocols, each tailored to specific use cases and scenarios. From the foundational HTTP governing web interactions to specialized protocols like MQTT for IoT communication and gRPC for high-performance RPC, these protocols form the backbone of modern computing. Their evolution continues to be shaped by the ever-changing landscape of technology, with an emphasis on security, efficiency, and adaptability to meet the evolving needs of software developers and end-users alike. The richness and diversity of communication protocols underscore their indispensable role in shaping the interconnected and dynamic world of software development.

Understanding the fundamentals of SSL/TLS encryption. The fundamentals of SSL/TLS (Secure Sockets Layer/Transport Layer Security) encryption form the bedrock of secure communication over the Internet, ensuring the confidentiality, integrity, and authenticity of data exchanged between clients and servers. SSL, the predecessor to TLS, was developed by Netscape in the mid-1990s to address the need for a secure protocol for online transactions. TLS, introduced as an improvement over SSL, is the modern and widely adopted standard for secure communication. The core purpose of SSL/TLS is to establish a secure channel between a client and a server, enabling encrypted data transfer. This is especially crucial in scenarios such as online banking, e-commerce transactions, and secure communication on the web.

The SSL/TLS protocol operates at the transport layer of the OSI model, facilitating secure communication over the Internet. It employs a combination of asymmetric and symmetric encryption, along with cryptographic hash functions and digital signatures, to achieve its security objectives. The initial phase of SSL/TLS communication involves a process known as the handshake. During the handshake, the client and server negotiate the cryptographic parameters and establish a shared secret key without transmitting it over the network. This shared secret key is then used for symmetric encryption, enhancing the efficiency of data encryption during the subsequent phases of communication.

Asymmetric encryption, also known as public-key cryptography, plays a pivotal role in the SSL/TLS handshake. Each party, the client, and the server possesses a pair of keys: a public key and a private key. The public key is shared openly, while the private key is kept confidential. During the handshake, the server presents its public key to the client, and the client generates a pre-master secret, encrypts it with the server's public key, and sends it back to the server. The server decrypts the pre-master secret using its private key, and both parties

use the pre-master secret to derive a shared secret key. This shared secret key becomes the cornerstone for symmetric encryption, enhancing the speed and efficiency of subsequent data transfer.

Symmetric encryption is employed for the bulk of data transmission after the handshake. Unlike asymmetric encryption, where
separate keys are used for encryption and decryption, symmetric encryption relies on a single shared secret key for both operations. This
symmetric key is derived during the handshake process and ensures
that the data exchanged between the client and server remains confidential. Common symmetric encryption algorithms used in SSL/
TLS include Advanced Encryption Standard (AES) and Triple DES
(3DES). These algorithms are selected based on the negotiated cryptographic parameters during the handshake, taking into account factors such as key length and algorithm strength.

To ensure the integrity of the transmitted data, SSL/TLS incorporates cryptographic hash functions. These functions generate
fixed-size hash values based on the content of the data. During the
data transfer phase, each transmitted message is hashed and the hash
value is appended to the message. Upon reception, the recipient
hashes the received message and compares the computed hash value
with the received hash value. If the two values match, it indicates
that the data has not been tampered with during transmission. Popular hash functions used in SSL/TLS include Secure Hash Algorithm
(SHA) variants.

Digital signatures are another essential component of SSL/TLS,
providing a mechanism for authentication and ensuring the origin
and integrity of the exchanged messages. Digital signatures involve
the use of asymmetric encryption to create a unique signature for a
message. During the handshake, the server presents its digital certificate, which includes its public key and is signed by a trusted Certificate Authority (CA). The client verifies the digital signature using
the CA's public key to establish the authenticity of the server. This

process ensures that the client is communicating with the intended server and not an imposter. The trust hierarchy established by CAs plays a crucial role in SSL/TLS, as clients implicitly trust the CAs to vouch for the authenticity of server certificates.

SSL/TLS is often associated with a set of protocols that specify the rules and procedures for secure communication. The specific protocol version negotiated during the handshake influences the security features and cryptographic algorithms used in the communication. Over the years, several versions of SSL and TLS have been developed, with each successive version addressing vulnerabilities and introducing improvements. SSL 2.0, SSL 3.0, TLS 1.0, TLS 1.1, TLS 1.2, and TLS 1.3 are notable versions, each refining the security mechanisms and cryptographic algorithms used in SSL/TLS.

The TLS 1.2 and TLS 1.3 versions represent significant milestones in the evolution of SSL/TLS. TLS 1.2, widely used in contemporary applications, enhances security by introducing stronger cryptographic algorithms and incorporating countermeasures against various attacks. TLS 1.3, the latest version at the time of this writing, builds upon the strengths of its predecessors and focuses on improving performance, reducing latency, and eliminating obsolete and insecure features. Notably, TLS 1.3 eliminates the use of outdated cryptographic algorithms, enhances the efficiency of the handshake process, and introduces mechanisms to resist certain types of attacks, providing a more robust and secure foundation for encrypted communication.

Key management is a critical aspect of SSL/TLS, encompassing the generation, distribution, storage, and destruction of cryptographic keys. The secure storage of private keys, especially on server systems, is paramount to preventing unauthorized access. Hardware Security Modules (HSMs) are often employed to securely store private keys and perform cryptographic operations, adding an additional layer of protection. The periodic rotation of cryptographic keys, known as key rotation, helps mitigate the risk associated with long-term key exposure. Effective key management practices contribute significantly to the overall security posture of SSL/TLS implementations.

In addition to its application in web browsing, SSL/TLS is integral to various secure communication protocols and applications. HTTPS, or HTTP Secure, employs SSL/TLS to secure data transfer between web browsers and servers, ensuring that sensitive information such as login credentials and financial transactions remains confidential. Secure email communication, often implemented using protocols like SMTPS and POP3S, relies on SSL/TLS for encrypting messages during transmission. Virtual Private Networks (VPNs) leverage SSL/TLS to establish secure communication channels for remote access and data transfer. SSL/TLS is also instrumental in securing application-layer protocols like FTPS (File Transfer Protocol Secure) and LDAPS (Lightweight Directory Access Protocol Secure).

Despite its widespread use and robust security features, SSL/TLS has faced challenges and vulnerabilities over the years. The discovery of vulnerabilities such as POODLE, BEAST, and Heartbleed prompted updates and refinements to the protocol. The deprecation of outdated cryptographic algorithms, support for Perfect Forward Secrecy (PFS), and ongoing efforts to address emerging threats demonstrate the commitment of the security community to continuously enhance the security of SSL/TLS.

In conclusion, the fundamentals of SSL/TLS encryption provide a robust framework for securing communication over the Internet. From the establishment of a secure channel through the handshake process to the use of asymmetric and symmetric encryption, cryptographic hash functions, and digital signatures, SSL/TLS ensures the confidentiality, integrity, and authenticity of data exchanged between clients and servers. The evolution of SSL/TLS versions, key management practices, and its widespread application in various secure communication protocols underscore its pivotal role in shaping the secure and trusted digital landscape. As technology continues to advance, SSL/TLS will undoubtedly remain a cornerstone in safeguarding sensitive information and enabling secure online interactions.

Common vulnerabilities associated with SSL.

SSL (Secure Sockets Layer) and its successor, TLS (Transport Layer Security), are critical protocols for securing communication on the Internet. However, like any technology, they are not immune to vulnerabilities, and understanding these vulnerabilities is crucial for maintaining a secure online environment. One of the well-known vulnerabilities associated with SSL is the POODLE (Padding Oracle On Downgraded Legacy Encryption) attack. Exploiting a vulnerability in the SSL 3.0 protocol, POODLE enables attackers to decrypt sensitive information, such as secure HTTP cookies, by exploiting the padding used in block ciphers. The solution to POODLE involves disabling SSL 3.0 support and adopting more secure TLS protocols.

Another significant vulnerability is the BEAST (Browser Exploit Against SSL/TLS) attack. BEAST targets the way block ciphers, such as AES-CBC (Advanced Encryption Standard in Cipher Block Chaining mode), operate in SSL/TLS. By leveraging JavaScript and a network sniffer, an attacker can decrypt parts of the encrypted communication. The solution to BEAST involves prioritizing the use of TLS 1.1 or higher and implementing patches and updates to mitigate the risk.

Heartbleed is a notorious vulnerability that affected the OpenSSL library, a widely used open-source implementation of SSL/TLS. Heartbleed allows attackers to read sensitive data from the memory of the affected server, potentially exposing cryptographic keys, login credentials, and other confidential information. The remediation for Heartbleed involves patching the vulnerable OpenSSL versions and reissuing SSL/TLS certificates.

The FREAK (Factoring attack on RSA-EXPORT Keys) vulnerability stems from the legacy export-grade cryptographic keys that were once mandated by the U.S. government. Attackers exploiting FREAK could force a downgrade of the encryption level, making it easier to break the encryption and intercept sensitive data. Mitigating FREAK involves disabling support for export-grade ciphers and ensuring that servers use strong, non-export-grade cryptographic keys.

DROWN (Decrypting RSA with Obsolete and Weakened eNcryption) is a vulnerability that targets servers supporting SSLv2 (SSL version 2). DROWN allows attackers to decrypt TLS sessions by exploiting weaknesses in the SSLv2 protocol, posing a threat even if the server primarily uses a more secure TLS version. To mitigate DROWN, server operators need to disable SSLv2 support and ensure that their private keys are not reused across different servers.

The POODLE vulnerability prompted the deprecation of SSL 3.0, but the subsequent discovery of the POODLE-bites vulnerability indicated that SSL 3.0 could still pose risks. POODLE-bites allows attackers to exploit weaknesses in SSL 3.0 to recover small amounts of plaintext from secure connections. The recommended solution is to disable SSL 3.0 support entirely and prioritize the use of modern TLS versions.

The CRIME (Compression Ratio Info-leak Made Easy) attack targets SSL/TLS compression mechanisms. By exploiting vulnerabilities in the compression algorithms, CRIME allows attackers to deduce information about the plaintext of encrypted messages. Disabling SSL/TLS compression is the primary mitigation strategy for CRIME, and modern servers and clients generally have compression disabled by default.

The Lucky 13 attack is a timing side-channel attack that targets the implementation of the CBC mode in TLS. By exploiting the timing differences in the processing of correctly and incorrectly formatted padding, attackers can deduce information about the plaintext. Mitigating Lucky 13 involves implementing countermeasures, such as adding random delays, to obscure the timing differences.

A more recent vulnerability is the ROBOT (Return of Bleichenbacher's Oracle Threat) attack, which targets servers supporting RSA key exchange and vulnerable to Bleichenbacher's original attack. ROBOT allows attackers to decrypt intercepted TLS sessions and impersonate the server. The remediation for ROBOT involves disabling support for RSA key exchange ciphers suites that are susceptible to Bleichenbacher's attack.

Forward Secrecy is an important security feature in SSL/TLS, but certain vulnerabilities, such as the Logjam attack, have targeted its implementation. Logjam allows attackers to downgrade the key exchange to a lower level of security, making it easier to decrypt intercepted communication. To counter Logjam, server operators should disable support for weak key exchange parameters and ensure that the key exchange uses sufficiently large prime numbers.

The SLOTH (Security Losses from Obsolete and Truncated Transcript Hashes) attack targets the use of hash functions in SSL/TLS handshakes. By exploiting weaknesses in hash functions, SLOTH can undermine the integrity of the handshake and potentially lead to the acceptance of compromised certificates. Mitigating SLOTH involves using strong hash functions and maintaining updated cryptographic libraries.

A vulnerability known as the Zombie POODLE attack combines elements of the original POODLE vulnerability with a padding oracle attack. This variant targets the TLS protocol and poses a threat even if SSL 3.0 is disabled. Mitigation strategies for Zombie POODLE involve disabling CBC cipher suites in TLS and prioritizing the use of modern cipher suites.

The Sweet32 attack is a vulnerability related to the use of 3DES (Triple Data Encryption Standard) cipher suites in SSL/TLS. By exploiting the predictable behavior of 3DES in certain conditions, attackers can decrypt parts of the communication. Mitigating Sweet32 involves disabling 3DES cipher suites and adopting more secure encryption algorithms.

As SSL/TLS vulnerabilities continue to emerge, it is crucial for organizations and system administrators to stay informed about the latest threats and promptly apply patches and updates to mitigate risks. Regular security audits, the use of strong cryptographic algorithms, and adherence to best practices for SSL/TLS configuration contribute to a more robust defense against potential vulnerabilities. Additionally, the adoption of the latest TLS versions and the deprecation of outdated protocols and cipher suites are essential steps in maintaining a secure and resilient SSL/TLS implementation.

Implementing the latest TLS versions for enhanced security.

Implementing the latest Transport Layer Security (TLS) versions is a critical and proactive measure for enhancing the security of network communication in the ever-evolving digital landscape. TLS, the successor to Secure Sockets Layer (SSL), is fundamental to securing data transmission over the Internet, ensuring confidentiality, integrity, and authenticity. TLS protocols continue to evolve in response to emerging security challenges and vulnerabilities, and organizations must prioritize the adoption of the latest versions to stay ahead of potential threats.

TLS 1.3 represents the most recent and significant advancement in the TLS protocol family. Introduced with the goal of improving performance, reducing latency, and enhancing security, TLS 1.3 builds upon the strengths of its predecessors while addressing known vulnerabilities. One notable feature of TLS 1.3 is the streamlined handshake process, which significantly reduces the number of round trips required to establish a secure connection. This not only improves the overall performance of secure communication but also mitigates the risk of certain attacks that target the handshake phase, such as the BEAST (Browser Exploit Against SSL/TLS) attack.

Furthermore, TLS 1.3 prioritizes Perfect Forward Secrecy (PFS), a cryptographic property that ensures each session key is derived independently, even if the long-term secret key is compromised. PFS adds an extra layer of security by preventing the decryption of past communications, even if the current session key is compromised. This is particularly crucial in protecting sensitive information over extended periods, as it limits the potential impact of a security breach.

Another significant enhancement in TLS 1.3 is the deprecation of outdated cryptographic algorithms and cipher suites. TLS 1.3 discards cryptographic algorithms with known vulnerabilities and weaknesses, promoting the use of stronger and more secure alternatives. The removal of obsolete algorithms aligns with best practices in cryptography and reduces the attack surface for potential adversaries. It also encourages the use of modern, secure algorithms like Elliptic Curve Cryptography (ECC), which offers strong security with shorter key lengths, contributing to overall efficiency.

In addition to the benefits of TLS 1.3, organizations should also consider the implications of earlier TLS versions, such as TLS 1.2 and TLS 1.1, which may still be in use. While TLS 1.2 is widely supported and considered secure, TLS 1.1 is now considered obsolete, and both have known vulnerabilities. Migrating to TLS 1.3 or, at a minimum, TLS 1.2 is crucial for maintaining a secure and resilient communication infrastructure. The use of TLS 1.1 and earlier versions poses a heightened risk due to identified vulnerabilities, making them susceptible to attacks that exploit weaknesses in their cryptographic implementations.

Implementing the latest TLS versions involves a comprehensive approach that encompasses both server and client configurations. Server operators play a pivotal role in ensuring a secure TLS implementation by configuring their servers to support the latest TLS versions. This includes enabling TLS 1.3 and disabling support for older, vulnerable versions. Server administrators should also prioritize the use of secure cipher suites and cryptographic algorithms, adhering to industry best practices and guidelines.

Clients, including web browsers and other applications, also need to be updated to support the latest TLS versions. Outdated clients that lack support for TLS 1.3 may default to older versions, potentially compromising the security of the communication. Organizations should encourage users to keep their software up to date, and developers should ensure that applications and services are designed to leverage the latest TLS capabilities.

Furthermore, the adoption of TLS 1.3 requires thorough testing to ensure compatibility with existing systems and applications. While TLS 1.3 is designed to be backward compatible with TLS 1.2, testing is essential to identify and address any potential issues that may arise during the transition. This includes assessing the compatibility of web servers, load balancers, and other infrastructure components with TLS 1.3.

As organizations transition to the latest TLS versions, they should also consider the broader context of their security posture. This includes the implementation of strong cryptographic configurations, adherence to security best practices, and the use of additional security mechanisms such as HTTP Strict Transport Security (HSTS) and secure cookie attributes. HSTS, for instance, enforces the use of secure, encrypted connections by web browsers, reducing the risk of man-in-the-middle attacks and enhancing overall web security.

Moreover, organizations should leverage the Online Certificate Status Protocol (OCSP) and Certificate Transparency (CT) to enhance the trustworthiness of digital certificates used in TLS connections. OCSP enables real-time validation of the status of digital certificates, preventing the use of compromised or revoked certificates. CT, on the other hand, provides transparency into the issuance of digital certificates, making it more difficult for attackers to misuse certificates for malicious purposes.

The importance of TLS extends beyond web browsing, encompassing various communication protocols such as email (SMTP, IMAP, POP3), file transfer (FTP), and virtual private networks (VPNs). Secure configurations for these protocols are paramount, and organizations should ensure that TLS is appropriately implemented across their entire network infrastructure. This includes secure configurations for mail servers, ensuring the use of secure protocols for file transfers, and securing VPN connections with the latest TLS versions.

In the context of cloud services and cloud-native architectures, the adoption of the latest TLS versions is equally crucial. Cloud service providers often offer TLS termination services, allowing organizations to offload the SSL/TLS processing to the cloud infrastructure. However, organizations must ensure that these services support the latest TLS versions and adhere to the recommended security practices.

While the benefits of implementing the latest TLS versions are clear, it is important to acknowledge that security is an ongoing process. Regular security audits, vulnerability assessments, and monitoring are essential components of a robust security strategy. Continuous updates to cryptographic libraries, operating systems, and applications are necessary to address emerging threats and vulnerabilities. Additionally, organizations should stay informed about industry developments, security advisories, and best practices to adapt their security measures to evolving threats.

In conclusion, the implementation of the latest TLS versions is a fundamental step toward enhancing the security of network communication. TLS 1.3, with its emphasis on improved performance, Perfect Forward Secrecy, and the elimination of outdated cryptographic algorithms, represents a significant advancement in secure communication protocols. Organizations should adopt a comprehensive approach, including server and client configurations, testing procedures, and additional security measures, to ensure a smooth transition to the latest TLS versions. By prioritizing security and staying vigilant in the face of evolving threats, organizations can build a resilient and secure communication infrastructure that protects sensitive data and maintains the trust of users and stakeholders.

Exploring protocols like SFTP and SCP for secure file transfers.

In the realm of secure file transfers, protocols such as SFTP (Secure File Transfer Protocol) and SCP (Secure Copy Protocol) play pivotal roles in providing a robust and encrypted framework for exchanging files between systems. SFTP, an extension of the SSH (Secure Shell) protocol, has emerged as a widely adopted and versatile solution for secure file transfers over a network. The primary advantage of SFTP lies in its integration with the SSH protocol, leveraging its strong encryption and authentication mechanisms. SFTP operates over a secure channel, encrypting both the command and data channels to ensure the confidentiality and integrity of the transferred files. This makes SFTP particularly well-suited for scenarios where the secure transmission of sensitive data is paramount.

One of the key strengths of SFTP is its platform independence, allowing users to perform secure file transfers between different operating systems seamlessly. The protocol supports a variety of authentication methods, including password-based authentication, public key authentication, and multi-factor authentication, offering flexibility to users based on their security requirements. Furthermore, SFTP includes a set of commands and features that enable users to perform various file operations, such as uploading, downloading, listing directory contents, and managing file permissions. Its ease of use, combined with strong security features, positions SFTP as a reliable choice for organizations seeking secure and efficient file transfer capabilities.

On a technical level, SFTP employs a client-server architecture. The client initiates a connection to the server, authenticates itself, and establishes a secure channel for data transfer. The encrypted communication prevents eavesdropping and man-in-the-middle attacks, ensuring that the contents of the transferred files remain confidential. Additionally, SFTP can be configured to use compression, improving the efficiency of data transfer, especially when dealing with large files.

SCP, or Secure Copy Protocol, is another secure file transfer protocol that shares its roots with the SSH protocol. SCP operates over SSH and provides a secure method for copying files between systems. While SFTP offers a broader range of file operations, SCP is focused specifically on secure copying, making it a straightforward and efficient solution for copying files securely between hosts. Like SFTP, SCP benefits from the encryption and authentication mechanisms inherent in the SSH protocol, ensuring a secure channel for file transfers.

The usage of SCP typically involves a command-line interface, making it suitable for both interactive and automated file transfer scenarios. To initiate a secure copy operation, users utilize the "scp" command, specifying the source file or directory and the destination. SCP supports both password and public key authentication, allowing users to choose the authentication method that aligns with their security policies. The secure copying process involves establishing an encrypted connection, verifying the user's identity, and securely transferring the specified files to the target system.

In comparison to SFTP, SCP has a more limited set of features as it primarily focuses on the secure copy operation. While this simplicity can be advantageous for straightforward file transfer requirements, organizations with more extensive file management needs may find that SFTP offers a more comprehensive solution. Additionally, SCP does not provide interactive directory listing functionality, and users need to specify the exact file paths for both source and destination during the copy operation.

Both SFTP and SCP contribute to secure file transfers in various contexts, and the choice between them depends on specific use cases and organizational requirements. Organizations often consider factors such as the need for additional file management capabilities, user familiarity with the protocols, and integration with existing workflows when deciding between SFTP and SCP.

In terms of security, both protocols benefit from the encryption and authentication mechanisms of SSH, offering protection against various security threats. The use of public key authentication, in particular, enhances security by eliminating the need for password-based authentication, reducing the risk of unauthorized access. Additionally, the ability to configure SSH to use specific cryptographic algorithms further allows organizations to tailor the security parameters to their specific needs.

When implementing secure file transfers, considerations extend beyond the choice of protocol to the overall security posture of the systems involved. This includes the configuration of firewalls, proper user access controls, regular security audits, and the use of secure channels for communication. Ensuring that systems are updated with the latest security patches and adhering to best practices in network security contribute to a robust and resilient environment for secure file transfers.

In conclusion, exploring protocols like SFTP and SCP for secure file transfers reveals two powerful solutions that leverage the security features of the SSH protocol. SFTP, with its broader set of file management capabilities, serves as a versatile choice for organizations with diverse file transfer needs. On the other hand, SCP's focused approach to secure copying makes it a straightforward and efficient option for specific use cases. Both protocols contribute to the secure exchange of files across networks, providing organizations with flexible and reliable tools to safeguard their sensitive data. As the digital landscape evolves, the emphasis on secure file transfers remains a cornerstone of information security, and protocols like SFTP and SCP continue to play essential roles in meeting these challenges.

Overview of security protocols for API communication (e.g., OAuth, JWT).

In the dynamic landscape of modern software development, secure communication between applications is paramount, and the use of robust security protocols for API communication is crucial. Two prominent protocols that have become integral to API security are OAuth (Open Authorization) and JWT (JSON Web Token), each serving distinct purposes within the authentication and authorization framework.

OAuth, designed to address the challenges of delegated access, is an open standard that enables secure authorization in a standardized and interoperable manner. OAuth facilitates third-party applications to access resources on behalf of a resource owner without exposing the owner's credentials. It employs a token-based approach, wherein access tokens are issued after the resource owner grants permission. OAuth defines different grant types, such as Authorization Code, Implicit, Resource Owner Password Credentials, and Client Credentials, providing flexibility to cater to various use cases. The Authorization Code flow, for instance, involves a multi-step process where the client obtains an authorization code and exchanges it for an access token, enhancing security by separating the authorization and token issuance steps.

The flexibility of OAuth is particularly evident in its use across diverse scenarios. OAuth is commonly employed in the context of web applications, mobile applications, and API integrations, facilitating secure and controlled access to resources. OAuth's wide adoption has contributed to its status as a robust and extensible standard, with various implementations and libraries available for different programming languages and platforms.

JWT, on the other hand, addresses the need for a compact, self-contained means of representing claims between parties in a secure manner. A JSON Web Token is a compact, URL-safe means of representing claims to be transferred between two parties. It consists of three parts: a header, a payload, and a signature. The header typically specifies the type of token and the signing algorithm, while the payload contains the claims. The signature, generated using a secret key, ensures the integrity of the token. JWTs are commonly used for authentication and information exchange between parties, such as between a client and a server or between different services within a microservices architecture.

One of the advantages of JWT is its statelessness, which is particularly valuable in distributed systems. As the token itself contains the necessary information, there is no need to query a centralized authentication server for each request, enhancing scalability and reducing the burden on the authentication infrastructure. JWTs are often used in conjunction with OAuth for transmitting information about the authenticated user or the authorization scope.

OAuth and JWT are often employed together to provide a comprehensive solution for securing API communication. In such scenarios, OAuth handles the authorization aspects, determining whether a client is permitted to access a specific resource, while JWT serves as the mechanism for representing and transmitting claims about the user or the resource owner. This combined approach leverages the strengths of each protocol, providing a robust and flexible framework for securing API communication in a variety of contexts.

OAuth's authorization server issues an access token to the client, and this access token, often in the form of a JWT, is then presented in subsequent API requests to access protected resources. The JWT, serving as a bearer token, is included in the request headers and provides a self-contained means of conveying the user's identity and the permissions associated with the access token. The statelessness of JWTs aligns well with the principles of RESTful API design, where each request from a client to a server is independent, and no session state is stored on the server.

The integration of OAuth and JWT introduces a layer of security to API communication by enforcing access controls, ensuring that only authorized clients can access protected resources. Additionally, the use of JWTs allows for the transmission of user information, such as user roles or claims, in a standardized and verifiable format, facilitating secure information exchange between parties.

While the combined use of OAuth and JWT provides a robust foundation for securing API communication, it is crucial to consider additional security measures to address potential threats. Token validation, secure token storage, and token expiration policies are vital aspects to mitigate risks associated with token-based authentication. The use of HTTPS to encrypt communication further safeguards the confidentiality and integrity of the transmitted tokens.

In conclusion, the use of OAuth and JWT in API communication represents a powerful and widely adopted approach to securing access to resources and transmitting information securely. OAuth's role in managing authorization, along with JWT's capability to represent and transmit claims, offers a comprehensive solution for ensuring secure, controlled, and stateless communication between applications and services. The symbiotic relationship between OAuth and JWT has become a cornerstone in the design and implementation of secure APIs, enabling developers to build scalable, interoperable, and secure systems in the ever-evolving landscape of distributed and interconnected applications. As the demand for secure API communication continues to grow, the principles and mechanisms introduced by OAuth and JWT remain integral to shaping the future of secure and collaborative digital ecosystems.

Risks associated with insecure DNS configurations.

Insecure Domain Name System (DNS) configurations pose significant risks to the security and reliability of the internet infrastructure, making it susceptible to various cyber threats. DNS, a fundamental component of the internet, translates human-readable domain names into IP addresses, facilitating the routing of data between devices. When DNS configurations lack proper security measures, several risks emerge, compromising the integrity, availability, and confidentiality of network communications.

One of the primary risks associated with insecure DNS configurations is DNS spoofing or cache poisoning. In this type of attack, malicious actors manipulate the DNS cache to associate legitimate domain names with incorrect IP addresses. This can lead to the redirection of user traffic to malicious sites, allowing attackers to launch phishing attacks, distribute malware, or conduct man-in-the-middle attacks. By corrupting the DNS cache, attackers can intercept communication between users and legitimate servers, compromising the confidentiality and authenticity of the transmitted data.

Another significant risk is DNS amplification attacks, where attackers exploit misconfigured DNS servers to amplify the volume of traffic directed towards a target. This form of distributed denial-of-service (DDoS) attack overwhelms the target server with a flood of DNS response packets, causing service disruptions. Misconfigured DNS servers that allow recursive queries from external sources without proper rate limiting or authentication become unwitting participants in these attacks. Securing DNS configurations involves implementing measures to prevent such misuse, such as limiting recursive queries to trusted sources and implementing rate limiting.

Cache poisoning can also result from insufficiently random transaction IDs in DNS queries, making it easier for attackers to predict and forge responses. When DNS servers generate predictable transaction IDs, attackers can more effectively inject malicious data into the cache. Strong randomness in transaction IDs, implemented through cryptographic techniques, is essential to thwarting these attacks and maintaining the integrity of the DNS resolution process.

Inadequate protection against DNS tunneling represents another risk associated with insecure DNS configurations. DNS tunneling is a technique used by malicious actors to bypass security controls by encapsulating non-DNS traffic within DNS requests and responses. This covert channel allows attackers to exfiltrate data or establish command and control channels without detection. Organizations with lax DNS security may inadvertently facilitate such tunneling, highlighting the importance of implementing solutions that can detect and block anomalous DNS traffic indicative of tunneling activities.

Furthermore, DNS-based Distributed Denial of Service (DDoS) attacks, specifically those leveraging reflection and amplification techniques, can exploit insecure configurations. In reflection attacks, attackers send DNS queries with a spoofed source IP address to open DNS resolvers, causing the responses to be directed towards the target. The amplification effect arises from the fact that DNS responses are typically larger than the corresponding queries, magnifying the impact of the attack. Mitigating these risks requires implementing best practices such as source IP validation, rate limiting, and the use of DNS response rate limiting (RRL) to prevent the abuse of open resolvers.

Insecure DNS configurations can also lead to DNS tunneling abuse in the context of data exfiltration and command-and-control activities. Malicious actors may leverage DNS requests and responses to covertly transmit information between compromised systems and external servers. Detecting and preventing DNS tunneling requires implementing advanced monitoring and analysis techniques to identify anomalous patterns in DNS traffic and block unauthorized communications.

Additionally, insufficiently protected DNS zones can expose organizations to zone transfer attacks. Zone transfers, intended for replicating DNS data across authoritative name servers, can be exploited by attackers to gain unauthorized access to sensitive information about an organization's DNS infrastructure. This information can be valuable for reconnaissance purposes and may aid in subsequent attacks. To mitigate zone transfer risks, organizations should implement access controls, limit zone transfer permissions, and regularly audit and monitor DNS configurations.

Pharming attacks represent another risk associated with insecure DNS configurations, involving the redirection of legitimate domain names to fraudulent websites. Attackers may manipulate DNS records to associate a trusted domain with a malicious IP address, leading users to unintended and potentially harmful destinations. This form of attack can compromise the integrity of online transactions, facilitate identity theft, and erode user trust. Protecting against pharming requires implementing secure DNS practices, including the use of DNS Security Extensions (DNSSEC) to cryptographically sign DNS records and ensure their authenticity.

Moreover, the lack of DNS security measures can expose organizations to the risk of domain hijacking. In domain hijacking, attackers gain unauthorized control over a domain by compromising the associated DNS credentials or exploiting vulnerabilities in the domain registrar's infrastructure. Once control is established, attackers can redirect traffic, manipulate DNS records, and disrupt services. To mitigate domain hijacking risks, organizations should implement strong authentication mechanisms for domain registration accounts, regularly monitor DNS settings, and use registrar features that enhance security.

In conclusion, insecure DNS configurations expose organizations and the broader internet ecosystem to a spectrum of risks ranging from DNS spoofing and cache poisoning to DDoS attacks, DNS tunneling, and domain hijacking. These risks can compromise the confidentiality, integrity, and availability of network communications, leading to various malicious activities. To mitigate these risks, organizations must prioritize DNS security measures, including the implementation of DNSSEC, robust access controls, rate limiting, transaction ID randomness, and continuous monitoring and auditing of DNS configurations. By addressing these vulnerabilities, organizations can fortify their DNS infrastructure, enhance resilience against attacks, and contribute to a more secure and trustworthy online environment.

Securing email communication through protocols like SMTPS and STARTTLS.

Securing email communication is of paramount importance in the digital age, where sensitive information is regularly exchanged over the Internet. Protocols such as SMTPS (Simple Mail Transfer Protocol Secure) and STARTTLS play critical roles in enhancing the security of email transmissions, ensuring the confidentiality and integrity of messages.

SMTPS is an extension of the traditional Simple Mail Transfer Protocol (SMTP) used for sending emails. SMTPS incorporates the security features of the Secure Sockets Layer (SSL) or its successor, the Transport Layer Security (TLS) protocol, to encrypt communication between the email client and the mail server. By encrypting the data in transit, SMTPS prevents eavesdropping and unauthorized access to the content of emails. This encryption is particularly crucial when emails contain sensitive information such as personal data, financial details, or confidential business communications. The use of SMTPS mitigates the risk of interception and tampering during the transmission of emails, providing a secure channel for communication.

STARTTLS is another mechanism designed to enhance the security of email communication. Unlike SMTPS, STARTTLS operates as an extension to the regular SMTP protocol, allowing servers to upgrade their connection to a secure, encrypted channel during the communication process. When a mail server supporting STARTTLS initiates communication with another server, it can request a secure connection, and if the receiving server also supports STARTTLS, they negotiate the use of encryption. This opportunistic approach to encryption ensures that even if both servers support STARTTLS, the communication can proceed in plaintext if either party does not request or support encryption. While STARTTLS provides a level of security, it is important to note that it may be susceptible to downgrade attacks, emphasizing the need for additional security measures.

The implementation of SMTPS and STARTTLS addresses some of the fundamental security challenges associated with email communication, but it is essential to understand their nuances and limitations. SMTPS, being a dedicated secure version of SMTP, ensures end-to-end encryption throughout the entire communication process. However, its usage has declined in favor of STARTTLS due to the latter's opportunistic and backward-compatible approach. STARTTLS, while providing encryption, is contingent on both the sending and receiving mail servers supporting the protocol and agreeing to establish a secure connection. This opportunistic nature makes STARTTLS vulnerable to Man-in-the-Middle (MitM) attacks, where an attacker can potentially intercept or manipulate the negotiation process to force plaintext communication.

To bolster the security of email communication further, organizations are increasingly adopting additional measures, such as Domain-based Message Authentication, Reporting, and Conformance (DMARC), DomainKeys Identified Mail (DKIM), and Sender Policy Framework (SPF). DMARC, in particular, helps prevent email spoofing and phishing attacks by enabling domain owners to specify how their emails should be authenticated, monitored, and enforced. DKIM allows the sender to digitally sign email messages, providing a mechanism for the recipient to verify the authenticity and integrity of the received emails. SPF, on the other hand, validates the originating IP address of an email, helping to combat email spoofing and phishing attempts.

Despite the advantages of SMTPS and STARTTLS, it is crucial to recognize that email security extends beyond the transport layer. End-to-end encryption, as provided by protocols like Pretty Good Privacy (PGP) or its open standard counterpart OpenPGP, can add an extra layer of protection by encrypting the content of the email itself. PGP relies on public-key cryptography, allowing users to encrypt messages with the recipient's public key and enabling the recipient to decrypt them using their private key. While PGP provides robust encryption, its widespread adoption has been limited by the complexity of key management and the need for both the sender and receiver to use compatible implementations.

The security landscape for email communication is continually evolving, with emerging standards such as the Mail Transfer Agent Strict Transport Security (MTA-STS) aiming to address some of the vulnerabilities associated with STARTTLS. MTA-STS allows domain owners to declare a policy stating that their mail servers must only be connected to over encrypted, authenticated channels. This proactive approach reduces the risk of downgrade attacks by explicitly specifying the security expectations for email communication.

To enhance email security further, organizations should consider the use of secure email gateways, which can inspect email traffic for malicious content, filter out phishing attempts, and enforce encryption policies. These gateways act as a frontline defense, complementing the security measures implemented at the transport layer. Additionally, user education and awareness programs play a crucial role in mitigating the human factor in email security. Users should be informed about the risks of phishing attacks, social engineering tactics, and the importance of verifying the authenticity of email sources.

In conclusion, securing email communication through protocols like SMTPS and STARTTLS represents a critical step in safeguarding sensitive information transmitted over the internet. While these protocols provide encryption during the transport of emails, their effectiveness depends on the support and implementation by both sending and receiving mail servers. Organizations should adopt a multi-layered approach to email security, incorporating end-to-end encryption, cryptographic standards like PGP, and additional measures such as DMARC, DKIM, SPF, and MTA-STS. By combining these technologies and best practices, organizations can create a resilient defense against email-based threats, ensuring the confidentiality, integrity, and authenticity of their communications in an increasingly interconnected and digitally reliant world.

Challenges and protocols for securing communication in the Internet of Things (IoT).

Securing communication in the Internet of Things (IoT) landscape presents a complex and multifaceted challenge, given the diverse and interconnected nature of IoT devices. As the number of connected devices continues to surge, the need for robust security measures becomes paramount to safeguard against potential threats and vulnerabilities. One of the primary challenges is the sheer heterogeneity of IoT devices, ranging from sensors and actuators to smart appliances and industrial machinery. This diversity introduces complexities in terms of device capabilities, communication protocols, and security requirements. Establishing a uniform security framework that accommodates various device types and communication patterns remains a persistent challenge for IoT ecosystems.

A crucial aspect of securing IoT communication is the protection of data at rest and in transit. Given that IoT devices often handle sensitive information, encryption plays a pivotal role in ensuring the confidentiality and integrity of data. Protocols such as Datagram Transport Layer Security (DTLS) and Secure Socket Layer (SSL)/Transport Layer Security (TLS) are commonly employed to encrypt data during transmission. DTLS is particularly relevant for the IoT due to its lightweight implementation, making it suitable for resource-constrained devices with limited processing power and memory.

In addition to encryption, authentication is a fundamental building block for securing communication in the IoT. Verifying the identities of devices and ensuring that they are authorized to communicate with each other is essential to prevent unauthorized access and data tampering. Protocols like OAuth and Mutual TLS (mTLS) are employed to facilitate secure authentication and authorization in IoT ecosystems. OAuth, known for its role-based access control, enables devices to obtain access tokens, allowing them to interact with authorized resources. mTLS, on the other hand, adds an extra layer of security by requiring both the client and server to present valid certificates, establishing a mutual trust relationship.

The deployment of Public Key Infrastructure (PKI) is integral to many IoT security architectures. PKI provides a framework for managing digital certificates, which are crucial for establishing trust between devices and ensuring the authenticity of communication. Certificate authorities issue digital certificates that bind public keys to specific entities, enabling secure identification and verification. However, the scalability and management of PKI for a vast number of IoT devices remain a challenge, especially considering the need for frequent certificate updates and revocations.

IoT devices often operate in resource-constrained environments, with limitations in processing power, memory, and energy resources. This poses challenges for implementing sophisticated security measures without compromising the device's functionality. Lightweight cryptographic algorithms, such as Elliptic Curve Cryptography (ECC) and Lightweight Cryptography (LWC), have gained prominence in the IoT domain due to their ability to provide strong security with reduced computational overhead. These algorithms strike a balance between security and efficiency, making them suitable for deployment in resource-constrained IoT devices.

Another critical challenge in securing IoT communication is the vulnerability of devices to physical attacks, tampering, or theft. Physical security measures, such as secure boot processes and hardware-based security modules, become imperative to protect IoT devices from unauthorized access or manipulation. Secure boot ensures that only authenticated and unaltered firmware is executed during device startup, preventing the installation of malicious software. Hardware-based security modules, like Trusted Platform Modules (TPMs) or Hardware Security Modules (HSMs), provide a secure enclave for cryptographic operations and key storage, enhancing the overall security posture of IoT devices.

The proliferation of IoT devices also raises concerns about the privacy of user data. As these devices collect and transmit a vast amount of personal information, ensuring that data is handled responsibly and in compliance with privacy regulations becomes a paramount consideration. Privacy-preserving protocols, such as Homomorphic Encryption and Differential Privacy, aim to enable secure data processing while preserving the privacy of individuals. Homomorphic Encryption allows computations to be performed on encrypted data without decrypting it, while Differential Privacy focuses on adding noise to data to protect individual privacy during data analysis.

Interoperability is a persistent challenge in the IoT landscape, particularly concerning the communication between devices from different manufacturers and ecosystems. The absence of standardized security protocols and communication standards can hinder the seamless integration of diverse devices into a cohesive and secure IoT environment. Initiatives like the Open Connectivity Foundation (OCF) and the Industrial Internet Consortium (IIC) work towards developing common standards and frameworks to address interoperability challenges, including security considerations.

As IoT devices often operate in distributed and dynamic environments, ensuring the continuous monitoring and management of security postures becomes a challenging task. Security Information and Event Management (SIEM) solutions, combined with anomaly detection and behavior analysis, are instrumental in identifying and responding to potential security incidents in real-time. Additionally, Over-The-Air (OTA) updates play a crucial role in maintaining the security of IoT devices by enabling manufacturers to patch vulnerabilities and update security configurations remotely.

In conclusion, securing communication in the Internet of Things is a multifaceted challenge that demands a holistic and adaptive approach. Encryption, authentication, physical security measures, and privacy-preserving protocols are integral components of a comprehensive security framework for IoT. The development and adoption of lightweight cryptographic algorithms, interoperability standards, and scalable PKI solutions are essential to addressing the unique challenges posed by the diverse and dynamic nature of IoT ecosystems. Continuous monitoring, incident response, and proactive measures, such as OTA updates, are crucial to maintaining the security and resilience of IoT devices in the face of evolving threats. As the IoT landscape continues to expand, collaboration among industry stakeholders, regulatory bodies, and standards organizations is paramount to shaping a secure and trustworthy IoT ecosystem for the future.

Exploring new and emerging communication protocols.

Exploring the realm of new and emerging communication protocols reveals a dynamic landscape characterized by innovations aimed at addressing the evolving needs of modern communication systems. Traditional protocols such as Transmission Control Protocol (TCP) and Internet Protocol (IP) have long served as the foundation for data exchange on the internet. However, as technology advances and new use cases emerge, there is a growing demand for protocols that can offer improved performance, security, and efficiency.

One notable entry in the arena of communication protocols is QUIC (Quick UDP Internet Connections), developed by Google. QUIC is designed to overcome some of the limitations of traditional protocols by combining the functionalities of both transport and security layers. Operating over User Datagram Protocol (UDP), QUIC aims to reduce latency by minimizing the connection establishment overhead through features like connection multiplexing. Moreover, QUIC incorporates encryption as an integral part of the protocol, enhancing security by default. This protocol is particularly relevant in the context of web applications and services where low-latency communication and robust security are crucial for delivering a seamless user experience.

In the context of real-time communication, Web Real-Time Communication (WebRTC) has emerged as a transformative protocol. WebRTC enables browser-based, peer-to-peer communication for voice and video, eliminating the need for third-party plugins or applications. Embraced by web developers and supported by major browsers, WebRTC facilitates secure and efficient real-time communication directly between users' devices. The protocol leverages standardized Application Programming Interfaces (APIs) to enable features like voice calling, video chat, and file sharing, making it a versatile solution for interactive applications and services.

In the context of the Internet of Things (IoT), the Constrained Application Protocol (CoAP) has gained prominence as a lightweight and efficient communication protocol. CoAP is designed for resource-constrained devices and networks, offering a simple Request-Response model over the User Datagram Protocol (UDP). With a focus on low overhead and efficient use of network resources, CoAP is well-suited for IoT scenarios where devices often operate with limited processing power and memory. CoAP's stateless design and support for multicast communication contribute to its suitability for resource-constrained environments, making it a preferred choice for IoT applications.

For scenarios where low latency and high throughput are paramount, the Datagram Congestion Control Protocol (DCCP) has emerged as an alternative to traditional transport protocols. DCCP is designed to provide congestion control without sacrificing performance, making it well-suited for applications like real-time streaming and online gaming. By allowing applications to negotiate congestion control mechanisms, DCCP provides flexibility for optimizing communication based on specific requirements. Its ability to adapt to varying network conditions positions DCCP as a protocol of interest in contexts where responsiveness and bandwidth efficiency are critical.

In the context of enhancing security in communication, the Transport Layer Security (TLS) protocol continues to evolve with new versions and enhancements. TLS, a successor to the deprecated Secure Sockets Layer (SSL), serves as the cornerstone for securing data in transit on the internet. The latest versions of TLS, such as TLS 1.3, introduce improvements in terms of speed, efficiency, and security. With a focus on minimizing handshake latency and removing obsolete cryptographic algorithms, TLS 1.3 represents a significant advancement in securing communication channels. Its adoption is crucial in mitigating vulnerabilities associated with older TLS versions and ensuring robust encryption for sensitive data.

As the demand for decentralized and censorship-resistant communication grows, protocols like InterPlanetary File System (IPFS) and Secure Scuttlebutt (SSB) have gained attention. IPFS, a peer-to-peer hypermedia protocol, reimagines the traditional client-server model by creating a distributed file system where content is addressed using cryptographic hashes. This decentralized approach to content distribution aims to provide resilience against network failures and censorship. Secure Scuttlebutt, on the other hand, is a decentralized social networking protocol that enables users to create and share content directly with their peers. By leveraging cryptographic signatures and a distributed feed architecture, SSB prioritizes privacy and user control over data in the realm of social communication.

In the pursuit of efficient and scalable communication for machine-to-machine interactions, the Message Queuing Telemetry Transport (MQTT) protocol has gained widespread adoption. MQTT is a lightweight and open messaging protocol designed for scenarios where low bandwidth, high-latency, or unreliable networks are common. With a publish-subscribe architecture, MQTT allows devices to exchange messages in a scalable and asynchronous manner. This protocol is particularly relevant in the context of IoT, where a multitude of devices need to communicate seamlessly in a resource-efficient manner.

The emerging concept of Named Data Networking (NDN) presents a paradigm shift from the traditional host-centric model to a data-centric approach. NDN reimagines communication by naming data rather than addressing hosts, making content the primary focus of the network. By directly requesting and caching named data, NDN aims to enhance content distribution, reduce latency, and improve overall network efficiency. This approach holds promise for scenarios where content retrieval and distribution are central, such as multimedia streaming and content delivery networks.

In conclusion, the exploration of new and emerging communication protocols unveils a vibrant landscape marked by innovations addressing the diverse requirements of contemporary communication systems. From protocols like QUIC and WebRTC, enhancing real-time communication, to CoAP catering to the specific needs of IoT devices, and TLS evolving to secure data in transit, each protocol reflects the dynamic nature of communication technology. The decentralization offered by IPFS and SSB, the efficiency of DCCP in low-latency scenarios, and the data-centric approach of NDN further highlight the diverse approaches to optimizing communication in various contexts. As technology continues to advance, these protocols play pivotal roles in shaping the future of communication, providing the foundation for secure, efficient, and decentralized interactions across the digital landscape.

Chapter 6: Authentication and Authorization

Differentiating between authentication and authorization.

Authentication and authorization are two fundamental concepts in the realm of information security, playing distinct yet interconnected roles in safeguarding systems, data, and resources. These concepts are often used in conjunction to establish a comprehensive security framework, ensuring that only authorized individuals or entities access specific resources and perform designated actions within a system.

Authentication is the process of verifying the identity of a user, device, or system entity. It is the means by which an entity proves its claimed identity to a system or service. The goal of authentication is to ensure that the entity seeking access is who or what it claims to be. This process typically involves the presentation of credentials, such as usernames and passwords, biometric data, smart cards, or cryptographic keys. Authentication methods can vary in strength, with multi-factor authentication (MFA) providing a higher level of assurance by requiring multiple forms of verification. The primary aim of authentication is to establish a trusted identity for entities interacting with a system, forming the foundation for subsequent authorization decisions.

Authorization, on the other hand, deals with granting or denying permissions to authenticated entities based on their verified identity. Once an entity's identity is established through authentication, authorization determines the actions and resources that the authenticated entity is permitted to access. Authorization is essentially the process of defining and enforcing policies that dictate what a user or system entity can or cannot do within a particular system or application. Authorization decisions are often based on roles, permissions, and access controls that are predefined and configured by system administrators. These controls help ensure that users are granted only the necessary privileges required for their roles or responsibilities, minimizing the risk of unauthorized access or misuse of resources.

To illustrate the distinction between authentication and authorization, consider the scenario of accessing a secure online banking application. Authentication comes into play when a user attempts to log in, providing a username and password as credentials. The system checks these credentials against stored records to verify the user's identity. If the authentication is successful, the system proceeds to the authorization phase, determining what actions the authenticated user is allowed to perform. For instance, an authenticated user may have authorization to view account balances, transfer funds between accounts, and pay bills, but they may not have authorization to modify account settings or perform administrative actions.

In practical terms, authentication serves as the gatekeeper, ensuring that only legitimate users or entities gain entry to a system or application. Once past this initial gate, authorization takes over to govern the actions and operations the authenticated entity can undertake. This separation of concerns is a fundamental principle in security design, promoting a layered approach that minimizes the impact of potential security breaches. Even if an attacker manages to compromise authentication credentials, robust authorization controls can limit the extent of unauthorized activities.

Authentication and authorization are integral components of access control systems, which are crucial in various domains, including information technology, physical security, and online services. In the context of web applications and services, technologies such as OAuth (Open Authorization) and OpenID Connect are commonly used to facilitate authentication and authorization processes. OAuth, specifically designed for delegated authorization, enables users to grant third-party applications limited access to their resources without exposing their credentials. OpenID Connect, built on top of OAuth, adds an identity layer, providing a standardized way for users to authenticate and obtain information about their identity, which can then be used for authorization decisions.

In enterprise environments, access control mechanisms often rely on role-based access control (RBAC) or attribute-based access control (ABAC) models for authorization. RBAC assigns permissions to roles, and users are assigned specific roles based on their job responsibilities. ABAC, on the other hand, considers a variety of attributes (such as user characteristics, environmental conditions, and resource properties) to make dynamic authorization decisions. These models enhance flexibility and scalability in managing permissions within complex organizational structures.

As technology evolves, so do the challenges associated with authentication and authorization. The rise of cloud computing, mobile devices, and the Internet of Things (IoT) introduces new considerations for securing identities and controlling access. Federated identity management, which enables users to use a single set of credentials across multiple systems or services, is one approach to address the complexities of authentication in distributed and interconnected environments. Additionally, advancements in biometric authentication, such as fingerprint recognition, facial recognition, and behavioral biometrics, contribute to enhancing the strength and user-friendliness of authentication mechanisms.

In conclusion, while authentication and authorization are distinct concepts, they work together seamlessly to establish and enforce secure access controls. Authentication verifies the identity of entities seeking access, while authorization determines the actions and resources that authenticated entities are permitted to access based on predefined policies. Together, these processes form the foundation of access control systems, safeguarding sensitive information and resources in diverse domains. As technologies continue to advance and security challenges evolve, the careful consideration and implementation of robust authentication and authorization mechanisms remain critical in ensuring the integrity, confidentiality, and availability of systems and data.

The importance of MFA in enhancing authentication security.

Multi-Factor Authentication (MFA) stands as a cornerstone in modern cybersecurity, playing a pivotal role in enhancing authentication security by adding layers of defense to verify the identity of users, devices, or systems. At its core, MFA addresses the limitations of traditional single-factor authentication methods, typically reliant on usernames and passwords. While these credentials have long been the standard for user authentication, their susceptibility to various attacks, such as phishing, credential stuffing, and brute-force attempts, underscores the necessity for a more robust and layered approach.

The significance of MFA lies in its ability to augment the authentication process with additional factors beyond the traditional username-password combination. By requiring users to provide multiple forms of identification, MFA substantially strengthens the security posture of systems and applications. The factors used in MFA are generally categorized into three types: something the user knows (knowledge-based factors), something the user has (possession-based factors), and something the user is (biometric factors).

Knowledge-based factors include elements that the user knows, such as passwords or personal identification numbers (PINs). While passwords remain a crucial component of authentication, their vulnerability to various attacks necessitates the integration of additional factors. MFA introduces the concept of possession-based factors, requiring users to possess something unique, typically a physical device like a smartphone, security token, or smart card. The possession of such items serves as an additional layer of validation, ensuring that even if a user's password is compromised, an attacker would still need the physical device to gain access.

Biometric factors add a dimension of uniqueness tied to the user's physiological or behavioral traits, such as fingerprints, retina scans, facial recognition, or voice patterns. Biometric authentication enhances security by leveraging the inherent uniqueness of these biological characteristics, making it significantly more challenging for unauthorized individuals to mimic or reproduce. Integrating biometrics into the MFA framework provides a high level of assurance regarding the user's identity, contributing to a robust defense against unauthorized access.

The holistic nature of MFA addresses the evolving threat landscape, where cyber adversaries employ increasingly sophisticated techniques to compromise authentication mechanisms. Phishing attacks, which involve tricking users into divulging their credentials through deceptive means, are mitigated by MFA's requirement for additional factors. Even if a user falls victim to a phishing attempt and provides their username and password, the lack of the secondary factor prevents unauthorized access.

Credential stuffing attacks, where attackers use stolen usernames and passwords from one service to gain unauthorized access to another, are thwarted by MFA's multi-layered approach. Even if an attacker manages to obtain a set of valid credentials, the absence of the additional authentication factors acts as a significant deterrent, preventing unauthorized entry.

The importance of MFA extends beyond thwarting external threats; it is equally critical in addressing insider threats and mitigating the impact of compromised credentials within organizations. In scenarios where employees inadvertently share or lose their credentials, MFA acts as a safeguard, requiring an additional layer of verification that extends beyond the compromised password. This additional layer introduces a proactive defense mechanism, reducing the risk of unauthorized access and potential data breaches resulting from internal security lapses.

The implementation of MFA aligns with the principles of the Zero Trust security model, which advocates for continuous verification and validation of user identities and devices, regardless of their location or network context. In a Zero Trust environment, the assumption is that no user or device should be automatically trusted, and MFA becomes an integral component in enforcing this principle. By incorporating multiple factors in the authentication process, MFA aligns with the Zero Trust philosophy, creating a more resilient and adaptive security posture.

As organizations increasingly migrate to cloud-based services and adopt remote work arrangements, the importance of MFA becomes even more pronounced. Cloud services, which store and process vast amounts of sensitive data, present lucrative targets for cybercriminals. MFA acts as a critical defense mechanism in such environments, ensuring that even if a user's credentials are compromised, an additional layer of verification is required to access cloud resources.

The convenience and ubiquity of mobile devices have contributed to the widespread adoption of MFA. Mobile-based authentication methods, such as one-time passcodes delivered through SMS, mobile apps, or push notifications, offer a seamless and user-friendly experience. Leveraging the possession factor, mobile-based MFA enhances security without imposing undue burden on users. Additionally, the integration of biometric authentication on mobile devices further augments the security of MFA, as users can authenticate using their fingerprints, facial recognition, or other biometric features.

While MFA significantly enhances authentication security, its successful implementation requires careful consideration of usability, scalability, and integration with existing systems. Striking the right balance between security and user experience is crucial to ensure that MFA does not become an impediment to productivity. Organizations need to educate users about the importance of MFA, provide clear guidance on its usage, and implement solutions that align with the specific needs and constraints of their user base.

In conclusion, the importance of Multi-Factor Authentication in enhancing authentication security cannot be overstated. In a landscape where cyber threats continue to evolve and traditional authentication methods are increasingly vulnerable, MFA provides a robust defense by requiring multiple forms of identification. Whether through knowledge-based factors like passwords, possession-based factors like mobile devices or security tokens, or biometric factors like fingerprints and facial recognition, MFA offers a layered approach that mitigates the risk of unauthorized access. Its role in addressing phishing attacks, credential stuffing, insider threats, and aligning with the Zero Trust security model positions MFA as a cornerstone in safeguarding digital identities and securing access to critical systems and data. As organizations navigate the complexities of cybersecurity, MFA emerges as a vital tool in building resilient defenses and adapting to the evolving threat landscape.

Understanding OAuth for authorization and OpenID Connect for authentication.

Understanding OAuth for authorization and OpenID Connect for authentication involves delving into the intricacies of modern identity and access management protocols that have become integral to securing applications, services, and resources in the digital landscape. OAuth, short for "Open Authorization," serves as a framework for delegated authorization, enabling users to grant third-party applications limited access to their resources without sharing their credentials. OAuth operates as an open standard that facilitates secure and standardized authorization workflows between different parties, such as users, applications, and resource servers.

The fundamental premise of OAuth is to allow users to delegate access to their protected resources without revealing their credentials to third-party applications. This is achieved through a process involving four key roles: the resource owner (the user who owns the protected resource), the client (the third-party application seeking access), the authorization server (responsible for authenticating the resource owner and obtaining authorization), and the resource server (hosting the protected resources).

The OAuth workflow typically begins with the client requesting authorization from the resource owner to access specific resources. To facilitate this, the client redirects the resource owner to the authorization server, initiating the authorization request. The resource owner, upon authenticating with the authorization server, grants or denies the requested permissions. If granted, the authorization server issues an authorization code to the client. This code is then exchanged for an access token, a credential that the client can present to the resource server to access the requested resources on behalf of the resource owner.

OAuth's flexibility and extensibility have led to its widespread adoption in various scenarios, including web and mobile applications, APIs, and cloud services. OAuth's versatility is evident in its support for various grant types, each catering to specific use cases. Common grant types include Authorization Code Grant, Implicit Grant, Resource Owner Password Credentials Grant, and Client Credentials Grant. Each grant type defines a different set of interactions between the client, resource owner, and authorization server, allowing OAuth to accommodate a wide range of authentication and authorization scenarios.

While OAuth excels at delegated authorization, it does not inherently address authentication concerns. This is where OpenID Connect (OIDC) comes into play. OpenID Connect is an identity layer built on top of OAuth 2.0, designed specifically for user authentication. OIDC extends OAuth by introducing additional mechanisms to verify the identity of users and obtain information about them. It simplifies the process of authenticating users while leveraging OAuth's authorization capabilities.

In the context of OpenID Connect, three main roles are defined: the end-user (an individual who uses the client's application), the relying party (the client application that relies on identity information), and the OpenID provider (the entity responsible for authenticating the end-user and providing identity information). The OpenID provider is often the same entity as the OAuth authorization server, streamlining the integration of authentication and authorization.

The OIDC authentication process builds upon the OAuth framework, introducing the concept of ID tokens. An ID token is a JSON Web Token (JWT) that contains claims about the authentication of the end-user. When an end-user authenticates with the OpenID provider, the provider issues an ID token along with the access token. The ID token serves as a secure and verifiable way for the client to obtain information about the authenticated user.

The OIDC authentication flow, known as the Authorization Code Flow, closely resembles the OAuth Authorization Code Grant. In this flow, the client redirects the end-user to the OpenID provider for authentication. After authentication, the OpenID provider issues an authorization code, which the client exchanges for both an access token and an ID token. The access token is then used to access protected resources, while the ID token provides identity information about the authenticated end-user.

One of the key benefits of OIDC is its standardization of identity information. The ID token contains standardized claims such as the subject (a unique identifier for the user), the issuer (the OpenID provider's identifier), and the audience (the intended recipient of the ID token). This standardization enhances interoperability, allowing clients to confidently interpret and use identity information across different OpenID providers.

The combination of OAuth and OpenID Connect provides a comprehensive solution for securing modern applications. OAuth addresses the delegation of authorization, allowing applications to access resources on behalf of users, while OpenID Connect focuses on authentication, providing a standardized way to verify user identities and obtain identity information. This separation of concerns aligns with the principles of security best practices, enabling organizations to build secure, scalable, and interoperable systems.

The OAuth and OpenID Connect frameworks are particularly well-suited for scenarios involving Single Sign-On (SSO), where users can authenticate once and then access multiple applications without re-entering their credentials. The use of standardized tokens, such as ID tokens and access tokens, enhances the efficiency of SSO implementations. Additionally, the frameworks accommodate the integration of social identity providers, enabling users to authenticate using accounts from popular platforms like Google, Facebook, or Microsoft.

Security considerations are paramount in the OAuth and OpenID Connect ecosystems. Threats such as token leakage, token replay attacks, and insecure communication channels must be addressed through proper implementation practices. The use of HTTPS, token expiration policies, secure storage of tokens, and adherence to best practices in token validation contribute to a robust security posture.

The adoption of OAuth and OpenID Connect is widespread across industries, with major identity providers and technology platforms supporting these standards. OAuth and OpenID Connect have become integral components of identity and access management strategies, providing a foundation for secure, scalable, and user-friendly authentication and authorization mechanisms. The frameworks' success is evidenced by their incorporation into industry-specific standards, such as Financial-grade API (FAPI) for the financial sector and Health Relationship Trust (HEART) for healthcare, further demonstrating their adaptability to diverse use cases.

In conclusion, OAuth and OpenID Connect collectively form a powerful duo in the realm of identity and access management. OAuth's focus on delegated authorization enables secure and standardized access to resources, while OpenID Connect's emphasis on authentication provides a standardized way to verify user identities and obtain identity information. The combination of these frameworks supports modern authentication and authorization scenarios, offering a robust and interoperable solution for securing applications, services, and APIs. As organizations navigate the complexities of identity management, understanding the synergy between OAuth and OpenID Connect becomes essential in building secure, scalable, and user-centric systems in the evolving landscape of digital identity.

The concept of tokens in authentication.

The concept of tokens in authentication is a fundamental aspect of modern identity and access management systems, playing a pivotal role in securing digital interactions and ensuring that only authorized entities gain access to protected resources. At its core, a token is a piece of data that represents the authorization granted to a user or system entity. Unlike traditional authentication methods that might involve the exchange of sensitive credentials like passwords, tokens offer a more secure and scalable approach by providing a temporary and revocable proof of authentication.

Tokens in the context of authentication are closely associated with token-based authentication systems, which have gained widespread adoption due to their efficiency, flexibility, and enhanced security features. In token-based authentication, the authentication process involves the exchange of a token rather than the sharing of sensitive credentials directly. This approach aligns with the principles of security best practices, mitigating the risks associated with common threats such as password theft, replay attacks, and man-in-the-middle attacks.

Tokens serve as digital credentials that encapsulate information about the authenticated entity, the granted permissions, and additional metadata. One of the key advantages of tokens is their ability to carry context-specific information, allowing for fine-grained access control and reducing the need for repeated authentication. The lifecycle of a token typically involves its issuance, usage, validation, and expiration, with each phase contributing to the overall security and effectiveness of the authentication process.

The issuance of tokens is a critical phase in the authentication workflow. When a user successfully authenticates, the authentication server generates a token containing relevant information, such as the user's identity, the scope of authorization, and a unique identifier. This process often involves the use of cryptographic techniques to ensure the integrity and confidentiality of the token. Commonly used token formats include JSON Web Tokens (JWT), Security Assertion Markup Language (SAML) tokens, and OAuth tokens, each catering to specific use cases and requirements.

Once issued, tokens become the currency of authentication, serving as the means by which a user proves their identity to access protected resources. Tokens are presented to resource servers or services during subsequent interactions to demonstrate that the bearer has been authenticated and possesses the necessary permissions. This decoupling of the authentication and authorization phases allows for more efficient and scalable authorization workflows, as resource servers can rely on the information encapsulated within the token without the need for direct communication with the authentication server.

Token validation is a critical step in the authentication process, ensuring that the presented token is legitimate, has not been tampered with, and remains within its validity period. The authentication server or resource server performs cryptographic verification to validate the token's signature, confirming its authenticity. Additionally, token validation may involve checks against token revocation lists or other mechanisms to ascertain the current status of the token. The robustness of token validation mechanisms is crucial in preventing unauthorized access and maintaining the integrity of the authentication system.

Token expiration is an essential aspect of token management, contributing to the security of the authentication process. Tokens are typically issued with a predefined expiration time, after which they become invalid. This time-based validity mitigates the risk associated with long-lived tokens and enhances the system's resilience against certain types of attacks, such as token replay attacks. Token expiration also aligns with the principle of least privilege, ensuring that access permissions are regularly revalidated, and users must reauthenticate to continue accessing protected resources.

The concept of refresh tokens adds an additional layer of flexibility to token-based authentication systems. Refresh tokens are long-lived credentials that, when presented to the authentication server, allow for the issuance of new access tokens without requiring the user to reauthenticate. This mechanism is particularly useful in scenarios where the user's credentials remain unchanged, but the access token needs to be periodically refreshed to maintain an active session. The use of refresh tokens strikes a balance between security and usability, reducing the frequency of full authentication while maintaining a dynamic and secure access control model.

Token-based authentication is widely employed in various authentication protocols and frameworks, each tailored to specific use cases and security requirements. OAuth 2.0, a widely adopted authorization framework, utilizes access tokens for resource access delegation and employs refresh tokens to enable secure token renewal.

OpenID Connect, built on top of OAuth 2.0, introduces the concept of ID tokens, which carry identity information about the authenticated user. These standardized token formats contribute to interoperability, allowing different systems and services to understand and process tokens consistently.

In the realm of web development, Single Sign-On (SSO) systems often rely on token-based authentication to enable seamless and secure user experiences across multiple applications. When a user authenticates with one application, the authentication server issues a token that can be presented to other applications within the same ecosystem, granting access without the need for repeated authentication. This not only enhances user convenience but also ensures a centralized and consistent approach to authentication and authorization.

As the digital landscape evolves, the concept of tokens in authentication continues to adapt to emerging technologies and security challenges. Mobile applications, APIs, and microservices increasingly rely on token-based authentication to facilitate secure communication and access control. The integration of biometric authentication and federated identity providers further expands the capabilities of token-based systems, enhancing both the security and user experience aspects of authentication.

In conclusion, tokens in authentication represent a crucial paradigm shift in securing digital interactions, providing a secure, scalable, and flexible approach to proving and managing user identity. Through token-based authentication, the risks associated with traditional credential-based systems are mitigated, and fine-grained access control becomes achievable. The issuance, usage, validation, and expiration of tokens collectively contribute to the robustness and effectiveness of modern authentication systems. As organizations embrace token-based authentication in various domains, from web applications to APIs and beyond, understanding and implementing secure token management practices becomes paramount in building resilient and user-friendly authentication mechanisms for the digital age.

Exploring the use of biometrics for user authentication.

Exploring the use of biometrics for user authentication unveils a transformative approach to verifying and validating individuals based on unique physiological or behavioral characteristics. In an era where traditional authentication methods, such as passwords and PINs, face increasing vulnerabilities, biometrics offer a promising alternative by leveraging the intrinsic features that distinguish one person from another. The rich tapestry of biometric modalities includes fingerprints, facial recognition, iris scans, voice patterns, palm prints, and even behavioral traits like keystroke dynamics and gait analysis. Each biometric modality presents distinct advantages, and the selection often depends on factors such as security requirements, user acceptance, and the specific use case.

Fingerprint recognition stands as one of the most widely adopted biometric modalities, leveraging the unique patterns of ridges and valleys on an individual's fingertips. Fingerprint scanners capture and analyze these patterns, creating a biometric template that serves as a digital representation of the fingerprint. The widespread use of fingerprint authentication in smartphones, laptops, and physical access systems attests to its reliability and user acceptance. Advances in sensor technology and image processing have significantly enhanced the accuracy and speed of fingerprint recognition, making it a mainstream choice for securing devices and applications.

Facial recognition, another prominent biometric modality, relies on analyzing facial features such as the distance between eyes, nose shape, and jawline to create a unique facial template. The ubiquity of cameras in smartphones and surveillance systems has fueled the proliferation of facial recognition applications. It finds application in various domains, from unlocking smartphones to airport security and law enforcement. However, concerns related to privacy, accuracy, and potential biases in certain implementations underscore the need for responsible deployment and ongoing refinement of facial recognition technologies.

Iris recognition, characterized by the unique patterns in the colored part of the eye, offers a high level of accuracy and security. Iris scanners capture intricate details that are difficult to forge or replicate, making it a robust biometric modality for access control and identity verification. Although less prevalent than fingerprint and facial recognition, iris recognition is gaining traction in applications where a higher level of security is paramount, such as border control and secure facilities.

Voice recognition leverages the distinct characteristics of an individual's vocal tract, including pitch, tone, and speech patterns, to create a unique voiceprint. Widely used in telephone-based authentication systems, voice recognition provides a natural and non-intrusive means of user verification. However, environmental factors, variations in speech due to illness or emotion, and the need for high-quality audio recordings pose challenges to its widespread adoption in certain scenarios.

Palm print recognition involves capturing and analyzing the unique patterns on an individual's palm, including the lines, ridges, and creases. Palm prints offer a larger surface area compared to fingerprints, potentially enhancing accuracy. While less common than other biometric modalities, palm print recognition finds applications in physical access control, particularly in environments where hygiene considerations may favor contactless authentication.

Behavioral biometrics introduce a unique dimension to user authentication by analyzing inherent patterns in an individual's behavior. Keystroke dynamics, for example, assess the rhythm and timing of typing on a keyboard, while gait analysis focuses on the unique way an individual walks. These behavioral traits can serve as additional layers of authentication or be used in scenarios where physical biometrics may not be practical. Behavioral biometrics are less intrusive and offer continuous authentication, adapting to changes in a user's behavior over time.

The adoption of biometrics for user authentication aligns with the shift towards user-centric and frictionless security experiences. Biometrics offer the advantage of being inherently tied to the individual, reducing the reliance on external tokens or memorized credentials. This not only enhances security but also addresses user fatigue associated with password management and the inconvenience of carrying physical tokens.

Despite the evident advantages of biometrics, several challenges and considerations must be addressed for their effective and ethical deployment. Privacy concerns, particularly regarding the storage and misuse of biometric data, necessitate robust data protection measures and adherence to privacy regulations. Biometric systems must prioritize transparency and user consent, providing individuals with clear information on how their biometric data will be used and stored.

The potential for bias in biometric systems, especially in facial recognition technology, has raised ethical and social concerns. Biases may arise from the underrepresentation of certain demographics in training datasets, leading to inaccuracies and unfair outcomes. Addressing biases requires diverse and representative datasets, ongoing monitoring, and continuous refinement of algorithms to ensure equitable and unbiased performance across diverse populations.

Security considerations in biometric systems extend beyond privacy and bias to encompass protection against spoofing or presentation attacks. Techniques such as using liveness detection to ensure the presence of a live and authentic user during biometric capture mitigate the risk of impersonation using replicas or digital media. Additionally, cryptographic measures, secure transmission protocols, and secure storage of biometric templates are essential components of a comprehensive biometric security strategy.

The integration of biometrics into multi-factor authentication (MFA) frameworks further enhances overall security. Combining biometrics with traditional authentication factors, such as passwords or PINs, creates a layered defense, requiring attackers to overcome multiple barriers. This multi-layered approach aligns with the principle of defense-in-depth and significantly raises the bar for unauthorized access.

The advent of mobile biometrics, embedded in smartphones and tablets, has democratized access to biometric authentication. Fingerprint sensors and facial recognition capabilities integrated into mobile devices have become commonplace, providing users with a seamless and secure means of unlocking their devices and authorizing transactions. The widespread adoption of biometrics in consumer devices has contributed to increased familiarity and acceptance among users.

In the enterprise context, biometrics are employed for securing access to sensitive systems, facilities, and data. Biometric authentication mitigates the risks associated with stolen or compromised passwords, as the biometric template is unique to each individual and challenging to replicate. The use of biometrics in conjunction with other authentication factors adds an extra layer of assurance, particularly in industries where stringent security requirements prevail.

As technology continues to advance, emerging trends in biometrics include the exploration of novel modalities, such as vein pattern recognition, earlobe geometry, and even brainwave-based authentication. The convergence of biometrics with artificial intelligence and machine learning holds the promise of improving accuracy, adaptability, and the ability to detect anomalies or suspicious patterns.

In conclusion, exploring the use of biometrics for user authentication reveals a dynamic landscape where the unique attributes of individuals become the key to secure access. From fingerprint and facial recognition to iris, voice, palm print, and behavioral biometrics, each modality offers distinct advantages in terms of accuracy, user experience, and security. The integration of biometrics into authentication systems requires a holistic approach, addressing privacy concerns, mitigating biases, and implementing robust security measures. As biometric technologies evolve and become more pervasive, they have the potential to redefine the future of user authentication, offering a balance between security, convenience, and user-centric experiences in the digital age.

Implementing RBAC for fine-grained authorization.

Implementing Role-Based Access Control (RBAC) for fine-grained authorization is a sophisticated approach to managing access rights within a system or application. RBAC is a well-established model that provides a structured and scalable method for defining, enforcing, and managing permissions based on roles assigned to users. In traditional RBAC implementations, users are assigned predefined roles, each associated with a set of permissions that determine what actions the users can perform within the system. However, for scenarios requiring more granular control over access, fine-grained RBAC extends this model by allowing the specification of permissions at a more detailed level, often down to the level of individual data records or specific operations.

The foundation of RBAC lies in the concept of roles, which represent sets of permissions that align with the responsibilities or functions within an organization. Fine-grained RBAC refines this concept by recognizing that not all users with the same role should have identical access to every resource or operation. Instead, it introduces the notion of attribute-based access control (ABAC) to allow for nuanced control based on user attributes, environmental conditions, or other contextual factors. This enables administrators to tailor access permissions with greater precision, addressing the need for more intricate authorization scenarios.

In a fine-grained RBAC system, the first step is to define the roles that reflect the various responsibilities or functions within the organization. These roles serve as the building blocks for access control policies. Unlike traditional RBAC, fine-grained RBAC emphasizes the importance of carefully defining not only what actions users can perform but also the specific context or conditions under which those actions are permitted. For example, a role might grant read access to certain sensitive data only during specific business hours or to users in a particular geographic location.

The next crucial aspect of implementing fine-grained RBAC is the definition of permissions at a granular level. Rather than associating a role with a broad set of permissions, administrators can specify permissions that pertain to specific attributes, fields, or operations within the system. For instance, a user with a finance role might have permissions to view salary information but only for employees within their department. This level of granularity ensures that access is restricted to the data or actions relevant to the user's role and responsibilities.

Fine-grained RBAC also introduces the concept of constraints, which allow administrators to define additional conditions that must be satisfied for a permission to be granted. These constraints can be based on user attributes, such as job title or department, as well as environmental factors like time of day or network location. Constraints add an extra layer of flexibility and control, enabling administrators to tailor access policies to the dynamic and context-dependent nature of modern organizations.

The assignment of roles and permissions is a crucial administrative task in fine-grained RBAC. User-role assignments must be made thoughtfully, considering the specific access needs of individuals within the organization. This process is typically guided by the principle of least privilege, ensuring that users are granted the minimum level of access required to fulfill their responsibilities. Moreover, administrators need to be vigilant in periodically reviewing and updating these assignments to reflect changes in organizational structure, personnel, or access requirements.

Fine-grained RBAC systems often incorporate the concept of hierarchy, allowing roles to be organized in a structured manner. A role hierarchy can simplify administration by inheriting permissions and constraints from higher-level roles to lower-level roles. This hierarchical structure streamlines the assignment of permissions, making it more intuitive and efficient, especially in large and complex organizations. Users with roles at different levels of the hierarchy inherit the permissions associated with their role and all the roles above it in the hierarchy.

The enforcement of fine-grained RBAC policies requires a robust access control mechanism integrated into the system architecture. This mechanism evaluates access requests against the defined roles, permissions, and constraints to determine whether the requested action should be allowed. Access control decisions take into account the user's assigned roles, the permissions associated with those roles, and any additional constraints that may be applicable. The enforcement mechanism acts as a gatekeeper, ensuring that users can only access resources and perform actions that align with their roles and the fine-grained access policies defined in the system.

Audit trails and logging play a crucial role in fine-grained RBAC implementations. The ability to trace access and actions performed by users is essential for security, compliance, and accountability. Detailed audit logs capture information such as who accessed what resource, when the access occurred, and whether the access was allowed or denied. This audit trail aids in forensic analysis, compliance reporting, and identifying potential security incidents. Additionally, periodic reviews of audit logs contribute to ongoing security assessments and help organizations maintain a proactive stance in managing access control.

Fine-grained RBAC is particularly beneficial in scenarios where data privacy and regulatory compliance are paramount. Industries such as healthcare, finance, and government, which handle sensitive and regulated information, can leverage fine-grained RBAC to ensure that access is precisely controlled to meet compliance requirements. The ability to enforce access policies at a granular level, including constraints based on data sensitivity or privacy considerations, aligns fine-grained RBAC with the stringent demands of regulatory frameworks.

The integration of fine-grained RBAC with identity management systems enhances the overall efficiency of access control. Centralized identity management allows for seamless synchronization of user attributes, roles, and permissions across different systems and applications. This integration simplifies the administration of access control policies and ensures consistency in user access across the organization. As employees change roles or responsibilities, the identity management system can automatically update their access privileges based on predefined rules.

While the benefits of fine-grained RBAC are evident, the successful implementation of such a system requires careful consideration of potential challenges and mitigations. Balancing the need for granularity with the risk of complexity is a key challenge. Administrators must strike a balance between providing detailed control over access and maintaining a system that is comprehensible, maintainable, and efficient. Excessive complexity can lead to administrative overhead, increased likelihood of misconfigurations, and challenges in troubleshooting access-related issues.

Additionally, user education and communication are critical aspects of implementing fine-grained RBAC. Users need to understand the access policies relevant to their roles, including any constraints or conditions that apply. Clear communication and training programs help ensure that users are aware of the access controls in place and understand how to request exceptions or escalate access-related issues. This proactive approach contributes to a positive user experience while maintaining the integrity of the access control system.

In conclusion, the implementation of fine-grained RBAC represents a sophisticated and powerful approach to access control, offering organizations the ability to define and enforce access policies at a highly detailed level. The combination of roles, permissions, constraints, and hierarchy creates a flexible and adaptable framework for managing access to resources, data, and functionalities within a system. While challenges exist in terms of complexity and user communication, the benefits of fine-grained RBAC, especially in industries with stringent regulatory requirements, make it a valuable tool in the arsenal of access control strategies. As organizations strive for precision, efficiency, and compliance in their access management practices, the adoption of fine-grained RBAC emerges as a strategic choice to meet these objectives in a dynamic and evolving security landscape.

Understanding ABAC and its benefits in dynamic access control.

Understanding Attribute-Based Access Control (ABAC) and its benefits in dynamic access control provides insights into a contemporary approach to managing access to resources and data within complex and evolving organizational landscapes. ABAC represents a departure from traditional access control models by introducing a more flexible and context-aware framework that leverages attributes associated with users, resources, and the environment to make access decisions. In contrast to Role-Based Access Control (RBAC), which relies on predefined roles and permissions, ABAC considers a broader set of attributes and conditions, allowing for a more nuanced and adaptive access control paradigm.

The core principle of ABAC is to evaluate access requests based on a set of attributes associated with the user, the resource, and the context in which the request occurs. User attributes may include role, department, location, and other characteristics, while resource attributes could encompass sensitivity, classification, and ownership. Contextual attributes, such as time of day, location, and device type, contribute to a more dynamic access control decision-making process. ABAC thus enables organizations to move beyond static, role-centric access policies and towards a more fine-grained and situation-aware approach.

One of the primary benefits of ABAC lies in its ability to adapt to the dynamic nature of modern organizations. In environments characterized by frequent personnel changes, diverse roles, and evolving data classifications, the rigid structure of traditional access control models can become a hindrance. ABAC addresses this challenge by allowing administrators to define policies that consider a multitude of attributes, enabling access decisions to align with the evolving needs and complexities of the organization. This adaptability is particularly valuable in industries where agility, scalability, and compliance with changing regulations are essential.

ABAC excels in scenarios where traditional models may struggle to accommodate the complexities of access control. For instance, in healthcare settings where access to patient records must be tightly controlled based on the patient's healthcare provider, the type of data, and the patient's consent, ABAC allows for the creation of policies that consider these granular attributes. This level of granularity ensures that access decisions are not only secure but also aligned with the specific requirements and constraints of the healthcare environment.

The incorporation of attributes in ABAC enables the implementation of fine-grained access policies that go beyond the binary notion of granting or denying access. ABAC allows for the specification of conditions or constraints that must be met for access to be granted. This nuanced approach is particularly relevant in situations where access may be contingent on specific circumstances, such as allowing access to sensitive data only during business hours or restricting access to certain resources based on the user's geographical location. By incorporating contextual attributes, ABAC provides a level of flexibility that is essential for today's dynamic and geographically dispersed organizations.

Another notable advantage of ABAC is its support for externalized and centralized policy decision points. In ABAC architectures, policy decisions are made by a Policy Decision Point (PDP), which can be a centralized component responsible for evaluating access requests against defined policies. This separation of policy decision from the application or resource allows for consistent and centralized policy management, simplifying the enforcement of access controls across diverse systems and applications. It also facilitates the maintenance of a single source of truth for access policies, reducing the likelihood of inconsistencies or conflicts in access control rules.

The integration of ABAC with external attribute sources further enhances its capabilities. ABAC systems can leverage information from external sources, such as identity providers, directory services, or even external databases, to enrich the set of attributes available for making access decisions. This integration ensures that access decisions are based on the most up-to-date and comprehensive information about users and resources. In dynamic environments where user attributes may change frequently, this real-time attribute retrieval enhances the accuracy and relevance of access control decisions.

ABAC aligns with the principles of least privilege and need-to-know, foundational concepts in information security. By considering a user's specific attributes and contextual factors, ABAC facilitates the enforcement of access policies that grant users the minimum level of access required to perform their tasks. This aligns with the principle of least privilege, reducing the risk of unauthorized access or misuse of resources. Additionally, the need-to-know principle is reinforced as access decisions are based on the specific attributes and conditions relevant to the user's role and the context of the access request.

The scalability of ABAC makes it well-suited for large and complex organizations with diverse user roles and a wide range of resources. As the number of users, roles, and data classifications grows, ABAC provides a scalable and manageable approach to access control. Its attribute-centric nature allows for the creation of policies that can be reused across different parts of the organization, streamlining administration and ensuring consistency in access control practices. This scalability is particularly advantageous in industries such as finance, where stringent access controls must be maintained across diverse business units and teams.

The dynamic nature of ABAC extends to its support for policy evolution and adaptation over time. In contrast to static access control models that may struggle to accommodate changes in organizational structure or data classifications, ABAC allows for the gradual refinement and evolution of access policies. This adaptability is crucial in industries where regulatory changes, mergers, acquisitions, or shifts in business processes necessitate continuous adjustments to access controls. ABAC's ability to accommodate evolving requirements positions it as a strategic choice for organizations seeking a future-proof access control solution.

The audit and reporting capabilities of ABAC contribute to compliance and accountability. ABAC systems typically generate detailed logs that capture information about access requests, policy decisions, and enforcement outcomes. These audit trails serve as valuable resources for compliance reporting, enabling organizations to demonstrate adherence to regulatory requirements and internal policies. The ability to trace access decisions back to specific attributes and contextual factors enhances transparency and supports organizations in meeting their compliance obligations.

However, the implementation of ABAC also comes with its set of considerations and challenges. Designing effective attribute structures and ensuring the accuracy of attribute data are critical aspects of a successful ABAC implementation. Inconsistencies or inaccuracies in attribute information can lead to incorrect access decisions, emphasizing the importance of robust identity management practices and data quality assurance.

Moreover, defining and managing a comprehensive set of attributes, policies, and conditions requires careful planning and ongoing governance. Organizations must invest in defining a clear taxonomy of attributes, establishing naming conventions, and ensuring that policies align with business objectives. Regular reviews and updates to attribute definitions and access policies are essential to maintaining the relevance and effectiveness of ABAC implementations over time.

In conclusion, understanding Attribute-Based Access Control (ABAC) and its benefits in dynamic access control provides organizations with a powerful framework for managing access to resources and data in a nuanced and context-aware manner. ABAC's departure from traditional access control models, its support for fine-grained policies, and its adaptability to changing organizational landscapes position it as a strategic choice for modern and dynamic environments. The incorporation of user attributes, resource attributes, and contextual factors in access decisions enhances precision, flexibility, and scalability, aligning ABAC with the evolving requirements of diverse industries. As organizations seek to balance security, compliance, and operational efficiency, ABAC emerges as a pivotal component in the arsenal of access control strategies for the digital age.

Configuring and implementing secure authorization policies.

Configuring and implementing secure authorization policies is a critical aspect of designing and maintaining a robust security posture within an organization's digital ecosystem. Authorization, a key component of the broader access control framework, governs the permissions and privileges granted to users, systems, or entities based on predefined policies. The goal is to ensure that only authorized individuals or entities can access specific resources, perform certain actions, or interact with sensitive data. In the realm of secure authorization, the process involves defining, configuring, and enforcing policies that align with the organization's security requirements, regulatory obligations, and operational needs.

The foundation of secure authorization policies lies in a clear understanding of the organization's structure, the nature of its data, and the roles and responsibilities of its users. A crucial initial step involves conducting a thorough access control analysis, identifying the various roles within the organization and mapping out the specific permissions required by each role. This analysis is essential for defining authorization policies that align with the principle of least privilege, ensuring that users are granted the minimum level of access necessary to perform their job functions. The process also involves classifying data based on sensitivity and criticality, enabling the creation of policies that reflect the appropriate level of protection for different types of information.

With a comprehensive understanding of the organization's structure and data landscape, the next step is to articulate and document authorization policies. These policies serve as a set of rules that dictate who can access what resources and under what conditions. Authorization policies often encompass a range of criteria, including user roles, data classifications, time of access, and contextual factors. For example, a policy might specify that only users with a certain role, such as financial analysts, can access financial data, and this access is permitted only during business hours. The documentation of these policies is crucial for transparency, auditability, and compliance purposes, providing a clear reference point for both administrators and auditors.

The implementation of secure authorization policies involves configuring access control mechanisms within the organization's systems, applications, and services. Role-Based Access Control (RBAC), a commonly used model, associates permissions with predefined roles and assigns users to these roles based on their job responsibilities. RBAC streamlines the administration of access control by grouping users into roles with similar access needs, simplifying the assignment and revocation of permissions. Additionally, organizations may choose to implement Attribute-Based Access Control (ABAC), which leverages user attributes, resource attributes, and contextual factors to make access decisions. ABAC provides a more dynamic and flexible approach, allowing for fine-grained control over access based on a broader set of criteria.

Centralized management of authorization policies enhances consistency and efficiency. Implementing a centralized authorization management system allows administrators to define, update, and enforce policies across multiple systems and applications from a single point. This centralization not only streamlines the administrative process but also ensures that access controls remain consistent and synchronized, reducing the risk of misconfigurations or discrepancies across different parts of the organization's IT infrastructure. Centralized management is particularly beneficial in large and distributed environments where maintaining a unified approach to access control is essential.

The enforcement of authorization policies is a crucial aspect of the implementation process. Access control mechanisms, whether embedded within applications, operating systems, or network devices, must effectively enforce the defined policies in real-time. This enforcement involves evaluating access requests against the configured policies and making access decisions based on the user's identity, assigned roles, attributes, and contextual factors. Robust enforcement mechanisms mitigate the risk of unauthorized access, protecting sensitive data and critical resources from potential security breaches.

Regular monitoring and auditing of access logs contribute to the ongoing effectiveness of secure authorization policies. Monitoring access logs allows organizations to track and analyze access patterns, detect anomalies, and identify potential security incidents. Auditing access logs is essential for compliance reporting, providing a historical record of access events that can be used to demonstrate adherence to regulatory requirements. Continuous monitoring also supports the identification of any deviations from the established policies, enabling administrators to take corrective actions promptly.

Secure authorization policies must be adaptive to accommodate changes in organizational structure, personnel, and technology. As organizations evolve, employee roles may change, new departments may be established, and the technology landscape may undergo transformations. Authorization policies need to be agile and capable of adapting to these changes without compromising security. This adaptability requires a proactive approach to policy management, involving regular reviews, updates, and adjustments to reflect the current state of the organization.

The integration of secure authorization with identity management systems enhances overall access control efficiency. Identity management systems maintain a centralized repository of user identities, roles, and attributes. Integrating authorization with identity management allows for seamless synchronization of user information, simplifying the administration of access controls. As employees join or leave the organization, change roles, or undergo other status changes, the identity management system can automatically update their access privileges based on predefined rules. This integration ensures that access controls remain synchronized with the organization's dynamic user landscape.

Multi-factor authentication (MFA) is a valuable complement to secure authorization policies, providing an additional layer of verification beyond traditional username and password credentials. MFA requires users to authenticate their identity through multiple factors, such as something they know (password), something they have (smart card or token), or something they are (biometric verification). The combination of secure authorization policies and MFA enhances the overall security posture, reducing the risk of unauthorized access even in the event of compromised credentials.

Continuous education and awareness programs are essential for promoting a culture of security and ensuring that users understand and comply with authorization policies. Employees need to be aware of the importance of following access control policies, safeguarding their credentials, and reporting any suspicious activities promptly. Training programs can include guidance on recognizing social engineering attempts, understanding the implications of unauthorized access, and adhering to organizational policies and procedures. Fostering a security-conscious culture is a proactive measure that reinforces the effectiveness of secure authorization policies.

The periodic review and assessment of authorization policies contribute to their effectiveness and relevance. As organizational dynamics evolve, it is essential to conduct regular reviews of access controls to ensure that policies align with current business needs, regulatory requirements, and security best practices. These reviews may involve assessing the accuracy of user roles and permissions, evaluating the appropriateness of data classifications, and validating the enforcement of contextual access conditions. Periodic assessments also provide an opportunity to identify and remediate any emerging risks or vulnerabilities in the access control framework.

Challenges in implementing secure authorization policies include balancing security with user convenience and addressing the potential for policy conflicts. Striking the right balance is crucial to avoid overly restrictive policies that impede productivity or excessively permissive policies that introduce security risks. User convenience is a key consideration to ensure that access controls do not hinder legitimate and necessary business operations. Additionally, careful policy design and testing are necessary to avoid conflicts that may arise when multiple policies intersect, potentially leading to unintended access outcomes.

In conclusion, configuring and implementing secure authorization policies is a multifaceted and ongoing process that requires a holistic approach to access control. From the initial analysis of organizational roles and data classifications to the documentation, configuration, enforcement, and ongoing management of policies, every stage contributes to the overall security posture. The adaptability of policies, integration with identity management, and the incorporation of additional security measures such as MFA contribute to a comprehensive and effective access control strategy. As organizations navigate the dynamic landscape of cybersecurity threats, maintaining secure authorization practices is foundational to protecting sensitive information, ensuring compliance, and fostering a culture of security awareness.

Overview of SSO and its advantages in user experience and security.

An overview of Single Sign-On (SSO) and its advantages in user experience and security provides insights into a transformative authentication model that addresses both convenience for users and enhanced security measures within digital ecosystems. Single Sign-On is a centralized authentication process that enables users to access multiple applications or services with a single set of login credentials. This departure from the traditional approach of requiring separate usernames and passwords for each system offers substantial benefits in terms of user experience and security.

One of the primary advantages of SSO lies in its positive impact on user experience. In a world where individuals interact with a multitude of applications and services daily, the burden of remembering and managing numerous sets of login credentials can lead to user frustration, password fatigue, and the risk of security lapses. SSO streamlines this experience by allowing users to authenticate themselves once and subsequently access various services without the need to repeatedly enter their credentials. This not only simplifies the user journey but also contributes to increased efficiency and productivity as users seamlessly move between applications without interruption.

Furthermore, the adoption of SSO aligns with the principle of usability, making it easier for users to comply with security best practices. Research has consistently shown that users are more likely to choose weak passwords or reuse passwords across multiple sites when confronted with the challenge of managing numerous credentials. SSO addresses this vulnerability by reducing the cognitive load on users, encouraging the creation and use of stronger, unique passwords for the single set of credentials they need to remember. This not only enhances the security of individual accounts but also reduces the risk associated with password-related attacks, such as credential stuffing.

From a security standpoint, SSO introduces several advantages that contribute to a more robust authentication ecosystem. The centralization of authentication means that organizations can implement stronger authentication methods, such as multi-factor authentication (MFA), more effectively. With SSO as the gateway to multiple services, implementing MFA at the single sign-on level significantly enhances the overall security posture. This approach ensures that even if an attacker gains access to the initial set of credentials, additional authentication factors act as a formidable barrier, providing an extra layer of protection against unauthorized access.

Moreover, SSO facilitates better management and enforcement of security policies. Organizations can implement and update security policies at the centralized authentication point, ensuring consistent application across all connected services. This centralized control is particularly valuable in ensuring that security measures, such as password complexity requirements or session timeout settings, are uniformly applied. This reduces the likelihood of vulnerabilities arising from inconsistent security configurations across diverse applications, creating a more cohesive and defensible security environment.

Another security advantage of SSO is its ability to streamline access revocation. In the event of an employee departure or a security incident, revoking access to multiple systems can be a complex and time-consuming process. With SSO, deactivating a user's access becomes more straightforward, as it can be accomplished at the centralized authentication point. This efficiency in access management minimizes the window of opportunity for unauthorized access and ensures a swift response to potential security threats, thereby enhancing the organization's overall resilience to security incidents.

SSO also contributes to better visibility and auditability. The centralized nature of SSO allows organizations to maintain comprehensive logs of user authentication and access events. This audit trail is invaluable for compliance purposes, enabling organizations to demonstrate adherence to regulatory requirements and internal security policies. Monitoring and analyzing these logs provide insights into user behavior, potential security incidents, and compliance gaps, fostering a proactive and data-driven approach to security management.

Furthermore, the adoption of SSO aligns with the growing trend of Zero Trust Security. In a Zero Trust model, trust is never assumed, and access is continuously verified, even for users inside the network. SSO, especially when combined with contextual information such as device health and user behavior analytics, reinforces the principles of Zero Trust by ensuring that users are authenticated and authorized based on the latest information and security context. This adaptive and continuous authentication approach is particularly relevant in today's dynamic and evolving threat landscape.

The integration of SSO with Identity and Access Management (IAM) systems enhances overall access control efficiency. IAM systems play a crucial role in managing user identities, roles, and access privileges. Integrating SSO with IAM ensures that user information is centralized, providing a single source of truth for user identities and access permissions. This integration simplifies the administration of access controls, ensuring that changes in user roles or access requirements are automatically reflected in the SSO environment. It also facilitates the synchronization of user attributes, streamlining the overall identity management process.

Despite these advantages, the implementation of SSO is not without challenges. One notable consideration is the risk of a single point of failure. If the SSO system experiences an outage or a security breach, users may be locked out of multiple services simultaneously. Organizations need to implement robust contingency plans, including redundancy measures and failover mechanisms, to mitigate this risk and ensure continuous access for users.

Additionally, interoperability and compatibility issues may arise when integrating SSO with various applications and services. Not all applications may support the same authentication protocols or be easily integrated into an SSO environment. This requires careful planning, testing, and potentially custom development to ensure a seamless and secure integration across the diverse landscape of an organization's IT infrastructure.

In conclusion, the overview of Single Sign-On (SSO) and its advantages in user experience and security underscores its pivotal role in modern authentication frameworks. SSO addresses the user experience challenges associated with managing multiple credentials while introducing robust security measures that align with contemporary best practices. The streamlined user journey, enhanced security through centralized management and policy enforcement, and integration with advanced authentication methods contribute to a more resilient and user-friendly authentication ecosystem. As organizations navigate the complexities of digital identity and access management, SSO emerges as a strategic enabler for achieving the delicate balance between user convenience and robust security in an increasingly interconnected and dynamic digital landscape.

Challenges and best practices for authentication and authorization in microservices.

Navigating the authentication and authorization landscape in microservices architecture poses a unique set of challenges and demands careful consideration of best practices to ensure a secure and seamless operational environment. Microservices, characterized by their decentralized and independently deployable nature, introduce complexities in managing user identities, access controls, and security protocols across a distributed system.

One of the foremost challenges in microservices authentication lies in the need for a cohesive and standardized approach across diverse services. With each microservice potentially employing different technologies, frameworks, or authentication mechanisms, achieving a unified authentication experience becomes a significant hurdle. This challenge is further exacerbated by the varying communication protocols and data formats utilized by microservices, requiring a thoughtful strategy to establish a common ground for authentication protocols.

Microservices often leverage token-based authentication mechanisms, with JSON Web Tokens (JWT) being a prevalent choice. While tokens offer advantages such as statelessness and scalability, they introduce the challenge of securely managing token issuance, validation, and expiration across multiple services. Best practices involve implementing robust token validation mechanisms, regularly rotating tokens to minimize the risk of compromise, and considering the use of token introspection to centralize token verification.

Maintaining a secure and reliable user identity across microservices is another considerable challenge. Traditional monolithic applications might rely on a centralized user database, but microservices often demand a decentralized approach. Implementing federated identity management or utilizing standards like OAuth 2.0 and OpenID Connect helps address this challenge by enabling secure and standardized user authentication and identity propagation across microservices. However, ensuring consistent identity across services requires meticulous design and alignment with the organization's security policies.

Authorization in microservices introduces complexities related to defining and enforcing access controls in a decentralized environment. Microservices typically follow the principle of data ownership, where each microservice manages its own data and associated access controls. This decentralized model challenges the traditional role of a centralized authorization server, demanding a shift towards a distributed and service-centric approach. Implementing Attribute-Based Access Control (ABAC) or using a policy engine can aid in defining fine-grained access policies that align with the microservices architecture.

A crucial challenge lies in securing inter-service communication, especially in a microservices architecture where services need to trust each other for seamless operation. Implementing mutual TLS (Transport Layer Security) for encrypting communication between microservices helps establish a secure and authenticated channel. Additionally, leveraging service meshes like Istio or Linkerd can provide a centralized control plane for managing secure communication, traffic routing, and enforcing policies without burdening individual microservices.

Microservices often require a robust strategy for handling authentication and authorization failures. Traditional monolithic applications might have a single point of failure, but in a microservices ecosystem, failures can cascade across services. Best practices involve implementing graceful degradation mechanisms, fallback authentication methods, and well-defined error-handling strategies to prevent widespread service disruptions in the face of authentication or authorization issues.

The dynamic nature of microservices, with services scaling up or down based on demand, poses a challenge in managing authentication and authorization at scale. Traditional approaches relying on session-based authentication may not align with the stateless and scalable nature of microservices. Leveraging stateless authentication mechanisms, such as JWT, and employing distributed caching or token validation services can help address scalability challenges while ensuring consistent security across the microservices ecosystem.

Ensuring that microservices are compliant with regulatory requirements and security standards is a persistent challenge. Microservices might handle sensitive data, and demonstrating compliance becomes complex when each service operates independently. Adopting a security-by-design approach, conducting regular security audits, and ensuring that each microservice adheres to relevant compliance standards are essential best practices. Integrating security into the microservices development lifecycle helps preemptively address compliance concerns.

The microservices paradigm introduces challenges in managing and synchronizing user roles and permissions across services. In monolithic architectures, a centralized database often handles user roles, but in microservices, this necessitates decentralized role management. Best practices involve adopting a role-based access control (RBAC) approach, using lightweight directory services or identity providers, and ensuring that role synchronization mechanisms are resilient and capable of handling dynamic changes in user roles.

Microservices authentication and authorization must align with the organization's overall security strategy. Ensuring consistency in security policies and practices across all microservices is a non-trivial challenge. Best practices include defining a comprehensive security framework, providing clear guidelines for microservices development teams, and regularly conducting security reviews to identify and rectify deviations from established security standards.

Implementing secure and user-friendly authentication mechanisms for external clients, such as mobile applications or third-party integrations, presents a distinctive challenge in microservices. Microservices might expose APIs that require secure and scalable authentication solutions. Leveraging OAuth 2.0 and OpenID Connect, providing secure token issuance and validation mechanisms, and employing API gateways with built-in authentication capabilities are essential best practices to address these challenges.

Microservices authentication and authorization demand a dynamic response to the evolving threat landscape. Traditional security measures may fall short in the face of sophisticated attacks or vulnerabilities specific to microservices architecture. Employing threat modeling, conducting regular security assessments, and staying informed about emerging security threats are vital best practices to enhance the resilience of microservices against potential security risks.

In conclusion, while microservices architecture offers scalability, flexibility, and agility, it introduces unique challenges in the realm of authentication and authorization. Addressing these challenges necessitates a combination of thoughtful design, adherence to best practices, and the adoption of technologies and standards that align with the principles of microservices. As organizations increasingly embrace the microservices paradigm, a proactive and holistic approach to securing authentication and authorization becomes paramount to realizing the full benefits of this architectural style while mitigating potential security risks.

Chapter 7: Testing for Security: Penetration Testing and Beyond

The role of security testing in the development life cycle.

The role of security testing in the development life cycle is indispensable, serving as a critical safeguard against vulnerabilities and threats that could compromise the integrity, confidentiality, and availability of software systems. Integrated seamlessly into the software development life cycle (SDLC), security testing is a proactive approach that aims to identify and address security weaknesses throughout the various stages of the development process, from inception to deployment.

During the requirements gathering and design phase of the SDLC, security considerations must be ingrained into the project's foundations. Security requirements, such as data encryption, access controls, and authentication mechanisms, need to be defined and documented. Security architects play a pivotal role in envisioning and planning the security posture of the system, ensuring that security is not an afterthought but an integral part of the software's design and functionality. This early integration of security principles sets the stage for more effective security testing in subsequent stages.

As development commences, security testing becomes an integral part of the coding and unit testing phase. Developers are tasked with adhering to secure coding practices, and automated tools can be employed to analyze code for common vulnerabilities such as injection flaws, cross-site scripting (XSS), and security misconfigurations. Static Application Security Testing (SAST) tools scan the source code for potential vulnerabilities, providing developers with early feedback on security issues. This proactive approach aids in identifying and rectifying security flaws at an early stage, minimizing the cost and effort required for remediation.

The iterative and collaborative nature of the Agile development methodology necessitates the inclusion of security testing in each sprint or development iteration. Security testing tools and methodologies are integrated into the continuous integration/continuous deployment (CI/CD) pipeline, enabling automated testing of code changes in near real-time. This automation not only accelerates the development process but also ensures that security checks are consistently applied, fostering a culture of security throughout the Agile development life cycle. Tools like Dynamic Application Security Testing (DAST) are employed to simulate real-world attacks and identify vulnerabilities that may not be apparent in static code analysis.

In parallel with functional testing, security testing extends to the system testing phase, where the entire application is evaluated for vulnerabilities and potential weaknesses. This holistic assessment involves a combination of automated tools, manual testing, and ethical hacking techniques to identify security vulnerabilities from an external perspective. Penetration testing, a crucial aspect of security testing, emulates the tactics of malicious actors to uncover vulnerabilities that may have been overlooked during the development process. By simulating real-world attack scenarios, penetration testing provides valuable insights into the resilience of the system against potential security threats.

As the development life cycle progresses towards the pre-deployment phase, security testing intensifies to ensure that the application is robust and secure before reaching the production environment. Security assessments, including vulnerability scanning and code reviews, are conducted rigorously to identify and remediate any lingering security issues. Compliance checks against industry standards and regulatory requirements are also performed to ensure that the application aligns with the relevant security benchmarks.

In the deployment and maintenance phase, security testing remains a continuous and dynamic process. Post-deployment monitoring, also known as runtime application self-protection (RASP), involves the continuous monitoring of applications in a live environment to detect and respond to security incidents in real-time. This proactive approach ensures that any emerging threats or vulnerabilities are promptly addressed, enhancing the overall security posture of the deployed application. Continuous security monitoring is crucial in today's rapidly evolving threat landscape, where new vulnerabilities and attack vectors emerge regularly.

Regular security updates and patch management are essential components of the ongoing maintenance phase. Security testing is employed to assess the impact of patches and updates on the overall security of the system. Regression testing, which ensures that new changes do not introduce security vulnerabilities or break existing security controls, becomes a critical part of the maintenance cycle. Automated tools assist in the identification of potential regressions, allowing for swift remediation and the prevention of security gaps.

The significance of security testing extends beyond the immediate development life cycle to include incident response and forensics in the event of a security breach. Organizations need to be prepared to respond effectively to security incidents, and security testing plays a role in evaluating the robustness of incident response plans and the organization's ability to contain and mitigate security threats. Post-incident analysis, often facilitated by forensic security testing, provides insights into the root causes of security incidents, allowing for improvements in security controls and strategies.

The integration of security testing into the entire development life cycle is underpinned by the concept of DevSecOps, an approach that emphasizes the collaboration between development, operations, and security teams. DevSecOps fosters a culture of shared responsibility for security, where security considerations are integrated into every phase of development and operations. This alignment ensures that security testing is not a standalone activity but an inherent and continuous part of the software development and deployment process.

In conclusion, the role of security testing in the development life cycle is multifaceted and essential for building resilient, secure, and trustworthy software systems. From the early stages of design and coding to the post-deployment monitoring and incident response, security testing permeates every facet of the software development life cycle. The proactive identification and remediation of security vulnerabilities, coupled with continuous monitoring and improvement, contribute to the creation of software that not only meets functional requirements but also adheres to the highest standards of security and resilience against evolving cyber threats. As organizations strive to deliver secure and robust applications in an increasingly interconnected and digital landscape, the integration of security testing into the fabric of the development life cycle becomes a strategic imperative.

Exploring various security testing types (penetration testing, code reviews, etc.).

The exploration of various security testing types reveals a comprehensive and layered approach to identifying, assessing, and mitigating vulnerabilities within software applications and systems. Penetration testing, commonly known as ethical hacking, stands as a foundational pillar in this realm. This dynamic testing type involves simulated attacks on a system to unearth potential vulnerabilities and weaknesses that malicious actors might exploit. By emulating real-world scenarios, penetration testing provides valuable insights into the security posture of a system, helping organizations understand their susceptibility to diverse cyber threats. Whether through network penetration testing, application penetration testing, or social engineering assessments, this proactive testing method aids in fortifying defenses and bolstering resilience against potential cyber threats.

Code reviews, another essential security testing type, delve into the very fabric of software development. Beyond the functional correctness of code, these reviews scrutinize the codebase for security vulnerabilities, adherence to secure coding practices, and potential weaknesses. Static Application Security Testing (SAST) tools automate this process by analyzing source code for common vulnerabilities, ensuring that developers receive timely feedback on security-related issues. SAST acts as a proactive gatekeeper, preventing potential security pitfalls before the code reaches the testing or production stages. This approach integrates security into the development life cycle, fostering a secure coding culture and reducing the likelihood of introducing vulnerabilities at the code level.

Dynamic Application Security Testing (DAST) provides a complementary perspective by evaluating applications from the outside-in. Instead of analyzing the source code, DAST interacts with the running application to identify vulnerabilities, misconfigurations, or weaknesses in real-time. This testing type mirrors the actions of potential attackers, probing the application's runtime behavior and assessing its resistance to various attack vectors. DAST is particularly effective in uncovering vulnerabilities that might be challenging to detect through static analysis alone, offering a holistic view of the security landscape and aiding in the identification of runtime-specific risks.

Security-focused architecture reviews take a broader view, examining the overall design and structure of a system to identify potential security flaws. This type of review assesses how different components interact, the flow of sensitive data, and the effectiveness of implemented security controls. Security architecture reviews play a crucial role in early threat modeling, helping organizations anticipate and mitigate potential security risks before they materialize. By aligning security considerations with the architectural design, this testing type lays the groundwork for a robust and resilient security foundation.

Fuzz testing, or fuzzing, represents a dynamic and automated approach to security testing that involves injecting malformed or unexpected data into an application to observe its behavior under stress. Fuzz testing aims to identify vulnerabilities related to input validation, boundary checks, and error handling by bombarding the system with unexpected inputs. This testing type is particularly valuable for uncovering unknown vulnerabilities that might be missed by more traditional testing methods. Fuzz testing can be applied at different levels, from protocol-level fuzzing for network security to application-level fuzzing for software applications, contributing to a comprehensive security testing strategy.

Web application security testing focuses specifically on the security aspects of web applications, given their prominence in modern software ecosystems. This testing type encompasses a range of techniques, including vulnerability scanning, penetration testing, and security code reviews, to identify and rectify potential threats specific to web applications. With the increasing prevalence of web-based services and the associated risks of cross-site scripting (XSS), SQL injection, and other web-centric vulnerabilities, web application security testing is instrumental in ensuring the robustness of web-based software against potential cyber threats.

Mobile application security testing addresses the unique challenges presented by the widespread use of mobile devices. As mobile applications store sensitive information and often interact with back-end services, security testing becomes paramount. This testing type includes assessments for vulnerabilities such as insecure data storage, insufficient encryption, and improper session management. Additionally, mobile application security testing evaluates the app's resilience against platform-specific risks and potential threats associated with device-specific functionalities. With the increasing ubiquity of mobile applications, ensuring their security through comprehensive testing is imperative for safeguarding user data and maintaining user trust.

Security testing in the context of the Internet of Things (IoT) is crucial, considering the proliferation of interconnected devices. IoT security testing involves assessing the security of devices, communication protocols, and the overall IoT ecosystem. This testing type explores potential vulnerabilities in device firmware, communication channels, and the interaction between devices and backend services. Given the diverse nature of IoT devices and the potential impact of security breaches on safety-critical systems, IoT security testing plays a pivotal role in identifying and mitigating risks associated with the expanding IoT landscape.

Cloud security testing addresses the security challenges inherent in cloud-based environments and services. As organizations migrate their infrastructure and applications to the cloud, security considerations become paramount. This testing type evaluates the security controls implemented by cloud service providers, assesses the configuration of cloud resources, and identifies potential misconfigurations that could expose sensitive data. Cloud security testing ensures that organizations can confidently leverage cloud services while maintaining a robust security posture in the shared responsibility model inherent in cloud computing.

Database security testing focuses on the secure management and protection of data stored in databases. This testing type involves assessing the security of database configurations, evaluating access controls, and identifying vulnerabilities related to data integrity and confidentiality. Database security testing is particularly crucial as databases often store sensitive information and are attractive targets for attackers seeking unauthorized access or data manipulation. By systematically assessing the security controls and configurations of databases, organizations can enhance the overall resilience of their data management systems.

Container security testing addresses the security considerations associated with containerized applications, a prevalent trend in modern software development using technologies like Docker and Kubernetes. This testing type evaluates the security of container images, the orchestration of containers, and the overall containerized infrastructure. Assessments include vulnerability scanning of container images, evaluating container runtime security, and ensuring secure configurations of orchestration platforms. Container security testing aligns with the principles of DevSecOps, emphasizing the integration of security measures into the containerized development and deployment pipeline.

Compliance testing ensures that software applications and systems adhere to relevant regulatory requirements, industry standards, and internal security policies. This testing type evaluates whether the implemented security controls align with specific compliance frameworks, such as PCI DSS, HIPAA, or GDPR. Compliance testing is essential for organizations operating in regulated industries, as it provides assurance that security measures are in place to protect sensitive information and maintain compliance with legal and industry-specific requirements.

In conclusion, the diverse landscape of security testing types reflects the dynamic and evolving nature of cybersecurity challenges. From the foundational penetration testing and code reviews to specialized assessments targeting web applications, mobile applications, IoT devices, and cloud-based environments, each testing type contributes to a comprehensive security strategy. The integration of these testing types into the software development life cycle ensures that security considerations are addressed proactively, minimizing the risk of vulnerabilities and enhancing the overall resilience of software applications and systems against an ever-expanding array of cyber threats. As organizations continue to prioritize security in the face of evolving risks, a multifaceted approach to security testing remains essential for safeguarding digital assets and maintaining user trust in an interconnected and rapidly changing technological landscape.

Understanding the objectives and methodologies of penetration testing.

Understanding the objectives and methodologies of penetration testing illuminates a crucial aspect of cybersecurity, wherein organizations employ simulated attacks to evaluate the security posture of their systems, networks, and applications. At its core, the primary objective of penetration testing is to identify vulnerabilities, weaknesses, and potential entry points that malicious actors could exploit to compromise the confidentiality, integrity, or availability of critical assets. The overarching goal is not only to discover these weaknesses but also to assess the effectiveness of existing security controls and measures in preventing or mitigating real-world threats. By adopting the perspective of a potential adversary, penetration testing provides valuable insights into the actual risk landscape faced by an organization, allowing for informed decision-making and targeted improvements in security defenses.

Penetration testing encompasses a variety of methodologies and approaches tailored to the specific assets and environments being assessed. One common methodology is the Open Source Security Testing Methodology Manual (OSSTMM), which defines a comprehensive framework for conducting penetration tests. OSSTMM emphasizes a holistic approach that goes beyond technical assessments to include elements such as operational security, human security, and data networks. Another widely recognized methodology is the Penetration Testing Execution Standard (PTES), which outlines a standardized process comprising seven stages: pre-engagement, intelligence gathering, threat modeling, vulnerability analysis, exploitation, post-exploitation, and reporting. This structured approach ensures a systematic and thorough examination of security controls and potential weaknesses.

The penetration testing process typically begins with the pre-engagement phase, where the objectives, scope, and rules of engagement are defined. Clear communication with stakeholders, including the organization's leadership, IT personnel, and relevant teams, is essential to establish a shared understanding of the testing goals, scope limitations, and any potential impact on operations. This phase also involves obtaining necessary approvals and ensuring compliance with legal and ethical considerations.

Intelligence gathering represents a crucial initial step in the penetration testing process. This phase involves collecting information about the target environment, including network infrastructure, system configurations, employee details, and potential points of entry. Open-source intelligence (OSINT) techniques, such as querying public databases and analyzing publicly available information, play a significant role in this phase. The goal is to gather insights that an actual attacker might leverage to tailor their approach, simulating a realistic and targeted attack scenario.

Threat modeling follows intelligence gathering and involves identifying and prioritizing potential threats based on the collected information. This phase aims to understand the risk landscape from the perspective of an adversary, mapping out potential attack vectors and vulnerabilities. By prioritizing threats, penetration testers can focus their efforts on the most critical areas, ensuring a targeted and risk-based approach to the subsequent stages of the testing process.

Vulnerability analysis is a core component of penetration testing, where testers actively seek and identify weaknesses in the target system. This involves utilizing automated scanning tools to identify known vulnerabilities and conducting manual assessments to discover nuanced or novel weaknesses that automated tools might miss.

Common vulnerabilities targeted during this phase include misconfigurations, outdated software, insecure coding practices, and weaknesses in network defenses. The objective is to comprehensively assess the attack surface and identify potential avenues for exploitation.

The exploitation phase involves attempting to actively exploit the identified vulnerabilities to gain unauthorized access or control over the target systems. This phase is conducted with extreme caution and adherence to the rules of engagement to prevent unintended disruptions to the organization's operations. Successful exploitation demonstrates the real-world impact of identified vulnerabilities and provides tangible evidence of potential risks. It also validates the effectiveness of existing security controls in preventing or mitigating exploitation attempts.

Post-exploitation activities focus on assessing the extent of access and control obtained during the exploitation phase. Penetration testers simulate the actions of a malicious actor who has successfully breached the system, exploring the potential for lateral movement, privilege escalation, and data exfiltration. This phase helps organizations understand the full implications of a successful attack and highlights areas where additional security measures or monitoring controls may be necessary to detect and respond to similar threats in a real-world scenario.

The final stage of penetration testing involves reporting and documentation. Testers provide a detailed report outlining the findings, including a description of vulnerabilities, the potential impact of exploitation, and recommendations for remediation. The report is typically tailored to different audiences, providing technical details for IT and security teams, executive summaries for leadership, and actionable insights for remediation efforts. A well-crafted report is a key deliverable, serving as a roadmap for improving security controls and addressing identified weaknesses.

Several types of penetration testing exist to address specific objectives and scenarios. External penetration testing focuses on assessing the security of externally facing systems, such as web applications and network infrastructure visible to the internet. Internal penetration testing, on the other hand, simulates attacks originating from within the organization's network, evaluating the security of internal systems and the potential for lateral movement by attackers with insider access. Web application penetration testing specifically targets vulnerabilities in web applications, including input validation flaws, injection attacks, and authentication bypass vulnerabilities. Wireless penetration testing assesses the security of wireless networks, identifying potential vulnerabilities in encryption protocols, access controls, and wireless devices.

Red teaming, while related to penetration testing, takes a broader and more adversarial approach. Red teaming involves simulating a realistic and sophisticated cyber threat, often over an extended period, to assess an organization's overall security posture. This approach goes beyond technical assessments to include social engineering, physical security assessments, and other tactics employed by advanced adversaries. Red teaming provides a holistic evaluation of an organization's ability to detect, respond to, and recover from a sophisticated and persistent cyber threat.

In conclusion, the objectives and methodologies of penetration testing serve as a cornerstone in the proactive defense against cyber threats. By simulating real-world attack scenarios, penetration testing provides organizations with actionable insights into their vulnerabilities and the effectiveness of their security controls. The structured and systematic approach, coupled with adherence to ethical considerations, ensures that penetration testing contributes not only to vulnerability identification but also to the ongoing improvement of an organization's overall security posture. As the cybersecurity landscape continues to evolve, penetration testing remains an indispensable tool for organizations seeking to fortify their defenses and stay one step ahead of potential adversaries.

Overview of popular security testing tools (e.g., OWASP ZAP, Burp Suite).

An overview of popular security testing tools reveals a rich landscape of solutions designed to assist cybersecurity professionals and developers in identifying, assessing, and mitigating vulnerabilities within software applications and systems. Among these tools, OWASP ZAP (Zed Attack Proxy) stands out as an open-source dynamic application security testing (DAST) tool. Renowned for its versatility, ZAP provides automated scanners, various tools for exploring security vulnerabilities, and a user-friendly interface. ZAP supports both automated and manual testing, making it suitable for a wide range of users, from beginners to experienced security professionals. With features such as automated scanners for common vulnerabilities like SQL injection and cross-site scripting (XSS), ZAP facilitates comprehensive testing and ensures the robustness of web applications against potential cyber threats.

Burp Suite, another prominent player in the security testing toolkit, is a comprehensive platform designed for web application security testing. Developed by PortSwigger, Burp Suite integrates a variety of tools that cover the entire web application security testing lifecycle. The tool is widely used for its proxy, which allows users to intercept and modify web traffic for analysis, and its scanner, which automates the identification of vulnerabilities. Burp Suite also includes features like an intruder for performing automated attacks, a repeater for manual testing and analysis, and a sequencer for assessing the randomness of session tokens. Its versatility and extensive feature set make Burp Suite a preferred choice for professionals engaged in web application security assessments.

Nmap, short for Network Mapper, is a powerful and flexible open-source tool for network discovery and security auditing. Although not exclusively a security testing tool, Nmap is widely used for reconnaissance and identifying potential vulnerabilities within networked systems. Nmap's capabilities extend beyond simple port scanning; it can detect open ports, identify services running on those ports, and even attempt to deduce the operating system in use. Nmap's scripting engine allows users to automate a variety of tasks, making it a valuable asset for both penetration testers and network administrators seeking to assess the security posture of their systems.

Metasploit, developed by Rapid7, is an advanced open-source penetration testing framework that facilitates the discovery, exploitation, and validation of security vulnerabilities. As a widely adopted tool in the cybersecurity community, Metasploit provides an extensive collection of exploits, payloads, and auxiliary modules, making it a comprehensive platform for penetration testing and ethical hacking. Metasploit's modular architecture enables users to customize and extend its capabilities, ensuring adaptability to evolving threat landscapes. Whether used for vulnerability validation, penetration testing, or red teaming exercises, Metasploit remains a powerful ally in the hands of security professionals aiming to assess and fortify the security defenses of systems and networks.

Wireshark, a network protocol analyzer, offers unparalleled visibility into the communication occurring over a network. While not primarily a security testing tool, Wireshark is instrumental in security assessments by allowing users to capture and analyze network traffic. Security professionals leverage Wireshark to identify anomalous patterns, detect potential security incidents, and gain insights into the behavior of networked applications. Its ability to capture and dissect packets in real-time makes Wireshark an invaluable tool for understanding the intricacies of network communications and uncovering potential security threats or vulnerabilities.

Nessus, developed by Tenable, is a widely used vulnerability scanning tool that automates the process of identifying security vulnerabilities within networks, systems, and applications. Nessus performs comprehensive scans, checking for known vulnerabilities, misconfigurations, and potential weaknesses that could be exploited by attackers. The tool supports a vast database of known vulnerabilities and offers both scheduled and on-demand scanning options. Nessus provides detailed reports with actionable insights, aiding organizations in prioritizing and addressing identified vulnerabilities based on their severity and potential impact.

Snort, an open-source intrusion detection and prevention system (IDS/IPS), is designed to monitor network traffic for suspicious patterns and potential security threats. While its primary function is intrusion detection, Snort can also be configured to act as a prevention system by blocking or alerting on identified threats. With its rule-based approach, Snort allows users to define custom rules or leverage pre-configured rules to detect known attack patterns. Snort's versatility and real-time analysis capabilities make it an essential tool for organizations seeking to enhance their network security and proactively identify and respond to potential threats.

Acunetix is a web vulnerability scanner that aids organizations in identifying and addressing security vulnerabilities within their web applications. Known for its accuracy and ease of use, Acunetix automates the scanning process, checking for a wide range of vulnerabilities, including SQL injection, cross-site scripting (XSS), and security misconfigurations. Acunetix supports both dynamic application security testing (DAST) and interactive application security testing (IAST), providing organizations with flexibility in their security testing approach. The tool also offers features for scanning APIs and detecting vulnerabilities in modern web technologies, making it a comprehensive solution for web application security assessments.

Sqlmap, an open-source penetration testing tool, specializes in automating the detection and exploitation of SQL injection vulnerabilities in web applications and databases. Widely recognized for its effectiveness, sqlmap allows security professionals to identify and exploit SQL injection vulnerabilities to assess the security robustness of web applications and underlying databases. Its features include automatic recognition of database management systems, the ability to perform deep database fingerprinting, and support for various attack techniques, ensuring thorough testing and validation of SQL injection vulnerabilities.

Security testing tools like OWASP ZAP, Burp Suite, Nmap, Metasploit, Wireshark, Nessus, Snort, Acunetix, and Sqlmap play pivotal roles in the cybersecurity landscape, providing professionals with the means to conduct comprehensive assessments of systems, networks, and applications. Each tool brings unique capabilities to the table, addressing specific aspects of security testing and contributing to a holistic approach in identifying and mitigating vulnerabilities. As the cybersecurity landscape continues to evolve, the effective use of these tools remains integral to proactively securing digital assets and staying ahead of emerging threats.

The role of static and dynamic code analysis in security testing.

The role of static and dynamic code analysis in security testing is paramount, representing two complementary approaches that collectively contribute to the identification, assessment, and mitigation of vulnerabilities within software applications. Static code analysis, also known as Static Application Security Testing (SAST), involves the examination of source code or compiled code without executing the program. This proactive method enables the early detection of potential security vulnerabilities by analyzing the codebase for patterns, coding practices, and configurations that might lead to exploitable weaknesses. SAST tools automatically scan the source code, identifying issues such as input validation flaws, insecure coding practices, and potential security misconfigurations. By conducting this analysis during the development phase, SAST aids developers in identifying and rectifying vulnerabilities before the code is even compiled, fostering a security-first mindset in the software development life cycle.

Dynamic code analysis, on the other hand, is a runtime testing method that involves analyzing the behavior of a running application to identify vulnerabilities and security weaknesses. Also known as Dynamic Application Security Testing (DAST), this approach simulates real-world attack scenarios, interacting with the application in a manner similar to how an external attacker would. DAST tools send requests to the application, analyze the responses, and identify potential vulnerabilities such as injection flaws, authentication bypass, and other runtime-specific issues. By assessing the application from the outside-in, DAST provides insights into how the application responds to potential attacks, offering a realistic perspective on its security posture and uncovering vulnerabilities that might be challenging to detect through static analysis alone.

The synergy between static and dynamic code analysis emerges as a comprehensive strategy for security testing, addressing different dimensions of the software development life cycle. Static analysis serves as a proactive measure, allowing developers to identify and rectify vulnerabilities in the early stages of development. Automated SAST tools scan the codebase for patterns indicative of security vulnerabilities, including but not limited to buffer overflows, code injection, and insecure coding practices. This enables developers to address security issues before the code is integrated into the larger system, reducing the likelihood of introducing vulnerabilities and minimizing the cost of remediation.

Dynamic analysis, in contrast, provides a realistic assessment of the application's security posture by evaluating its behavior in a runtime environment. DAST tools simulate potential attacks by interacting with the application through its external interfaces, identifying vulnerabilities that may only manifest during actual usage. This approach is particularly valuable for uncovering issues related to input validation, session management, and other runtime-specific vulnerabilities that may not be apparent in the static codebase.

The integration of static and dynamic code analysis into the software development life cycle aligns with the principles of a secure software development process. Static analysis initiates the security assessment at the earliest stages, empowering developers to adopt secure coding practices and address potential vulnerabilities in the source code. Automated SAST tools streamline this process, providing rapid feedback to developers and enabling them to make informed decisions about security improvements. By fostering a proactive approach to security, static analysis contributes to the creation of a robust and secure codebase, reducing the likelihood of security incidents and vulnerabilities in the final product.

Dynamic analysis complements static analysis by providing a real-world perspective on the application's security posture. As applications evolve and interact with external components, their behavior in a runtime environment becomes a critical aspect of security testing. DAST tools simulate attacks and interactions with the application, uncovering vulnerabilities that may arise from the complex interplay of components during actual usage. This dynamic approach ensures that security assessments consider the application's response to diverse inputs, user interactions, and potential attack scenarios. By evaluating the application in a realistic environment, dynamic analysis provides a valuable layer of validation, confirming the effectiveness of security controls and identifying vulnerabilities that might not be evident in the static codebase.

The iterative and cyclical nature of the software development life cycle necessitates continuous security testing to adapt to evolving requirements and address emerging threats. Static and dynamic code analysis contribute to this iterative process by providing ongoing assessments at different stages of development. In the early phases, static analysis identifies and mitigates vulnerabilities at the source code level, promoting secure coding practices and reducing the likelihood of introducing new vulnerabilities. As the application progresses to later stages, dynamic analysis ensures that the evolving codebase interacts securely with external components and remains resilient to potential runtime-specific vulnerabilities.

Furthermore, the integration of static and dynamic code analysis aligns with the principles of DevSecOps, emphasizing the collaboration between development, operations, and security teams throughout the software development life cycle. By incorporating security testing into the continuous integration and continuous deployment (CI/CD) pipeline, organizations ensure that both static and dynamic analyses are consistently applied to code changes in near real-time. Automated tools facilitate this integration, allowing for rapid feedback to developers and enabling the swift remediation of identified vulnerabilities. This collaborative and automated approach fosters a culture of shared responsibility for security, where security considerations become an integral part of the development process rather than a separate and isolated activity.

While static and dynamic code analysis play crucial roles in security testing, it's essential to recognize their respective strengths and limitations. Static analysis excels in identifying potential vulnerabilities at the source code level, offering early insights into insecure coding practices and configuration issues. However, it may face challenges in comprehensively assessing runtime-specific behaviors and interactions. Dynamic analysis, on the other hand, provides a realistic view of an application's security posture in a live environment, uncovering vulnerabilities that may only manifest during actual usage. However, dynamic analysis may not have the same depth of visibility into the codebase as static analysis.

To maximize the effectiveness of security testing, organizations often adopt a hybrid approach that combines both static and dynamic analyses. This hybrid approach, often referred to as Interactive Application Security Testing (IAST), seeks to leverage the strengths of both methods by integrating runtime analysis into the static analysis process. IAST tools instrument the application during runtime, providing insights into its behavior while still utilizing static analysis techniques to examine the codebase. This integrated approach aims to provide a more comprehensive and accurate assessment of an application's security posture, combining the early detection capabilities of static analysis with the realism and context of dynamic analysis.

In conclusion, the role of static and dynamic code analysis in security testing is essential for building secure and resilient software. By integrating both approaches into the software development life cycle, organizations can proactively identify and address vulnerabilities at the source code level while also validating the application's security posture in a realistic runtime environment. This comprehensive strategy aligns with modern development practices, promotes a culture of security throughout the development process, and contributes to the creation of robust and trustworthy software in the face of evolving cyber threats.

Integrating security testing into continuous integration/continuous deployment (CI/CD) pipelines.

Integrating security testing into Continuous Integration/Continuous Deployment (CI/CD) pipelines is a critical and transformative practice that aligns with the principles of DevSecOps, aiming to seamlessly incorporate security measures throughout the software development life cycle. In the dynamic landscape of modern software development, where agility and rapid releases are paramount, the integration of security testing into CI/CD pipelines becomes imperative for identifying and mitigating vulnerabilities at an early stage. This integration not only ensures that security considerations are an integral part of the development process but also facilitates the swift and automated remediation of security issues, fostering a proactive and collaborative approach to software security.

The CI/CD pipeline represents the backbone of modern development workflows, automating the build, test, and deployment processes. The integration of security testing into this pipeline enhances its capability to deliver secure software continuously. The initial phase of the CI/CD pipeline involves source code management, where developers commit code changes. By incorporating static code analysis or Static Application Security Testing (SAST) tools at this stage, vulnerabilities and coding flaws can be identified as soon as code is committed. Automated SAST tools scan the codebase for security issues, providing rapid feedback to developers and enabling them to address vulnerabilities before they progress further into the pipeline. This early detection reduces the cost and effort associated with remediation, as issues are resolved closer to their point of origin in the development life cycle.

As the CI/CD pipeline progresses to the build and integration phases, dynamic code analysis or Dynamic Application Security Testing (DAST) tools can be seamlessly integrated. These tools assess the application at runtime, simulating real-world attack scenarios and identifying vulnerabilities related to inputs, authentication, and potential runtime-specific issues. Automated DAST scans can be triggered as part of the CI/CD pipeline, ensuring that applications are not only built efficiently but also undergo dynamic testing to uncover vulnerabilities that may only manifest during execution. This dynamic testing phase adds a layer of realism to the security assessment, aligning with the evolving nature of applications and their runtime behaviors.

Containerization technologies, such as Docker and Kubernetes, have become integral to modern CI/CD pipelines, facilitating consistent and scalable deployment environments. Security testing within CI/CD can extend to container security, ensuring that container images are free from vulnerabilities and adhering to secure configuration practices. Container security scanning tools can be integrated into the pipeline to automatically analyze container images for known vulnerabilities, misconfigurations, and adherence to security best practices. This proactive approach prevents the deployment of insecure containers, minimizing the attack surface and enhancing the overall security posture of the application.

The automated nature of CI/CD pipelines allows for the integration of security testing not only at specific stages but also throughout the entire pipeline. This continuous and iterative testing approach aligns with the philosophy of continuous security, where security measures are applied continuously and consistently rather than as isolated events. Integrating security testing into each stage of the pipeline ensures that security checks are not merely gatekeepers but active contributors to the development process. Automated testing tools provide real-time feedback, allowing developers to address security issues promptly, iterate on code changes, and deliver secure software incrementally.

Security testing in CI/CD pipelines is not confined to traditional application security; it extends to infrastructure as code (IaC) and cloud configurations. As organizations embrace cloud-native architectures and infrastructure automation, the security of infrastructure code becomes pivotal. Static analysis tools designed for IaC, such as Terraform or AWS CloudFormation linters, can be integrated into the CI/CD pipeline to assess the security of cloud infrastructure configurations. This ensures that cloud environments are provisioned securely, adhere to least privilege principles, and are free from misconfigurations that could expose sensitive data or resources.

In addition to SAST, DAST, container security, and IaC security, other security testing types can also be seamlessly integrated into CI/CD pipelines. Vulnerability scanning tools, which assess systems and dependencies for known vulnerabilities, can be incorporated to identify and remediate security issues in third-party libraries and dependencies. Compliance testing tools can verify whether applications and infrastructure configurations comply with regulatory requirements and industry standards. Each of these testing types contributes to a multifaceted and comprehensive security strategy, ensuring that software is not only functionally correct but also resilient against a spectrum of security threats.

The success of integrating security testing into CI/CD pipelines relies on collaboration between development, operations, and security teams. This collaborative model, often referred to as DevSecOps, emphasizes shared responsibility for security and the seamless integration of security measures into the development workflow. Security professionals work hand-in-hand with developers and operations teams to define security requirements, select appropriate testing tools, and establish policies that govern the security posture of applications throughout the CI/CD pipeline. The automation of security testing within CI/CD also aligns with the broader principles of automation, scalability, and repeatability that characterize modern software development practices.

Continuous monitoring and feedback are integral components of the CI/CD pipeline, ensuring that security testing results are continuously assessed, and any emerging issues are promptly addressed. Security information and event management (SIEM) systems, along with continuous monitoring tools, can be integrated to provide visibility into security events and anomalies. Real-time dashboards and alerts can notify teams of potential security incidents, enabling rapid response and remediation. This ongoing feedback loop reinforces the continuous improvement of security measures, allowing organizations to adapt to evolving threats and emerging vulnerabilities.

The integration of security testing into CI/CD pipelines aligns with the principles of shift-left security, where security measures are pushed earlier into the development life cycle. This proactive approach reduces the time and resources required for remediation, as security issues are identified and addressed closer to their origin. The iterative and automated nature of CI/CD pipelines fosters a culture of continuous improvement, where security measures are not viewed as impediments but as essential components of the development process. This cultural shift is fundamental to building a resilient and secure software development practice in an era of rapid release cycles and evolving cyber threats.

In conclusion, integrating security testing into CI/CD pipelines is a strategic imperative for organizations seeking to deliver secure software at the speed of modern development. By seamlessly embedding security measures into the development workflow, organizations can identify and remediate vulnerabilities at an early stage, reducing the risk of security incidents and enhancing the overall security posture of their applications. The collaboration between development, operations, and security teams, coupled with the automation of security testing, forms the foundation of a DevSecOps approach that aligns security with the principles of agility, collaboration, and continuous improvement.

As organizations continue to navigate the dynamic landscape of software development, the integration of security testing into CI/CD pipelines remains a key enabler for building and maintaining secure, resilient, and high-quality software.

Focusing on security testing specific to web applications.

Security testing for web applications is a critical discipline in the realm of cybersecurity, given the increasing prevalence of web-based services and the persistent threat landscape. Web applications, ranging from e-commerce platforms to social networking sites, are often prime targets for malicious actors seeking to exploit vulnerabilities for unauthorized access, data breaches, or other nefarious activities. To safeguard the confidentiality, integrity, and availability of sensitive data processed by web applications, a comprehensive security testing approach is essential, encompassing various techniques and methodologies.

Static Application Security Testing (SAST) plays a pivotal role in the security testing of web applications by examining the source code or compiled code without execution. Automated SAST tools scan the application's codebase to identify potential vulnerabilities and coding flaws during the early stages of development. Common vulnerabilities such as SQL injection, cross-site scripting (XSS), and insecure coding practices can be detected proactively, enabling developers to address issues before the code is even compiled. This preventive approach aligns with the principles of secure coding and contributes to the creation of a robust and secure foundation for web applications.

Dynamic Application Security Testing (DAST) complements SAST by assessing the security of web applications in a runtime environment. Unlike SAST, which analyzes code without execution, DAST simulates real-world attack scenarios by interacting with the running application. DAST tools send requests to the application, analyze responses, and identify vulnerabilities related to runtime behaviors, input validation, and authentication mechanisms. By assessing the application from the outside-in, DAST provides insights into how the application responds to potential attacks and uncovers vulnerabilities that may only manifest during actual usage. This dynamic approach adds a layer of realism to the security assessment, ensuring that the application's security posture is evaluated comprehensively.

Web applications often rely on databases to store and manage data, making database security a crucial aspect of overall web application security. Database Security Testing involves assessing the security of database systems, including access controls, encryption, and data integrity measures. Common database vulnerabilities, such as SQL injection and insecure configurations, can have severe consequences, leading to unauthorized access or manipulation of sensitive data. Database Security Testing tools and methodologies aim to identify and remediate such vulnerabilities, strengthening the overall security of web applications that rely on backend databases.

Web application security testing also extends to the realm of secure coding practices. Developers play a central role in building secure web applications, and fostering a security-conscious mindset is essential. Secure Code Review involves manual or automated assessments of the codebase to ensure adherence to secure coding practices and compliance with security standards. This proactive approach enables organizations to identify and rectify potential security issues during the development phase, reducing the likelihood of introducing vulnerabilities into the final application.

In the context of web applications, Cross-Site Scripting (XSS) and Cross-Site Request Forgery (CSRF) are prevalent vulnerabilities that can have significant security implications. XSS occurs when an attacker injects malicious scripts into web pages viewed by other users, potentially leading to the theft of sensitive information or the hijacking of user sessions. CSRF involves tricking a user's browser into performing actions on a web application without the user's knowledge or consent. Security testing for web applications includes the identification and mitigation of XSS and CSRF vulnerabilities, employing techniques such as input validation, output encoding, and the use of anti-CSRF tokens.

Web application firewalls (WAFs) are integral components of the defense-in-depth strategy for web application security. WAFs are designed to filter and monitor HTTP traffic between a web application and the Internet, providing an additional layer of protection against various attacks, including SQL injection, XSS, and other common web application vulnerabilities. WAFs can be tested and configured to ensure they effectively block malicious traffic while allowing legitimate requests to pass through. This proactive testing approach ensures that WAFs serve as robust safeguards against known and emerging threats targeting web applications.

As web applications increasingly leverage APIs (Application Programming Interfaces) to facilitate data exchange and integration with external services, API Security Testing becomes crucial. APIs, if not properly secured, can expose sensitive data and functionalities to potential attackers. API Security Testing involves assessing the authentication mechanisms, authorization controls, and data integrity measures implemented in APIs. Security testing tools and methodologies can be applied to identify and remediate vulnerabilities in API endpoints, ensuring that data transmitted between the web application and external services remains secure.

The prevalence of third-party components, libraries, and frameworks in web applications introduces additional considerations for security testing. Open-source components may contain vulnerabilities that, if left unaddressed, can be exploited by attackers to compromise the security of the entire application. Software Composition Analysis (SCA) involves the identification and assessment of third-party components for known vulnerabilities. Automated SCA tools scan dependencies and libraries used in web applications, providing insights into potential security risks and enabling organizations to apply timely updates or patches.

Web applications often handle sensitive user authentication and authorization processes, making Identity and Access Management (IAM) a critical aspect of security testing. IAM Security Testing involves evaluating the effectiveness of authentication mechanisms, password policies, session management, and access controls implemented in web applications. Testing methodologies aim to identify weaknesses in user authentication and authorization processes, such as weak password policies, insecure session management, or insufficient access controls that could lead to unauthorized access.

Secure File Upload Testing is particularly relevant for web applications that allow users to upload files. Insecure file upload functionalities can be exploited to execute arbitrary code, leading to remote code execution or other security breaches. Security testing for file uploads involves assessing the validation and processing of uploaded files to prevent malicious payloads. Techniques such as file type verification, size limits, and proper sanitization of file names contribute to secure file upload functionalities in web applications.

The emergence of client-side technologies, including JavaScript frameworks and Single Page Applications (SPAs), introduces new considerations for security testing. Client-Side Security Testing involves evaluating the security of client-side code and interactions to identify vulnerabilities such as DOM-based XSS, insecure data storage, or inadequate input validation on the client side. Automated testing tools, in conjunction with manual assessments, contribute to the overall security of client-side components, ensuring that web applications remain resilient against client-side attacks.

Continuous Security Monitoring for web applications is a proactive approach that involves the ongoing assessment of security controls, configurations, and user activities. Security monitoring tools can detect anomalous patterns, potential security incidents, or deviations from established security policies. Continuous monitoring provides organizations with real-time insights into the security posture of web applications, enabling rapid response to emerging threats and vulnerabilities.

The integration of security testing into the Software Development Life Cycle (SDLC) is essential for building and maintaining secure web applications. Adopting

a DevSecOps approach encourages the collaboration between development, operations, and security teams throughout the SDLC. By integrating security testing into the CI/CD pipeline, organizations ensure that security measures are applied continuously and consistently, fostering a culture of shared responsibility for security.

In conclusion, security testing for web applications is a multifaceted discipline that addresses diverse threats and vulnerabilities. From static and dynamic analysis to database security, secure coding practices, and API security testing, the comprehensive security testing approach is vital for ensuring the resilience of web applications against evolving cyber threats. As organizations navigate the digital landscape, prioritizing web application security through systematic and proactive testing becomes paramount to safeguarding sensitive data, maintaining user trust, and mitigating potential security risks.

Challenges and strategies for testing the security of mobile applications.

Testing the security of mobile applications poses unique challenges in the ever-evolving landscape of mobile technology, where the ubiquity of smartphones and the sophistication of mobile applications make them attractive targets for cyber threats. One of the primary challenges is the diverse ecosystem of mobile platforms, including iOS and Android, each with its own security models, app store policies, and user demographics. Developing security testing strategies that account for these platform-specific nuances is crucial. The fragmentation within the Android ecosystem, where multiple device manufacturers and versions of the operating system coexist, adds an additional layer of complexity. Security testing must adapt to this diversity to ensure the broadest coverage and identify vulnerabilities that may be specific to certain devices or Android versions.

The pervasive use of third-party libraries and frameworks in mobile app development introduces another layer of complexity and risk. Mobile developers often leverage pre-built components to expedite the development process, but these third-party elements may harbor vulnerabilities that could compromise the security of the entire application. Integrating strategies for Software Composition

Analysis (SCA) into the security testing process helps identify and mitigate risks associated with third-party dependencies, ensuring that the entire application stack adheres to security best practices.

Mobile applications heavily rely on network communication to interact with servers and external services, making data transmission security a critical concern. The adoption of secure communication protocols, such as HTTPS, is essential to protect sensitive data during transit. However, ensuring the correct implementation of secure communication and guarding against vulnerabilities like Man-in-the-Middle (MitM) attacks requires comprehensive testing. Security professionals must employ techniques like network traffic analysis and penetration testing to assess the resilience of mobile applications against eavesdropping, tampering, or other network-related threats.

The dynamic nature of mobile environments introduces challenges in securing user authentication and authorization processes. Mobile applications often handle sensitive user data and transactions, requiring robust authentication mechanisms. Testing the security of user authentication involves evaluating factors such as password policies, session management, and the effectiveness of biometric authentication methods where applicable. Ensuring that authorization controls are implemented correctly to prevent unauthorized access and privilege escalation is equally critical. Security testing strategies should include assessments of authentication and authorization mechanisms specific to mobile contexts, considering factors like device identifiers, push notifications, and multi-factor authentication.

The prevalence of mobile applications that collect, process, and store sensitive user information raises concerns about data security and privacy. Mobile Security Testing must encompass assessments of how applications handle Personally Identifiable Information (PII), financial data, or other sensitive data types. Techniques such as static and dynamic analysis, as well as penetration testing, help identify vulnerabilities related to data storage, encryption, and data leakage. Compliance with data protection regulations, such as the General Data Protection Regulation (GDPR) or the Health Insurance Portability and Accountability Act (HIPAA), further complicates the testing process, requiring organizations to implement strategies for ensuring regulatory compliance.

Mobile applications often incorporate functionalities like geolocation services, camera access, and other sensors, introducing privacy considerations. The challenge lies in ensuring that these features are implemented securely to prevent unauthorized access or misuse. Security testing strategies for mobile applications should encompass the assessment of permissions and privacy controls, examining how applications handle sensitive functionalities and whether they adhere to the principle of least privilege. Additionally, strategies for testing the security of mobile applications should consider scenarios where malicious applications attempt to exploit permissions or sensors for unauthorized activities.

The user interface and user experience (UI/UX) of mobile applications are critical components of their success, but they also present security challenges. Mobile Security Testing needs to evaluate the resilience of applications against common UI-based attacks, such as clickjacking, screen overlay, or phishing attempts. Assessing the security of mobile application interfaces involves scrutinizing input validation, secure coding practices, and the prevention of UI-based attacks that could deceive users or manipulate app behavior. Effective security testing strategies must strike a balance between ensuring a seamless user experience and safeguarding against potential UI-related vulnerabilities.

The rise of mobile banking, mobile payments, and other financial services delivered through mobile applications amplifies the impact of security vulnerabilities. Mobile financial applications handle sensitive financial transactions and personal information, making them lucrative targets for attackers. Security testing in this context must be rigorous, covering aspects such as secure communication, authentication, and encryption of financial data. The testing process should also evaluate the resilience of financial applications against a spectrum of attacks, including those aimed at compromising transaction integrity, intercepting financial data, or exploiting vulnerabilities in third-party payment gateways.

Mobile applications often rely on backend servers, APIs, and cloud services to provide dynamic content, functionality, and data storage. The security of these backend components is integral to the overall security of mobile applications. Mobile Backend Security Testing involves assessing the security of APIs, server configurations, and data storage mechanisms. Techniques such as API security testing, penetration testing of backend systems, and cloud security assessments contribute to a comprehensive evaluation of the entire mobile ecosystem. Ensuring the secure interaction between mobile applications and backend services is vital for preventing data breaches, unauthorized access, or compromise of sensitive information.

The constantly evolving threat landscape and the emergence of new attack vectors pose ongoing challenges for mobile application security testing. Threat intelligence plays a crucial role in staying ahead of potential threats, understanding new attack techniques, and proactively fortifying mobile applications against emerging vulnerabilities. Security testing strategies should incorporate threat modeling, where potential threats and attack vectors are identified and assessed systematically. This proactive approach enables organizations to prioritize security measures based on the likelihood and potential impact of various threats, enhancing the resilience of mobile applications against both current and future threats.

The proliferation of mobile applications, coupled with the rapid release cycles and frequent updates characteristic of the mobile app ecosystem, demands a shift-left approach to security testing. Integrating security into the entire Software Development Life Cycle (SDLC) ensures that security considerations are addressed from the earliest stages of development. This includes secure coding practices, static analysis of code, and security testing in development and testing environments. Automated testing tools that seamlessly integrate into the Continuous Integration/Continuous Deployment (CI/CD) pipeline enable organizations to conduct security testing early and often, identifying and addressing vulnerabilities throughout the development life cycle.

Security testing for mobile applications must be conducted in diverse testing environments that mimic real-world scenarios. Emulation of different mobile devices, operating systems, and network conditions ensures that security testing is representative of the varied environments in which mobile applications operate. This diversity is essential for identifying platform-specific vulnerabilities, understanding the impact of different network conditions on application security, and assessing the overall resilience of mobile applications across a spectrum of usage scenarios.

The collaboration between security professionals, developers, and quality assurance teams is instrumental in addressing the multifaceted challenges of mobile application security testing. A culture of security awareness and shared responsibility fosters effective communication and collaboration throughout the development life cycle. Security training for developers helps them adopt secure coding practices, understand common security pitfalls, and actively contribute to the security of mobile applications. Collaboration ensures that security testing is not an isolated activity but an integral part of the development process, aligning with the principles of DevSecOps.

In conclusion, testing the security of mobile applications is a complex and dynamic process that requires a multifaceted approach.

From addressing platform-specific nuances to securing data transmission, authentication, and backend services, effective security testing strategies must be comprehensive and adaptive. Overcoming challenges associated with diverse ecosystems, third-party dependencies, privacy considerations, and emerging threats requires a proactive and collaborative mindset. As organizations continue to innovate in the mobile space, prioritizing robust security testing practices is paramount to building and maintaining secure, resilient, and trustworthy mobile applications in an ever-evolving digital landscape.

Ensuring the security of cloud-based applications and infrastructure.

Ensuring the security of cloud-based applications and infrastructure is a multifaceted and critical undertaking in the contemporary digital landscape. Cloud computing offers unparalleled benefits in terms of scalability, flexibility, and cost efficiency, but it also introduces a complex set of security considerations that require careful attention and strategic approaches.

One of the foundational aspects of securing cloud-based applications is understanding the shared responsibility model inherent in most cloud service providers (CSPs). In this model, the CSP is responsible for the security of the cloud infrastructure itself, including the physical data centers, networking, and the hypervisor layer. However, customers are responsible for securing their data, applications, identities, and configurations within the cloud. This shared responsibility necessitates a clear delineation of responsibilities and a robust security strategy on the part of the cloud customer.

Identity and Access Management (IAM) is a cornerstone of cloud security, addressing the challenge of managing and securing user identities, roles, and permissions within cloud environments. IAM controls should be implemented to ensure the principle of least privilege, granting users and services the minimum permissions necessary for their tasks. Multi-Factor Authentication (MFA) adds an extra layer of security, mitigating the risks associated with compromised credentials and unauthorized access. IAM policies should be regularly reviewed and updated to align with evolving business requirements and to revoke unnecessary privileges.

Securing data in transit and at rest is paramount in cloud environments. Transport Layer Security (TLS) protocols should be employed to encrypt data during transmission, protecting it from interception and tampering. For data at rest, robust encryption mechanisms should be implemented, and encryption keys must be managed securely. Cloud-native encryption services, such as Key Management Services (KMS), play a vital role in simplifying key management and ensuring the integrity and confidentiality of sensitive data.

The configuration of cloud resources is a crucial factor influencing security. Misconfigurations can expose vulnerabilities and create avenues for unauthorized access. Cloud Security Posture Management (CSPM) tools are instrumental in continuously assessing and remediating misconfigurations. Automation is key in ensuring that configurations align with security best practices, and Infrastructure as Code (IaC) tools, such as Terraform or AWS CloudFormation, enable the consistent and secure provisioning of resources.

Vulnerability management is an ongoing process to identify, prioritize, and remediate vulnerabilities within the cloud environment. Continuous monitoring, automated scanning tools, and regular vulnerability assessments contribute to a proactive approach. Patch management for cloud-based resources is essential, ensuring that software and systems are up-to-date with the latest security patches to address known vulnerabilities.

As cloud environments often rely on virtualization and containerization technologies, securing these technologies is imperative. Hypervisor and container security measures should be implemented to isolate workloads and prevent unauthorized access or lateral movement. Container orchestration platforms, like Kubernetes, should be configured securely, and container images must be scanned for vulnerabilities before deployment. Runtime security solutions further enhance the protection of containers during execution.

Network security within cloud environments involves implementing robust controls for traffic segmentation, firewall rules, and network access controls. Virtual Private Clouds (VPCs) or Virtual Networks provide isolated network environments, and security groups or Network Security Groups (NSGs) define and enforce network traffic policies. Intrusion Detection and Prevention Systems (IDPS) contribute to monitoring and mitigating malicious activities within the cloud network.

Logging and monitoring are integral components of cloud security, providing visibility into user activities, resource changes, and potential security incidents. Cloud-native monitoring services, such as AWS CloudWatch or Azure Monitor, offer centralized logging and real-time insights. Security Information and Event Management (SIEM) solutions aggregate and analyze logs from various cloud services, facilitating threat detection, incident response, and compliance monitoring.

Incident response planning is essential for cloud security, outlining the steps to be taken in the event of a security incident. Cloud environments may require unique considerations, such as coordination with the CSP's incident response team. Security teams should conduct regular simulations and drills to ensure a swift and effective response to security incidents, minimizing the impact on the business.

Compliance with regulatory requirements and industry standards is a critical aspect of cloud security. Cloud customers must understand the specific compliance obligations relevant to their industry and geography. CSPs typically offer compliance certifications for their services, and customers should leverage these certifications to demonstrate adherence to regulatory requirements. Regular audits and assessments help ensure ongoing compliance and identify areas for improvement.

As organizations increasingly adopt cloud-native architectures, serverless computing introduces new security considerations. Serverless functions, executed in response to events, require specific security measures. Access controls, secure coding practices, and runtime security monitoring become crucial to mitigate risks associated with serverless computing. Understanding the unique security challenges of serverless architectures is essential for organizations embracing this paradigm.

Threat intelligence plays a pivotal role in anticipating and mitigating potential security threats. Continuous monitoring of threat intelligence feeds enables organizations to stay informed about emerging threats, vulnerabilities, and attack techniques. Threat intelligence can be leveraged to enhance security controls, update incident response plans, and fortify defenses against specific threats targeting cloud environments.

As organizations increasingly adopt multi-cloud or hybrid cloud strategies, where they use services from multiple cloud providers or combine cloud services with on-premises infrastructure, ensuring consistent security across environments becomes paramount. Security policies, IAM configurations, and security controls should be harmonized to maintain a unified security posture. Interconnecting security solutions, such as cloud access security brokers (CASBs), can provide centralized visibility and control across diverse cloud environments.

The human factor is a critical aspect of cloud security. Security awareness training for employees, developers, and administrators is essential to foster a security-conscious culture. Employees should be educated on phishing threats, social engineering tactics, and best practices for securing their interactions with cloud resources. DevOps teams should integrate security into the development life cycle, emphasizing secure coding practices and collaboration with security teams.

Cloud security governance involves the establishment of policies, procedures, and frameworks to guide and oversee security activities within the cloud environment. Security governance ensures that security measures align with organizational objectives, risk appetite, and compliance requirements. Regular audits and assessments, conducted internally or by third-party assessors, provide assurance that security controls are effective and that the cloud environment adheres to established security policies.

As cloud technologies evolve, security measures must adapt accordingly. Cloud security is not a one-time effort but a continuous process of improvement and adaptation to emerging threats and technologies. Organizations should stay informed about advancements in cloud security, update their security strategies accordingly, and leverage the latest security features and services provided by CSPs.

In conclusion, ensuring the security of cloud-based applications and infrastructure is a comprehensive and dynamic endeavor. The combination of robust IAM, encryption, configuration management, vulnerability management, and incident response practices forms the foundation of a secure cloud environment. Collaboration with CSPs, adherence to compliance requirements, and a proactive stance toward emerging threats contribute to a resilient and trustworthy cloud security posture. As organizations navigate the complexities of the cloud, a holistic and adaptive approach to security is essential for safeguarding data, maintaining compliance, and fostering the trust of users and stakeholders in the digital era.

Responding to emerging threats and vulnerabilities post-deployment.

Responding to emerging threats and vulnerabilities post-deployment is a critical aspect of maintaining the security and resilience

DIPHARSH

of software systems in the constantly evolving landscape of cyber threats. Despite rigorous pre-deployment testing and security measures, the dynamic nature of technology and the sophistication of malicious actors mean that new threats and vulnerabilities can emerge even after the deployment of a system. The post-deployment phase requires a proactive and adaptive security strategy to identify, assess, and mitigate these emerging risks effectively.

A key element of an effective post-deployment response is the establishment of a robust incident response plan. This plan serves as a structured framework for the organization to follow in the event of a security incident. It outlines the roles and responsibilities of key personnel, the steps to be taken during an incident, and the communication protocols to ensure a coordinated and efficient response. Incident response planning involves anticipating various scenarios, from data breaches to service disruptions, and devising specific actions to contain, eradicate, and recover from each type of incident.

Continuous monitoring is fundamental to the early detection of emerging threats and vulnerabilities. Post-deployment, organizations should implement a comprehensive monitoring infrastructure that tracks system activities, network traffic, and user behaviors. Security Information and Event Management (SIEM) solutions play a crucial role in aggregating and analyzing logs from various sources, providing real-time insights into potential security incidents. Anomalies, suspicious patterns, or unexpected changes in system behavior should trigger immediate investigation, enabling organizations to respond promptly to emerging threats.

Vulnerability management remains an ongoing process in the post-deployment phase. Regular vulnerability assessments and scans help identify weaknesses in software, configurations, or third-party components. These assessments should be conducted at regular intervals to stay ahead of emerging threats. Automated scanning tools, combined with manual assessments, contribute to a comprehensive understanding of the system's security posture. Prioritizing and addressing identified vulnerabilities based on their severity is essential for effective risk mitigation.

Adopting a threat intelligence-driven approach enhances the organization's ability to respond to emerging threats. Threat intelligence involves the collection, analysis, and dissemination of information about current and potential cyber threats. By staying informed about the tactics, techniques, and procedures employed by threat actors, organizations can proactively adjust their security measures to counteract evolving attack methods. Collaborating with external threat intelligence sources, such as Information Sharing and Analysis Centers (ISACs), enhances the breadth and depth of threat intelligence.

In the post-deployment phase, organizations should maintain a comprehensive inventory of their assets, including hardware, software, and data repositories. This asset management framework is crucial for understanding the attack surface and prioritizing security efforts. Regularly updating the asset inventory ensures that new deployments, changes, or decommissioned assets are reflected accurately. This knowledge is instrumental in responding to emerging threats effectively, allowing organizations to focus on protecting their most critical assets.

Communication and collaboration are key components of an effective post-deployment response strategy. Establishing clear lines of communication among security teams, IT personnel, executives, and external stakeholders is essential. Timely and transparent communication helps disseminate information about emerging threats, ongoing incident response efforts, and the potential impact on the organization. Collaborating with industry peers, sharing threat intelligence, and participating in information-sharing communities contribute to a collective defense against emerging cyber threats.

Post-deployment security requires a proactive approach to secure coding practices and software development. Developers play a crucial role in addressing vulnerabilities that may emerge post-deployment. Regular code reviews, secure coding training, and the integration of security into the Software Development Life Cycle (SDLC) contribute to the creation of resilient software. Implementing automated security testing tools, such as Static Application Security Testing (SAST) and Dynamic Application Security Testing (DAST), during the development process helps identify and address vulnerabilities before they reach production.

Patch management is an integral part of responding to emerging vulnerabilities post-deployment. Software vendors regularly release patches to address known vulnerabilities, and organizations must have a structured process for applying these patches promptly. Automated patch management tools can streamline the process of identifying, testing, and deploying patches across the organization's infrastructure. Prioritizing critical patches and applying them in a timely manner reduces the window of exposure to potential exploits.

Emphasizing a culture of security awareness among employees is crucial in the post-deployment phase. Human factors, such as social engineering attacks or insider threats, can contribute to emerging security risks. Security awareness training programs educate employees about the latest threats, phishing tactics, and best practices for maintaining a secure working environment. Encouraging a security-conscious culture fosters a sense of responsibility among employees, making them active participants in the organization's defense against emerging threats.

In the post-deployment phase, organizations should conduct regular penetration testing and red teaming exercises. These simulated attacks help identify potential vulnerabilities and weaknesses in the security architecture. Penetration testers emulate the tactics of real-world attackers, providing valuable insights into the effectiveness of security controls and the organization's ability to detect and respond to advanced threats. The results of these exercises inform adjustments to security measures, ensuring that the organization remains resilient to emerging threats.

As organizations increasingly rely on third-party services, APIs, and integrations, managing the security of these external dependencies becomes crucial in the post-deployment phase. Regularly assessing the security posture of third-party vendors, conducting security reviews of APIs, and monitoring the security practices of external partners contribute to a holistic security strategy. Establishing Service Level Agreements (SLAs) that include security requirements and regularly auditing third-party security practices help mitigate risks associated with external dependencies.

In the post-deployment phase, organizations should be prepared for regulatory compliance audits. Compliance requirements may evolve, and ensuring ongoing adherence to relevant regulations is essential. Organizations must maintain documentation, conduct internal audits, and demonstrate compliance with applicable data protection laws, industry standards, and regulatory frameworks. Proactive compliance management helps avoid legal repercussions and enhances the overall security posture of the organization.

In conclusion, responding to emerging threats and vulnerabilities in the post-deployment phase requires a comprehensive and adaptive security strategy. The combination of incident response planning, continuous monitoring, vulnerability management, threat intelligence, and collaboration forms the foundation of an effective post-deployment security posture. By integrating security into every aspect of the organization, fostering a culture of awareness, and embracing proactive measures, organizations can navigate the ever-changing threat landscape and respond effectively to emerging risks, ensuring the ongoing security and resilience of their systems and data.

Chapter 8: Continuous Vigilance: Maintaining a Secure Codebase

Recognizing the dynamic nature of security threats.

Recognizing the dynamic nature of security threats is a fundamental aspect of navigating the complex and ever-evolving landscape of cybersecurity. In an interconnected and digitized world, where technological advancements bring unprecedented opportunities, the corresponding increase in sophistication and diversity of security threats presents a continuous challenge for individuals, organizations, and societies at large. This dynamic nature underscores the importance of adopting a proactive and adaptive approach to cybersecurity, acknowledging that the threat landscape is not static but constantly shifting in response to technological innovations, geopolitical developments, and the evolving tactics of malicious actors.

The cyber threat landscape is characterized by its multifaceted and dynamic nature, with threats manifesting in various forms, including but not limited to malware, phishing attacks, ransomware, advanced persistent threats (APTs), and zero-day vulnerabilities. Malicious actors leverage a range of techniques to exploit vulnerabilities and infiltrate systems, reflecting an ongoing game of cat and mouse with cybersecurity defenders. The dynamic nature of these threats demands continuous vigilance, as new attack vectors emerge, and threat actors adapt their strategies to bypass existing security measures.

Technological innovation, while driving progress and efficiency, simultaneously introduces new attack surfaces and vulnerabilities. Emerging technologies such as the Internet of Things (IoT), cloud computing, artificial intelligence (AI), and quantum computing present both unprecedented opportunities and potential security challenges. Recognizing the dynamic nature of security threats entails understanding how these innovations can be exploited by threat actors and staying ahead of the curve in implementing security measures that account for the unique risks associated with evolving technologies.

Cyber threat actors are not static entities; they continuously refine and adjust their tactics, techniques, and procedures (TTPs) to circumvent security defenses. Threat actors range from individual hackers to sophisticated state-sponsored groups, each with distinct motivations and capabilities. The fluidity of the threat landscape means that defenders must be agile, anticipating the next move of threat actors and adapting security strategies accordingly. This requires a deep understanding of threat intelligence, gained through continuous monitoring of indicators of compromise, analysis of attack patterns, and collaboration within the cybersecurity community to share insights and countermeasures.

The interconnected nature of global networks amplifies the impact of security threats, transcending geographical boundaries and organizational borders. Recognizing the dynamic nature of these threats involves acknowledging the interdependencies between different entities and understanding that a security breach in one part of the world can have ripple effects across industries and sectors. Collaborative efforts, information sharing, and international cooperation are crucial in addressing the global nature of cybersecurity threats, as defending against these threats requires a collective response that transcends individual capabilities.

Social engineering, a tactic that exploits human psychology to manipulate individuals into divulging sensitive information or performing actions that compromise security, adds a human dimension to cybersecurity threats. Phishing attacks, pretexting, and other social engineering techniques evolve alongside changes in human behavior, current events, and societal trends. Recognizing the dynamic nature of these threats requires ongoing education and awareness programs to empower individuals to identify and resist social engineering attempts. Moreover, it involves understanding that threat actors continually refine their social engineering tactics to exploit human vulnerabilities and adapting security measures accordingly.

The proliferation of data and its increasing value make data-centric attacks a prominent facet of the dynamic threat landscape. Cybercriminals seek to compromise and exploit sensitive data, ranging from personally identifiable information (PII) to intellectual property and financial records. Recognizing the dynamic nature of data-centric threats involves implementing robust data protection measures, including encryption, access controls, and data loss prevention (DLP) solutions. As data usage patterns evolve, security strategies must continually evolve to safeguard data throughout its lifecycle, from creation and storage to transmission and disposal.

The regulatory landscape adds another layer of dynamism to cybersecurity, as new data protection laws and compliance requirements emerge. Organizations must navigate a complex web of regulations that vary by industry, region, and jurisdiction. Recognizing the dynamic nature of regulatory compliance involves staying informed about changes in legislation, understanding the implications for data handling practices, and adjusting security measures to ensure ongoing adherence to evolving compliance requirements. Compliance should be viewed not only as a legal obligation but as a crucial component of a comprehensive cybersecurity strategy.

The threat landscape is also influenced by geopolitical factors, with state-sponsored cyber attacks becoming increasingly prevalent. Nation-states leverage cyber capabilities to achieve political, economic, or military objectives, contributing to the dynamic nature of global cybersecurity. Recognizing the geopolitical dimension of security threats requires organizations and governments to factor in geopolitical tensions, alliances, and cyber warfare considerations when developing and updating cybersecurity strategies. This involves understanding the motivations and capabilities of nation-state actors and implementing measures to detect and mitigate state-sponsored cyber threats.

The dark web and underground cybercriminal forums serve as breeding grounds for the development and exchange of malicious tools, services, and information. Recognizing the dynamic nature of the cybercriminal ecosystem involves monitoring these forums for emerging threats, understanding the economics of cybercrime, and anticipating the commoditization of hacking tools and services. Cyber threat intelligence from these sources provides insights into the tactics and tools favored by threat actors, enabling defenders to proactively adjust their security postures.

Machine learning and AI, while offering advancements in cybersecurity through anomaly detection and behavioral analysis, also introduce new risks. Threat actors are increasingly incorporating AI into their attack strategies, automating tasks and evading traditional security measures. Recognizing the dynamic nature of AI-driven threats requires the development of AI-powered defenses that can adapt and learn from evolving attack patterns. This cat-and-mouse game between AI-driven defenses and AI-powered attacks underscores the need for continuous innovation in cybersecurity.

The dynamic nature of security threats necessitates a shift from a reactive to a proactive cybersecurity posture. Traditional signature-based approaches to security, while still valuable, must be complemented by proactive measures such as threat hunting, anomaly detection, and behavior analytics. Recognizing that threats may not always follow known patterns, organizations must invest in technologies and practices that can identify deviations from normal behavior and indicators of compromise in real-time.

In conclusion, recognizing the dynamic nature of security threats is a foundational principle in modern cybersecurity. It involves understanding that the threat landscape is in a constant state of flux, shaped by technological advancements, human behavior, geopolitical factors, and the ever-evolving tactics of cybercriminals. A proactive and adaptive approach to cybersecurity, informed by threat intelligence, collaborative efforts, and a commitment to ongoing education, is essential for organizations and individuals to effectively navigate and mitigate the risks posed by the dynamic and multifaceted world of cybersecurity threats.

Developing a robust strategy for timely application of security patches.

Developing a robust strategy for the timely application of security patches is a critical imperative in the realm of cybersecurity, where the constant evolution of threats demands a proactive and adaptive defense posture. The application of security patches serves as a primary line of defense against vulnerabilities that could be exploited by malicious actors to compromise systems, exfiltrate sensitive data, or disrupt critical operations. A comprehensive strategy for timely patch management encompasses various facets, ranging from vulnerability identification and prioritization to testing and deployment, ensuring that organizations can effectively fortify their digital infrastructure against emerging threats.

The foundation of a robust patch management strategy lies in the timely identification of vulnerabilities within software, operating systems, and applications. Continuous monitoring of vendor advisories, security bulletins, and threat intelligence feeds is crucial for staying abreast of newly discovered vulnerabilities. Automation tools that scan networks and systems for vulnerabilities contribute to the efficiency of this process, enabling organizations to maintain an up-to-date inventory of potential security risks. Establishing channels for receiving notifications from software vendors, open-source communities, and security forums ensures that organizations are promptly informed about newly disclosed vulnerabilities relevant to their infrastructure.

Prioritizing identified vulnerabilities is a key aspect of an effective patch management strategy, recognizing that not all vulnerabilities pose an equal level of risk. Vulnerability severity, the potential impact on business operations, and the likelihood of exploitation are factors that should inform the prioritization process. Common Vulnerability Scoring System (CVSS) scores and other risk assessment frameworks aid in categorizing vulnerabilities based on their criticality. This prioritization allows organizations to focus their resources on addressing high-risk vulnerabilities promptly, mitigating the most significant threats to their security posture.

Testing plays a pivotal role in the patch management process, ensuring that applying patches does not inadvertently introduce system instability or compatibility issues. Organizations should establish a structured testing environment that mirrors their production environment, allowing for the simulation of patch deployments before they are applied to live systems. Automated testing tools, along with manual verification procedures, contribute to a thorough evaluation of the patches' impact on system functionality. Testing should encompass a range of scenarios, including different operating systems, network configurations, and application dependencies, to provide a comprehensive assessment of the patches' compatibility.

The timely deployment of patches is a critical element in closing the window of exposure to potential exploits. Organizations should establish a well-defined process for patch deployment that includes a predetermined schedule, change management procedures, and contingency plans. Automation tools that facilitate the systematic rollout of patches across multiple systems contribute to the efficiency of deployment efforts. Continuous monitoring of patch deployment status and automated reporting mechanisms help ensure that all systems are brought up to the desired patch level within the established timeframe.

In environments with diverse technologies and third-party dependencies, coordination with vendors and partners is essential for a synchronized approach to patch management. Collaborative efforts enable organizations to align their patching schedules with those of their suppliers, ensuring that vulnerabilities across interconnected systems are addressed collectively. Engaging in information-sharing initiatives, such as Information Sharing and Analysis Centers (ISACs), facilitates the exchange of threat intelligence and best practices, contributing to a collective defense against emerging threats.

Recognizing that some systems may be more challenging to patch than others, organizations should implement compensating controls to mitigate the risks associated with delayed patching. This involves employing intrusion detection and prevention systems, network segmentation, and additional security measures to fortify systems that cannot be patched immediately. Risk assessments should guide the determination of acceptable levels of risk for systems that may operate with temporary vulnerabilities, allowing organizations to balance the need for security with the practical constraints of certain environments.

Communication is a cornerstone of effective patch management, both internally within an organization and externally with stakeholders. Establishing clear lines of communication between IT teams, security personnel, and relevant business units ensures that patching activities are aligned with business priorities and operational requirements. Regularly informing end-users and stakeholders about the importance of applying patches promptly fosters a culture of security awareness, encouraging active participation in the organization's defense against cyber threats.

In addition to routine patch management activities, organizations should be prepared to respond swiftly to the emergence of zero-day vulnerabilities—previously unknown vulnerabilities for which patches have not yet been released. Developing a rapid response plan, including the deployment of temporary mitigations and enhanced monitoring, allows organizations to mitigate the risks associated with zero-day vulnerabilities until official patches are available. Collaboration with industry peers and government agencies can provide early warnings about zero-day threats and facilitate a coordinated response.

Automation is a force multiplier in the realm of patch management, streamlining routine tasks and enhancing the efficiency of the overall process. Organizations should leverage automation tools for vulnerability scanning, patch deployment, and compliance monitoring. Automated workflows can help orchestrate patching activities across diverse systems, reducing the manual effort required and minimizing the likelihood of human error. Additionally, automation contributes to the establishment of a continuous monitoring and improvement cycle, allowing organizations to adapt their patch management strategy based on evolving threat landscapes and technological advancements.

Regular audits and assessments of the patch management process contribute to ongoing improvement and adherence to best practices. Internal and external audits help organizations evaluate the effectiveness of their patch management strategy, identify areas for enhancement, and ensure compliance with industry standards and regulatory requirements. Continuous feedback loops, involving incident response analyses and lessons learned from previous patching activities, contribute to a culture of continuous improvement, enabling organizations to refine their strategies based on real-world experiences.

In conclusion, developing a robust strategy for the timely application of security patches is a multifaceted endeavor that requires a proactive, systematic, and adaptive approach. From vulnerability identification and prioritization to testing, deployment, and continuous improvement, each stage of the patch management process plays a crucial role in fortifying organizations against the dynamic and ever-evolving landscape of cybersecurity threats. By establishing clear processes, leveraging automation, fostering collaboration, and embracing a culture of continuous improvement, organizations can navigate the complexities of patch management with agility and resilience, mitigating risks and safeguarding their digital assets.

Conducting regular code reviews for ongoing security assessment.

Conducting regular code reviews for ongoing security assessment is a fundamental practice that plays a pivotal role in fortifying software applications against evolving cyber threats. Code review, as an integral component of the Software Development Life Cycle (SDLC), serves not only as a mechanism for identifying and rectifying coding errors but also as a proactive means of assessing and enhancing the security posture of software systems throughout their development and maintenance phases. This systematic and iterative process involves the collaborative examination of source code by peers, architects, and security experts to uncover vulnerabilities, adherence to secure coding practices, and overall robustness of the application's security measures.

The overarching goal of integrating regular code reviews into the software development process is to identify and address security issues at an early stage, reducing the likelihood of vulnerabilities persisting into the production environment. By fostering a culture of continuous improvement and accountability, organizations can instill security consciousness among development teams, ensuring that security considerations are woven into the fabric of code development rather than being treated as an afterthought. This proactive approach aligns with the principles of secure coding and enables developers to learn from identified issues, fostering skill development and knowledge transfer within the team.

During code reviews, a multifaceted set of security considerations is examined, encompassing authentication mechanisms, authorization controls, input validation, data encryption, error handling, and adherence to coding standards. The process extends beyond identifying common vulnerabilities, such as SQL injection or cross-site scripting, to encompass a comprehensive understanding of the application's architecture and potential attack surfaces. Threat modeling, an integral part of security-focused code reviews, involves identifying potential threats and vulnerabilities based on the application's design and functionality, contributing to a holistic assessment of security risks.

The collaborative nature of code reviews facilitates knowledge sharing and mentorship within development teams. By providing a platform for experienced developers and security experts to share insights, best practices, and lessons learned, code reviews become a mechanism for skill development and the propagation of secure coding principles throughout the organization. This knowledge transfer ensures that security considerations become ingrained in the development culture, empowering developers to make informed decisions and write more resilient and secure code.

Automation tools and static code analysis play a complementary role in enhancing the effectiveness of code reviews. Automated scanners can quickly identify common coding mistakes, potential vulnerabilities, and deviations from coding standards, allowing developers to focus their manual review efforts on more complex security issues. Static code analysis tools provide an additional layer of scrutiny by analyzing the source code without executing it, offering insights into code quality, potential security vulnerabilities, and areas for improvement. Integrating these tools into the code review process streamlines the identification of security issues and accelerates the overall review cycle.

The frequency of code reviews should align with the development cadence and the criticality of the application being developed. Regular, ongoing code reviews are particularly crucial in agile and iterative development environments where code changes are frequent. In such environments, code reviews become an intrinsic part of each iteration, ensuring that security considerations are continuously integrated into the evolving codebase. Additionally, incorporating code reviews into the Continuous Integration/Continuous Deployment (CI/CD) pipeline allows for automated checks and feedback on code changes before they are merged into the main codebase, providing an additional layer of defense against potential security vulnerabilities.

The effectiveness of code reviews relies on a structured and well-defined process that establishes clear expectations for reviewers and developers. A checklist of security best practices, coding standards, and common vulnerabilities serves as a reference guide during reviews, ensuring that all relevant aspects are considered. Code review meetings provide an opportunity for collaborative discussions, clarifications, and knowledge exchange. Defining roles and responsibilities, establishing coding guidelines, and incorporating security-focused metrics into performance evaluations contribute to the overall success of the code review process.

The scope of code reviews extends beyond traditional web applications to include mobile applications, APIs, and other software components. Mobile application security, for instance, involves considerations such as secure data storage, secure communication, and protection against reverse engineering. Code reviews for APIs encompass assessing authentication mechanisms, input validation, and proper handling of sensitive data. Tailoring code reviews to the specific characteristics of different types of applications ensures a comprehensive assessment of security measures across diverse technological landscapes.

Incorporating threat modeling into the code review process adds a proactive layer to security assessments. Threat modeling involves identifying potential threats, vulnerabilities, and attack vectors based on the application's design and functionality. By systematically analyzing the application from an adversary's perspective, threat modeling guides developers and reviewers in identifying and mitigating potential security risks before they materialize. This forward-looking approach complements the retrospective nature of traditional code reviews, contributing to a holistic understanding of the application's security posture.

Code reviews serve as a continuous feedback loop for developers, enabling them to learn from identified issues and apply security principles to future code development. Security training and awareness programs further augment the effectiveness of code reviews by ensuring that developers are well-versed in secure coding practices, common vulnerabilities, and emerging threats. Regular training sessions, workshops, and access to up-to-date security resources empower developers to make informed decisions during the code development process, reducing the likelihood of introducing security vulnerabilities.

The feedback generated during code reviews contributes to the creation and refinement of secure coding guidelines and best practices within the organization. By analyzing common patterns of vulnerabilities and root causes, organizations can update coding standards, incorporate new security controls, and enhance developer training programs. This continuous improvement cycle strengthens the overall security posture of applications and promotes a culture of security awareness and excellence within the development teams.

Code reviews also play a crucial role in compliance with industry regulations and standards. Many regulatory frameworks mandate the incorporation of secure coding practices into software development processes. Regular code reviews, coupled with documentation of security considerations and remediation efforts, provide a tangible record of an organization's commitment to security and compliance. This documentation serves as valuable evidence in audits and assessments, demonstrating due diligence in addressing security concerns throughout the development life cycle.

In conclusion, conducting regular code reviews for ongoing security assessment is a cornerstone of building robust and resilient software applications in the face of evolving cyber threats. The iterative and collaborative nature of code reviews ensures that security considerations are woven into the fabric of software development, fostering a proactive and adaptive approach to addressing vulnerabilities. By combining manual reviews, automated tools, threat modeling, and ongoing training, organizations can create a comprehensive code review process that not only identifies and mitigates security risks but also contributes to the development of a security-conscious culture within the entire development ecosystem.

Continuous education for development teams on emerging threats.

Continuous education for development teams on emerging threats is a paramount strategy in the ever-evolving landscape of cybersecurity, where staying ahead of new and sophisticated threats is imperative for the resilience of software applications. The dynamic nature of cyber threats necessitates a proactive approach to security education, ensuring that development teams are equipped with the knowledge and skills required to identify, mitigate, and respond to emerging risks. This ongoing education encompasses a multifaceted approach, including awareness programs, training sessions, hands-on exercises, and access to up-to-date resources, fostering a culture of security consciousness within development teams.

Security awareness programs serve as a foundational element of continuous education, providing a broad understanding of the current threat landscape, common attack vectors, and the importance of incorporating security considerations into the development process. These programs aim to cultivate a sense of responsibility among development team members, emphasizing their role as guardians of the organization's digital assets. By raising awareness about the consequences of security breaches, the financial and reputational impact on organizations, and the evolving tactics of cyber adversaries, awareness programs create a baseline understanding that forms the groundwork for more in-depth training initiatives.

Training sessions tailored to the specific needs of development teams are instrumental in deepening their understanding of emerging threats and enhancing their technical skills. These sessions cover a spectrum of topics, ranging from secure coding practices and vulnerability analysis to threat modeling and incident response. Incorporating real-world examples and case studies allows developers to contextualize theoretical knowledge, providing practical insights into the consequences of security lapses. Hands-on exercises, such as simulated phishing campaigns, penetration testing labs, and secure coding challenges, offer a practical and interactive learning experience, reinforcing theoretical concepts and fostering a proactive mindset.

The continuous education process should adapt to the rapidly changing threat landscape, ensuring that development teams are informed about the latest attack techniques, vulnerabilities, and defensive measures. Regular updates on emerging threats, security advisories, and industry trends are vital components of ongoing education. Access to curated threat intelligence feeds, forums, and industry publications provides developers with a real-time understanding of evolving cyber threats. Integrating threat intelligence into the education curriculum enables teams to anticipate potential risks and adjust their security practices accordingly, transforming them into proactive defenders against emerging threats.

The adoption of secure coding practices is a fundamental aspect of continuous education for development teams. Training programs should instill the principles of secure coding, emphasizing practices that mitigate common vulnerabilities such as injection attacks, cross-site scripting, and insecure direct object references. In-depth knowledge of secure coding standards, language-specific security considerations, and the secure use of frameworks and libraries enables developers to write resilient code from the outset, reducing the likelihood of introducing vulnerabilities that could be exploited by attackers. Code reviews, as part of the development process, serve as a practical application of secure coding principles, providing developers with constructive feedback and opportunities for continuous improvement.

Threat modeling, as an integral part of continuous education, empowers development teams to think proactively about potential security risks during the design phase of software development. This structured approach involves identifying potential threats, vulnerabilities, and attack vectors based on the application's design and functionality. By systematically analyzing the security implications of architectural decisions, data flows, and user interactions, development teams gain a holistic understanding of the threat landscape specific to their application. Integrating threat modeling into the development life cycle ensures that security considerations are ingrained from the earliest stages of application design, preventing security issues from becoming systemic.

Continuous education for development teams should extend beyond technical aspects to encompass broader security concepts, compliance requirements, and privacy considerations. Understanding the regulatory landscape and industry-specific compliance standards is crucial for aligning development practices with legal and regulatory requirements. Education programs should cover topics such as data protection laws, secure handling of personally identifiable information (PII), and the implications of privacy breaches. This broader perspective ensures that development teams are not only technically adept but also well-versed in the ethical and legal dimensions of cybersecurity.

The integration of secure development practices into the Software Development Life Cycle (SDLC) is a cornerstone of continuous education. By incorporating security checkpoints at key stages of the SDLC, such as requirements gathering, design, coding, testing, and deployment, development teams embed security into the fabric of the development process. This holistic approach ensures that security is not treated as a standalone consideration but rather as an intrinsic part of each phase of application development. Automation tools that support secure coding practices, conduct static and dynamic code analysis, and provide real-time feedback during the development process contribute to the seamless integration of security into the SDLC.

Continuous education should empower development teams to understand and counteract the evolving threat landscape associated with cloud computing and containerized applications. As organizations increasingly migrate to cloud environments and adopt containerization technologies, developers need to be well-versed in the unique security challenges posed by these paradigms. Training programs should cover topics such as secure configuration of cloud services, identity and access management in cloud environments, and the security considerations specific to container orchestration platforms. With the proper education, development teams can leverage the advantages of cloud computing while mitigating associated risks.

Collaboration and knowledge sharing within development teams and across the organization enhance the collective capability to respond to emerging threats. Establishing internal forums, community-driven initiatives, and collaborative platforms allows developers to share experiences, discuss challenges, and disseminate knowledge gained from ongoing education efforts. Cross-functional collaboration, involving security teams, operations, and other stakeholders, creates a synergy of expertise that is invaluable in addressing the multidimensional nature of cybersecurity challenges. Regular knowledge-sharing sessions, workshops, and collaborative projects contribute to a culture of continuous learning and improvement.

The effectiveness of continuous education initiatives is reinforced by establishing key performance indicators (KPIs) and metrics that measure the impact of education programs on the security posture of development teams. Metrics could include the reduction in the number of security vulnerabilities introduced during the development process, the speed at which vulnerabilities are remediated, and the overall improvement in the security awareness of team members. Regular assessments, surveys, and feedback mechanisms allow organizations to gauge the efficacy of education efforts, identify areas for improvement, and tailor future programs to address specific needs.

In conclusion, continuous education for development teams on emerging threats is an essential and dynamic component of a robust cybersecurity strategy. By fostering a culture of security awareness, providing targeted training sessions, integrating secure coding practices into the SDLC, and embracing a collaborative and adaptive approach, organizations can empower development teams to navigate the ever-changing threat landscape effectively. This ongoing education not only enhances technical skills but also cultivates a proactive and security-conscious mindset, positioning development teams as integral contributors to the overall cybersecurity resilience of the organization.

Preparing for and responding to security incidents.

Preparing for and responding to security incidents is a critical aspect of modern information technology management, given the increasing frequency and sophistication of cyber threats. To effectively address this challenge, organizations must adopt a comprehensive and proactive approach that encompasses both pre-incident preparation and timely response strategies. The preparatory phase involves establishing a robust cybersecurity framework, which includes developing policies, procedures, and guidelines to govern information security practices. This framework should be aligned with industry standards and best practices, such as those outlined by ISO 27001, NIST, or CIS. Furthermore, organizations should conduct regular risk assessments to identify potential vulnerabilities and threats specific to their environment, considering factors like the nature of their business, the sensitivity of data, and the regulatory landscape.

A key element in incident preparation is the implementation of security controls and technologies that can detect, prevent, and mitigate potential threats. This involves deploying firewalls, intrusion detection systems (IDS), intrusion prevention systems (IPS), antivirus solutions, and other advanced security tools. Security awareness training for employees is equally important, as human error remains a significant contributor to security incidents. Employees should be educated on recognizing phishing attempts, using strong passwords, and adhering to security policies to minimize the risk of inadvertent security breaches. Regular drills and simulations can help organizations evaluate the effectiveness of their incident response plans and ensure that employees are well-prepared to handle real-life security incidents.

Establishing an incident response plan (IRP) is a fundamental component of preparedness. The IRP outlines the procedures and roles that need to be followed when a security incident occurs. It should define the chain of command, communication protocols, and the steps to be taken during each phase of incident handling, including detection, analysis, containment, eradication, recovery, and lessons learned. The plan should be dynamic and updated regularly to reflect changes in the threat landscape, the organization's infrastructure, and the evolving regulatory environment. Additionally, organizations should collaborate with relevant external entities, such as law enforcement agencies, industry groups, and information-sharing forums, to stay informed about emerging threats and trends.

In the event of a security incident, a rapid and effective response is paramount to minimize damage and protect sensitive information. The first phase, detection, relies on the organization's monitoring and alerting systems. Anomalies and suspicious activities should be promptly identified, and incident responders should be notified to initiate the response process. Once an incident is confirmed, the organization must move swiftly to analyze the incident, understanding its scope, impact, and the techniques employed by the adversaries. This phase often involves collaboration between IT security teams, legal counsel, and, in some cases, external forensics experts.

Containment is the next critical step, aiming to prevent further spread of the incident and mitigate its impact. This may involve isolating affected systems, blocking malicious network traffic, and disabling compromised user accounts. Simultaneously, organizations must begin the process of eradicating the threat, which entails removing malicious code, closing vulnerabilities, and ensuring that the adversary no longer has access to the organization's systems. The eradication phase often requires a delicate balance between swiftly addressing the incident and preserving evidence for legal or investigative purposes.

Recovery is the subsequent phase, where organizations work towards restoring normal operations and mitigating any lingering effects of the incident. This involves restoring data from backups, verifying the integrity of systems, and implementing additional security measures to prevent a recurrence. Communication is crucial during the recovery phase, as organizations must keep stakeholders informed about the incident, its impact, and the steps being taken to address it. Transparency builds trust and demonstrates a commitment to addressing the situation responsibly.

The final phase of incident response is the post-incident analysis or lessons learned. This retrospective examination aims to identify areas for improvement in the incident response plan, security controls, and overall cybersecurity posture. Conducting a thorough analysis helps organizations understand the root causes of the incident, whether they be technical, procedural, or human-related, and provides insights for enhancing resilience against future threats. Organizations should document their findings, update their incident response plans accordingly, and share the lessons learned with relevant stakeholders. This continuous improvement cycle is essential for staying ahead of the ever-evolving threat landscape.

In conclusion, preparing for and responding to security incidents requires a multifaceted and dynamic approach that spans both proactive measures and reactive strategies. Organizations must invest in comprehensive cybersecurity frameworks, robust security controls, and ongoing employee training to minimize the risk of security breaches. Simultaneously, having a well-defined incident response plan is crucial for navigating the complexities of a security incident when it occurs. The ability to detect, contain, eradicate, and recover from incidents is vital, and organizations should prioritize communication and collaboration both internally and externally throughout the incident response process. Finally, the post-incident analysis is a key component for continuous improvement, helping organizations learn from each incident and adapt their strategies to the evolving threat landscape. By integrating these elements into their cybersecurity practices, organizations can enhance their resilience and better protect their digital assets in an increasingly challenging security environment.

Continuous monitoring for suspicious activities and security incidents.

Continuous monitoring for suspicious activities and security incidents is a fundamental practice in contemporary cybersecurity, essential for maintaining the integrity and resilience of an organization's digital infrastructure. This proactive approach involves the real-time scrutiny of network traffic, system logs, and user activities to promptly identify and respond to potential threats. The digital landscape is rife with diverse and evolving risks, ranging from sophisticated cyber-attacks to insider threats, making continuous monitoring a critical component of a robust cybersecurity strategy.

To effectively implement continuous monitoring, organizations must deploy a comprehensive set of tools and technologies that can capture and analyze vast amounts of data generated by their IT infrastructure. Security Information and Event Management (SIEM) systems play a pivotal role in this regard, aggregating and correlating log data from various sources, such as firewalls, intrusion detection systems, and servers. Advanced analytics and machine learning capabilities within these systems enable the identification of patterns indicative of suspicious or malicious activities, enhancing the ability to detect threats that may otherwise go unnoticed.

One of the primary benefits of continuous monitoring is its capacity to provide real-time visibility into the organization's digital environment. By monitoring network traffic, organizations can detect anomalies, unauthorized access attempts, or unusual patterns that may signal a potential security incident. This proactive stance allows security teams to respond swiftly, minimizing the dwell time of adversaries within the network and reducing the potential impact of an incident.

Continuous monitoring is not limited to external threats; it also addresses insider threats, which can be equally detrimental. Monitoring user activities, access patterns, and behavior can help identify anomalies that may indicate a compromised account or malicious insider activity. By establishing baselines for normal behavior, organizations can more effectively pinpoint deviations that may require further investigation. This approach is crucial for maintaining a balance between protecting sensitive data and respecting the privacy of legitimate users.

Automated alerting is a key feature of continuous monitoring systems, enabling security teams to receive immediate notifications when suspicious activities are detected. However, the sheer volume of alerts generated can be overwhelming. To address this challenge, organizations are increasingly leveraging artificial intelligence and machine learning algorithms to prioritize alerts based on their severity and relevance. This allows security analysts to focus their attention on the most critical threats, improving the efficiency of incident response efforts.

In addition to identifying and responding to security incidents, continuous monitoring contributes significantly to threat intelligence gathering. By analyzing patterns and trends in the data, organizations can gain valuable insights into the tactics, techniques, and procedures employed by adversaries. This intelligence enhances the organization's ability to proactively defend against emerging threats and adjust security controls accordingly. Collaborating with external threat intelligence feeds further enriches the organization's understanding of the global threat landscape.

Compliance with regulatory requirements is another driver for the adoption of continuous monitoring practices. Many industry regulations and data protection laws mandate organizations to implement measures for monitoring and safeguarding sensitive information. Continuous monitoring not only helps organizations meet these compliance requirements but also strengthens their overall security posture by providing a proactive defense against potential threats.

An essential aspect of continuous monitoring is the integration of vulnerability management. Regularly scanning and assessing the organization's systems and applications for vulnerabilities ensures that security teams can identify and remediate weaknesses before they are exploited by malicious actors. This proactive approach aligns with the principle of "security by design," where vulnerabilities are addressed in the early stages of system development or deployment.

While continuous monitoring is a powerful tool, it is not a one-size-fits-all solution. Organizations must tailor their monitoring strategies to their specific needs, taking into account the nature of their business, the sensitivity of their data, and the regulatory environment in which they operate. Regular risk assessments assist in identifying critical assets, potential threats, and the most effective monitoring techniques for mitigating risks. This customized approach allows organizations to allocate resources efficiently and prioritize monitoring efforts based on the areas of greatest concern.

Continuous monitoring is most effective when integrated into a broader cybersecurity framework that includes incident response, threat intelligence, and risk management. The synergy between these components creates a dynamic and adaptive defense strategy capable of addressing both known and emerging threats. Organizations should view continuous monitoring not as a standalone practice but as an integral part of their cybersecurity posture, working in concert with other security measures to create a resilient and responsive defense system.

In conclusion, continuous monitoring for suspicious activities and security incidents is an indispensable practice in the modern cybersecurity landscape. It enables organizations to detect and respond to threats in real-time, reducing the risk of data breaches and minimizing the impact of security incidents. By leveraging advanced technologies such as SIEM systems, machine learning, and threat intelligence, organizations can enhance their ability to identify both external and insider threats. Continuous monitoring not only contributes to regulatory compliance but also provides valuable insights into the evolving threat landscape. When integrated into a comprehensive cybersecurity framework, continuous monitoring becomes a cornerstone of an organization's proactive defense strategy, allowing it to adapt to the dynamic nature of cyber threats and safeguard its digital assets effectively.

Integrating security into the DevOps culture. Integrating security into the DevOps culture is a vital and evolving paradigm that seeks to harmonize the traditionally distinct domains of development and operations with robust security practices. DevOps, a collaborative and agile approach to software development and IT operations, prioritizes speed, efficiency, and continuous delivery. However, this accelerated pace can inadvertently introduce security vulnerabilities if not addressed proactively. Therefore, embedding security into the DevOps culture is imperative to ensure that security considerations are seamlessly woven into every stage of the development lifecycle.

The traditional perception of security as a separate and often bottlenecked phase in the software development process is challenged by the DevOps philosophy. The integration of security into DevOps, often referred to as "DevSecOps," promotes a cultural shift that aligns security objectives with the overarching goals of DevOps – rapid delivery, collaboration, and agility. This involves breaking down silos between development, operations, and security teams, fostering a shared responsibility for security throughout the development pipeline.

At the heart of DevSecOps is the concept of "shifting left," which entails moving security practices and considerations to the earliest stages of the development process. By integrating security from the outset, organizations can identify and address potential vulnerabilities and compliance issues earlier in the development lifecycle, reducing the likelihood of security-related defects reaching production. This approach aligns with the agile principle of iterative development, allowing teams to adapt and refine security measures throughout the software delivery lifecycle.

One key practice in integrating security into DevOps is the automation of security testing and compliance checks. Automated security testing tools, such as static application security testing (SAST) and dynamic application security testing (DAST), can be seamlessly integrated into the DevOps pipeline. These tools scan code for vulnerabilities, assess the security of dependencies, and identify potential weaknesses in the application or infrastructure. Automated testing not only accelerates the identification of security issues but also ensures consistency and repeatability in the evaluation process.

Collaboration and communication are foundational to DevOps, and extending this collaborative ethos to security practices is a central tenet of DevSecOps. Security teams actively engage with development and operations teams, sharing expertise and collaborating on security requirements. This collaborative model facilitates a mutual understanding of each team's objectives and challenges, fostering a culture where security is not seen as a hindrance but as an integral part of the development process.

Implementing security as code is another critical aspect of DevSecOps. This involves codifying security policies and configurations alongside application code, infrastructure as code (IaC), and other development artifacts. Security as code allows organizations to manage and version security controls in a manner consistent with the principles of DevOps. It also ensures that security measures are applied consistently across diverse environments, reducing the risk of misconfigurations and vulnerabilities.

Continuous integration and continuous delivery (CI/CD) pipelines serve as the backbone of DevOps practices, automating the process of building, testing, and deploying applications. Embedding security controls directly into these pipelines enables organizations to enforce security policies at every stage of development, reducing the surface area for potential attacks. Security gates can be implemented to halt the deployment process if predetermined security criteria are not met, ensuring that only secure code is released into production.

Monitoring and feedback loops are essential components of the DevOps philosophy, and integrating security requires continuous monitoring for vulnerabilities and threats. Security teams leverage real-time monitoring tools and log analysis to detect and respond to security incidents promptly. This proactive approach aligns with the DevOps principle of rapid feedback, allowing teams to address security issues in near real-time and continuously improve security measures.

Education and awareness play a crucial role in fostering a security-aware culture within DevOps teams. Training programs and awareness initiatives ensure that developers, operations personnel, and security professionals are equipped with the knowledge and skills needed to identify and address security issues. By empowering individuals with a security mindset, organizations can create a collective responsibility for security within the DevOps culture.

DevSecOps is not a one-size-fits-all solution, and its successful implementation requires tailoring security practices to the specific needs and context of each organization. Risk assessments and threat modeling help identify the unique security challenges associated with the organization's technology stack, business processes, and regulatory environment. This contextual understanding enables organizations to prioritize security measures that align with their specific risk profile and compliance requirements.

In conclusion, integrating security into the DevOps culture represents a transformative approach to addressing the inherent tension between speed and security in software development. DevSecOps advocates for a cultural shift that embraces security as an integral part of the development process, emphasizing collaboration, automation, and continuous improvement. By shifting security left in the development lifecycle, leveraging automation, and fostering a collaborative mindset, organizations can effectively balance the need for rapid delivery with the imperative to build secure and resilient software. The journey towards DevSecOps requires a commitment to cultural change, ongoing education, and the adoption of technologies that enable seamless integration of security into the DevOps pipeline. Ultimately, DevSecOps is not merely a set of practices but a cultural evolution that harmonizes the traditionally separate worlds of development, operations, and security, leading to more secure and resilient software delivery.

Establishing key performance indicators (KPIs) for security.

Establishing key performance indicators (KPIs) for security is a crucial undertaking that plays a pivotal role in the effective management and evaluation of an organization's cybersecurity posture. KPIs serve as measurable metrics that enable organizations to assess the effectiveness of their security initiatives, identify areas of improvement, and make informed decisions to enhance overall security resilience. The landscape of cyber threats is dynamic and multifaceted, necessitating a strategic and comprehensive approach to defining KPIs that align with the organization's objectives, risk tolerance, and regulatory requirements.

One foundational aspect of security KPIs lies in aligning them with the organization's overarching business goals. This alignment ensures that security measures are not perceived in isolation but are integrated into the broader context of organizational success. KPIs should be reflective of the organization's mission, values, and strategic priorities, emphasizing the importance of a holistic and business-centric approach to cybersecurity. By demonstrating the impact of security on the achievement of business objectives, organizations can garner support and investment for security initiatives from key stakeholders.

A critical category of security KPIs revolves around the identification and management of vulnerabilities within the organization's digital infrastructure. Metrics related to vulnerability management provide insights into the organization's ability to proactively identify and remediate potential weaknesses that could be exploited by malicious actors. KPIs in this domain may include the average time to patch vulnerabilities, the percentage of critical vulnerabilities remediated within a specified timeframe, and the frequency of vulnerability assessments. These metrics are essential for maintaining a robust defense against evolving cyber threats.

Incident response and resolution times are integral KPIs for evaluating the organization's ability to detect, respond to, and recover from security incidents. The mean time to detect (MTTD) and mean time to respond (MTTR) are key indicators that measure the efficiency of the organization's incident response capabilities. A low MTTD signifies a rapid detection of security incidents, while a low MTTR indicates a swift and effective response. These KPIs are essential for minimizing the impact of security incidents, reducing downtime, and enhancing overall cybersecurity resilience.

User awareness and training are pivotal components of a comprehensive security strategy, and corresponding KPIs play a central role in evaluating their effectiveness. Metrics such as the completion rates of security training programs, the frequency of simulated phishing exercises, and the reduction in security incidents attributable to human error provide insights into the organization's success in fostering a security-aware culture. These KPIs help measure the effectiveness of educational initiatives and highlight areas where additional training or awareness efforts may be needed.

Monitoring and detection capabilities are paramount in the face of sophisticated cyber threats, making KPIs related to threat detection and response essential. Metrics such as the number of false positives, the accuracy of threat detection tools, and the time taken to investigate and remediate confirmed threats contribute to a comprehensive understanding of the organization's threat detection capabilities. These KPIs aid in fine-tuning security controls, optimizing detection strategies, and improving the overall efficacy of the organization's security infrastructure.

The effectiveness of access controls and identity management is a critical dimension of security, and KPIs in this realm focus on metrics that assess the organization's ability to manage and control user access to systems and data. KPIs may include the average time to provision or deprovision user accounts, the frequency of access reviews, and the number of unauthorized access attempts. These metrics contribute to the organization's efforts to maintain the principle of least privilege and reduce the risk of unauthorized access.

Measuring the resilience of the organization's systems and networks against external threats is another important category of security KPIs. Metrics related to network security, such as the number of detected intrusions, the effectiveness of firewall rules, and the frequency of security assessments, provide insights into the organization's ability to safeguard its digital assets from external threats. These KPIs are instrumental in gauging the efficacy of perimeter defenses and adjusting security strategies in response to emerging threats.

Compliance with regulatory requirements and industry standards is a fundamental aspect of cybersecurity, and corresponding KPIs help organizations assess their adherence to applicable frameworks. Metrics may include the percentage of systems compliant with specific regulations, the number of security incidents leading to compliance violations, and the timeliness of reporting security incidents to regulatory authorities. Compliance-related KPIs contribute to the organization's ability to meet legal obligations, build trust with stakeholders, and avoid potential financial and reputational repercussions.

Risk management is an overarching theme that encompasses various aspects of security, and corresponding KPIs provide a quantitative assessment of the organization's risk posture. Metrics related to risk assessment, risk mitigation, and risk monitoring contribute to a comprehensive understanding of the organization's risk landscape. These KPIs assist in prioritizing security investments, aligning security measures with business objectives, and demonstrating the organization's commitment to effective risk management practices.

Continuous improvement is a fundamental principle in cybersecurity, and KPIs related to the effectiveness of security programs contribute to this ethos. Metrics such as the percentage reduction in security incidents over time, the frequency of security program assessments, and the success rate of security initiatives highlight the organization's commitment to learning from past experiences and adapting to evolving threats. These KPIs support a culture of continuous learning and improvement within the cybersecurity domain.

In conclusion, establishing key performance indicators for security is a dynamic and multifaceted process that requires careful consideration of the organization's business goals, risk landscape, and regulatory environment. Security KPIs serve as quantitative measures that enable organizations to assess their cybersecurity posture, identify areas for improvement, and make informed decisions to enhance overall security resilience. By aligning KPIs with business objectives, organizations can foster a holistic approach to cybersecurity that integrates security seamlessly into the fabric of their operations. From vulnerability management to incident response, user awareness, and risk management, the diverse categories of security KPIs contribute to a comprehensive understanding of an organization's security posture, facilitating a proactive and adaptive approach to cybersecurity.

Communicating security updates and best practices to end-users.

Communicating security updates and best practices to end-users is a critical component of any organization's cybersecurity strategy, as the human factor remains a significant contributor to security incidents. Effectively conveying important information about the latest security updates and best practices is essential for empowering end-users to play an active role in safeguarding sensitive data and digital assets. This communication process requires a thoughtful and user-centric approach, recognizing the diverse backgrounds, technical proficiency, and roles of end-users within the organization.

One foundational element of successful communication with end-users is the development of clear and accessible messages. Security updates and best practices can often be complex, laden with technical jargon, and challenging for non-technical users to understand. Therefore, translating technical information into plain language is crucial. The use of simple and straightforward language, devoid of unnecessary technical terms, ensures that the communication is comprehensible to a broad audience. This approach not only aids in conveying the intended message but also fosters a sense of inclusivity, making security updates and best practices accessible to all users, regardless of their technical expertise.

The mode of communication is equally important in reaching and engaging end-users. Organizations should leverage a variety of communication channels to disseminate security information effectively. Traditional channels, such as email notifications and in-house newsletters, can serve as reliable means for reaching a broad audience. However, organizations should also explore modern and interactive channels, such as webinars, video tutorials, and online forums, to cater to diverse learning preferences. The use of multiple channels ensures that security updates and best practices are communicated in a manner that resonates with different segments of the user population.

Tailoring communications to specific user groups is a key consideration in ensuring relevance and impact. Recognizing that not all users have the same roles, responsibilities, or technical requirements, organizations should segment their user base and tailor messages accordingly. For example, IT administrators may require detailed technical information about system updates, while non-technical staff may benefit from simplified instructions focused on practical actions they can take to enhance security. This targeted approach increases the likelihood that users will engage with and act upon the provided information, fostering a sense of personal responsibility for security.

Regularity and consistency in communication are essential elements of an effective strategy for conveying security updates and best practices. Security is an evolving landscape, with new threats and vulnerabilities emerging regularly. As such, organizations should establish a predictable and consistent schedule for communication, ensuring that users receive timely updates without being inundated with information. Regular communication helps build a culture of awareness and responsiveness, reinforcing the importance of staying informed about security matters as an ongoing responsibility.

In addition to communicating updates and best practices reactively, organizations should also proactively educate users about the broader cybersecurity landscape. This includes raising awareness about common threats, such as phishing attacks, malware, and social engineering tactics. By providing users with a foundational understanding of potential risks, organizations empower them to recognize and respond to security threats more effectively. Regularly sharing real-world examples and case studies can make abstract security concepts more tangible, enhancing users' ability to apply best practices in practical scenarios.

Interactive training sessions and workshops can be valuable tools for engaging end-users and reinforcing security best practices. These sessions provide opportunities for users to ask questions, seek clarification, and actively participate in the learning process. Simulated phishing exercises, where users receive mock phishing emails to test their ability to recognize and report phishing attempts, are particularly effective in enhancing users' awareness and resilience against social engineering attacks. These hands-on experiences contribute to a culture of continuous learning and improvement, making security practices more ingrained in users' daily routines.

Establishing a feedback loop is crucial for gauging the effectiveness of communication efforts and addressing user concerns. Organizations should encourage users to provide feedback on the clarity, relevance, and helpfulness of security communications. This can be facilitated through surveys, feedback forms, or open forums where users can share their thoughts and experiences. Actively seeking and incorporating user feedback helps refine communication strategies, ensuring that they align with user needs and preferences.

Incentivizing positive security behavior among end-users can be a powerful motivator for compliance with best practices. Recognition programs, such as "Security Champion" awards or acknowledgment of individuals who consistently adhere to security guidelines, create a positive reinforcement mechanism. Incentives could also include gamification elements, where users earn badges or rewards for completing security training modules or reporting potential security incidents. These approaches not only motivate individuals to actively engage with security communications but also contribute to fostering a culture where security is valued and celebrated.

Personalizing communication efforts by incorporating real-world examples and case studies relevant to the organization's industry or specific threats can enhance the relatability of security updates and best practices. By connecting security concepts to tangible scenarios that resonate with end-users, organizations make the information more memorable and actionable. This personalized approach helps users understand the direct impact of their actions on the organization's security posture, reinforcing a sense of shared responsibility.

In conclusion, communicating security updates and best practices to end-users is a multifaceted endeavor that requires a thoughtful and user-centric approach. Clear and accessible language, diverse communication channels, and tailored messages contribute to effective communication. Regular and proactive education, interactive training sessions, and the establishment of feedback loops further enhance the impact of communication efforts. Incentivizing positive security behavior and personalizing communication make security updates and best practices more relatable and actionable for end-users. Ultimately, a holistic communication strategy fosters a culture of awareness, responsibility, and continuous improvement, positioning end-users as active contributors to the organization's overall cybersecurity resilience.

Strategies for staying ahead of evolving cybersecurity threats.
Staying ahead of evolving cybersecurity threats is a perpetual challenge that requires a dynamic and proactive approach, as the landscape of cyber threats continually evolves in complexity and sophistication. Organizations must adopt multifaceted strategies that encompass technological advancements, threat intelligence, risk management, and a robust cybersecurity culture to effectively mitigate and respond to emerging threats.

A foundational element in staying ahead of cybersecurity threats is the continuous assessment and enhancement of an organization's cybersecurity posture. Regular risk assessments, vulnerability assessments, and penetration testing provide valuable insights into the organization's susceptibility to potential threats. By identifying and addressing vulnerabilities in systems, networks, and applications, organizations can significantly reduce their attack surface and fortify their defenses against evolving threats. These assessments should be conducted systematically and in conjunction with evolving business processes and technology deployments to ensure ongoing relevance.

Implementing a comprehensive and adaptive cybersecurity framework is essential for staying ahead of threats. Standards such as ISO 27001, NIST Cybersecurity Framework, and CIS Controls offer guidance for organizations to establish a robust cybersecurity foundation. Adhering to these frameworks provides a structured approach to managing risk, implementing security controls, and continuously improving cybersecurity practices. The framework should be regularly reviewed and updated to align with emerging threats, technological advancements, and changes in the organization's risk profile.

An integral aspect of staying ahead of cybersecurity threats is the proactive integration of threat intelligence into an organization's security strategy. Threat intelligence involves gathering and analyzing information about current and emerging cyber threats, including the tactics, techniques, and procedures employed by malicious actors. By leveraging threat intelligence feeds, organizations can anticipate potential threats, identify indicators of compromise, and adjust their security controls accordingly. Collaborating with information-sharing platforms and industry groups enhances the organization's access to timely and relevant threat intelligence, contributing to a more informed and adaptive defense strategy.

The adoption of advanced cybersecurity technologies is paramount for staying ahead of evolving threats. Artificial intelligence (AI), machine learning, and automation play pivotal roles in augmenting human capabilities and improving the efficiency of threat detection and response. AI-driven security solutions can analyze vast amounts of data in real-time, identifying patterns indicative of malicious activities and enabling organizations to respond swiftly to potential threats. Endpoint detection and response (EDR) solutions, intrusion detection systems (IDS), and next-generation firewalls are examples of technologies that leverage advanced capabilities to bolster an organization's cybersecurity defenses.

In the face of evolving threats, organizations should prioritize the implementation of a zero-trust security model. Zero trust assumes that threats may exist both outside and inside the network and requires continuous verification of user identities, devices, and activities. This model reduces the reliance on traditional perimeter defenses and emphasizes the importance of continuous monitoring, least privilege access, and strong authentication mechanisms. Implementing zero trust architecture contributes to a more resilient security posture that aligns with the dynamic nature of modern cybersecurity threats.

Ensuring the security of third-party relationships is a critical component of staying ahead of cybersecurity threats. As organizations increasingly rely on external vendors and partners, the security posture of these third parties directly impacts the overall security resilience of the organization. Conducting thorough security assessments of third-party vendors, establishing clear security expectations in contracts, and regularly monitoring and auditing their security practices help mitigate the risk of supply chain attacks and ensure that the extended ecosystem adheres to robust cybersecurity standards.

A proactive incident response capability is paramount for staying ahead of cybersecurity threats. Organizations should develop and regularly test incident response plans to ensure swift and effective responses to security incidents. Conducting tabletop exercises, simulations, and red teaming exercises helps organizations identify gaps in their incident response processes and improve their ability to handle real-time security incidents. The lessons learned from each incident should be used to refine and enhance the incident response plan continuously.

Educating and raising awareness among employees is a fundamental strategy for staying ahead of evolving cybersecurity threats. Human factors remain a significant attack vector, and employees are often targeted through phishing attacks, social engineering, and other manipulation tactics. Security awareness training programs, regular communication about emerging threats, and simulated phishing exercises empower employees to recognize and respond to potential threats effectively. Cultivating a security-aware culture within the organization enhances the collective ability to thwart evolving threats.

Engaging in cybersecurity threat hunting activities enables organizations to actively seek out potential threats within their environment before they manifest into full-fledged security incidents. Threat hunting involves the proactive analysis of network and system data to identify abnormal patterns or behaviors indicative of potential threats. Skilled threat hunters leverage their expertise and threat intelligence to uncover hidden threats that automated security tools may not detect. Integrating threat hunting into the cybersecurity strategy contributes to a proactive and anticipatory defense posture.

Collaboration and information-sharing within the cybersecurity community are vital for staying ahead of evolving threats. Organizations should actively participate in industry-specific forums, share threat intelligence with peers, and collaborate with law enforcement agencies and cybersecurity organizations. The collective knowledge and experiences shared within these communities contribute to a more comprehensive understanding of emerging threats and enable organizations to prepare for and respond to new attack vectors more effectively.

Regularly reviewing and updating security policies, procedures, and controls is a crucial aspect of staying ahead of cybersecurity threats. As the threat landscape evolves, so should an organization's security governance framework. Conducting regular audits and assessments to ensure compliance with security policies and industry regulations helps identify areas for improvement and alignment with emerging threats. A flexible and adaptive security policy framework ensures that security measures remain effective in the face of changing threat landscapes.

In conclusion, staying ahead of evolving cybersecurity threats requires a holistic and adaptive approach that encompasses technology, threat intelligence, risk management, and a strong cybersecurity culture. By continuously assessing and enhancing the organization's cybersecurity posture, integrating advanced technologies, leveraging threat intelligence, adopting a zero-trust model, securing third-party relationships, and prioritizing incident response capabilities, organizations can establish a proactive defense against the dynamic and sophisticated nature of modern cyber threats. Additionally, fostering collaboration within the cybersecurity community, engaging in threat hunting, educating employees, and regularly reviewing and updating security policies contribute to a comprehensive strategy that positions organizations to anticipate, adapt to, and effectively counter evolving cybersecurity threats.

****